An Introduction to
COASTAL NAVIGATION

A Seaman's Guide

Published by

Morgans Technical Books Limited

P.O. Box 5, Wotton-under-Edge,
Gloucestershire. GL12 7BY

ISBN 0 948254 02 5

4th Edition 1989 (Incorporating the IALA Maritime Buoyage System 'A' for UK waters)
2nd Impression 1989

Acknowledgements

Extracts from British Admiralty charts 31, 32, 109, 148, 152, 734, 777, 871, 883, L(D1) 1156, 1178, 1185, 1190, 1267, 1607, 1634, 1828, 1892, 2345, 2693, 3315, D6067 are reproduced with the sanction of the Controller, Her Majesty's Stationery Office and of the Hydrographer of the Navy.

The Publisher also wishes to acknowledge with thanks the permissions given by the Controller, Her Majesty's Stationery Office, for the reproduction of illustrations and tables from pages 20, 25 and 115 the *Admiralty Manual of Navigation - Volume 1 (1964);* page 28 the *Admiralty Manual of Navigation - Volume 2 (1964);* pages 14 and 15 the *Tidal Stream Atlas - The Channel Islands and Adjacent Coasts of France (1970);* pages 17, 18, 19 and 20 the *Admiralty List of Lights and Fog Signals - Volume A (1981);* Diagrams 1, 2, 3 and 5 *NP 735 IALA Maritime Buoyage System 'A';* pages 27, 46, 48, 50, 51, 103, 146 and 148 the *Admiralty Tide Tables - Volume 1 (1985).*

Printed and bound by View Publications (Bristol) Ltd., Wickwar, Nr. Bristol, England.

Foreword
by
The Captain, H.M.S. Dryad, The Royal Naval School of Maritime Operations

"Good fixes bring their comfort with them; doubt in Navigation is apt to become the forerunner of sorrow."

A Seaman Officer must be capable of navigating a ship safely both across the oceans and in coastal waters under all conditions. Making a coastal passage involves many of the seaman's basic navigation skills; the study and interpretation of the chart, the prediction of tidal streams and a variety of other considerations must precede the practical planning and safe execution of the passage whatever the visibility and weather.

While there is no short cut to careful planning and no substitute for practical experience at sea, much can be learnt from this book which sets out to combine in a logical sequence and an easily assimilated form lessons on coastal navigation from a variety of publications.

The student who has worked conscientiously through this book will have acquired a good "Introduction to Coastal Navigation" before going to sea, from then on a strict adherence to the basic principles given in this book, practical experience and vigilance will bring confidence and comfort when navigating in confined waters.

Technical Advice

The Publisher would like to acknowledge the detailed and constructive help given at every stage of this project by Lieutenant Commander D. Hart Dyke, Navigating Officer, Britannia Royal Naval College, Dartmouth. The help given by Instructor Lieutenant J. Wheatley, Senior Instructor Officer, Amphibious Training Unit, Royal Marines, Poole, is also acknowledged.

Validation

The first edition of this programmed text was tested on two classes of New Entry Officers undergoing pre-sea training at the Britannia Royal Naval College.

After study of the programme, the average test mark was 74%, and the average study time 6 hours 30 minutes. The students were in the first month of training, and had not been to sea. Age span was 18 - 23, minimum educational qualifications, 2 'A' levels.

Contents

Preface

This book was written at the request of the Captain, Britannia Royal Naval College, Dartmouth who gave full co-operation in its preparation.

Scope of the Book

The book is designed to teach those theoretical aspects of coastal navigation that need to be acquired before practical chartwork can be undertaken.

The initial sections cover the representation of the Earth on a chart, and at an early stage the student is instructed in the method of correcting compass readings for variation and deviation. From there he goes on to learn the significance to the navigator of tides, tidal streams, tidal levels, buoys and lights. Having progressed this far he is now ready to learn the basic tasks of fixing the ship's position and plotting the ship's course; these topics are covered in the final sections. At relevant points throughout the book the student learns the important chart symbols and abbreviations.

On completion of the book he is adequately prepared for lessons on practical chartwork.

Intended Readership

The book is designed for use by New Entry Officers in the first month of training at Britannia Royal Naval College, Dartmouth.

It will, however, be found equally valuable to any private person needing an introduction to coastal navigation.

Previous Knowledge Needed

No knowledge of navigation is needed to begin studying the book.

To the Student

Because of the concentrated form of learning offered by this book you may find when studying from it that working for too long is tiring. You should find what length of study time suits you best – an hour is probably a good time to start with.

There are self-tests at the end of each section and you will find it helpful to complete them as a check on your learning.

If you wish to study in more depth, references to the *Admiralty Manual of Navigation-Volume 1* are provided for this purpose. You will also find the *Mariner's Handbook* of considerable value.

Note to the Private Student

You will find in this book references to:

Admiralty Tide Tables, Volume 1.
Admiralty List of Lights and Fog Signals, Volume A.

These books are needed for:

a) Multiplication tables for tidal calculations (Section 4).
b) Heights of tidal levels (Section 5).
c) Geographical ranges of lights (Section 7).

If you do not wish to buy these books you will still get full value from the text as you will be able to do the calculations in a) above, by simple arithmetic, and the principles of b) and c) can be understood without working the calculations.

If you require the books they may be bought from your local Admiralty Chart Agent.

Section 1: Latitude and Longitude

For safe navigation it is essential that you are able to plan the passage of your ship in coastal waters and make sure that the ship follows the planned track. To do this, the chart is the main tool of your trade and this programme will give you the background knowledge that is necessary for using the chart. You will learn some basic facts about chart symbols, compasses, lights, buoyage and tidal streams.

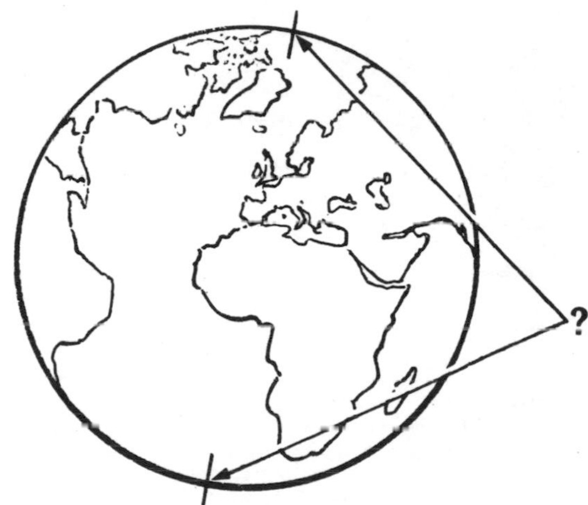

Firstly, though, there are some facts about the Earth itself which are important for navigation.

The Earth, as you know, rotates on its axis. The extremities of the axis of rotation are called the ________.

poles

The drawing below shows how sunlight falls on the Earth's surface. Which of the two arrows indicates the direction of rotation of the Earth?

Is it this direction?

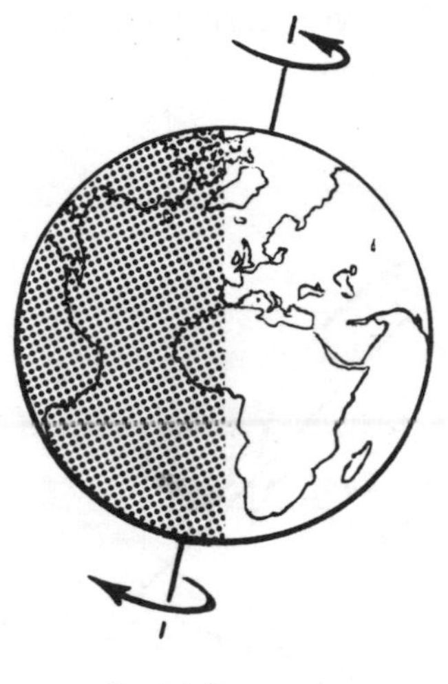

Or this?

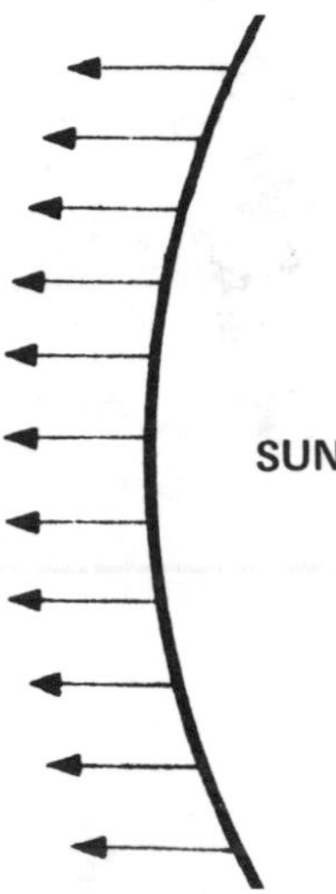

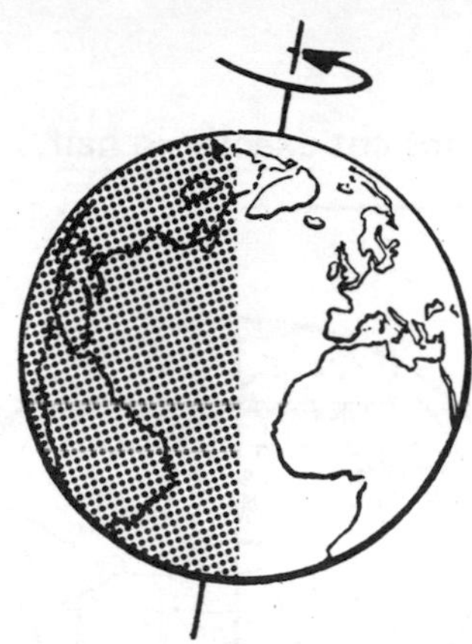

The Earth rotates in this direction (i.e. the Sun rises in the east).

____

The Earth is slightly flattened at the poles, and so it is not a perfect sphere. However, for navigational purposes it can be regarded as spherical. A sphere can be cut exactly in half in any number of directions. Each of these cuts passes through the centre of the sphere and the resulting line on the Earth's surface is known as a *great circle.*

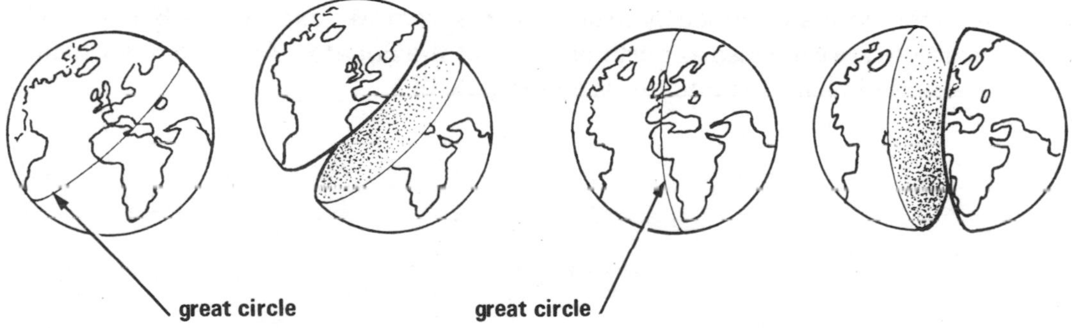

A sphere can also be cut to produce a *small circle.* Here are some examples:

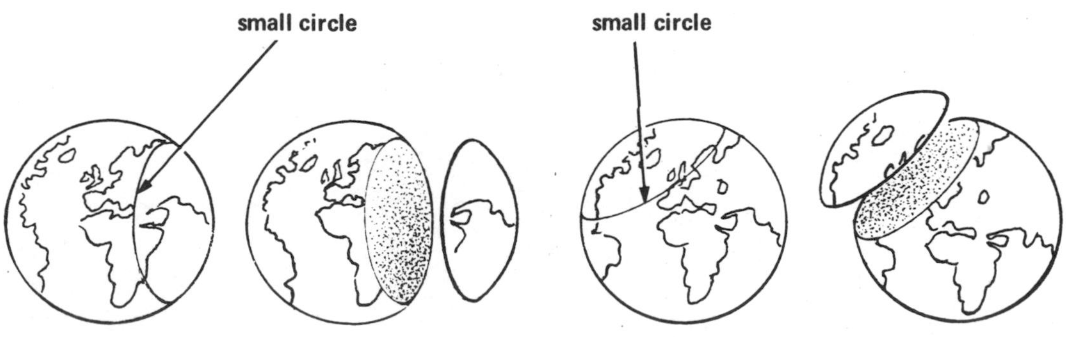

The difference between a great circle and a small circle is that with a small circle the sphere is not cut ________________.
(Complete the sentence.)

With a small circle the sphere is not cut exactly in half.

___

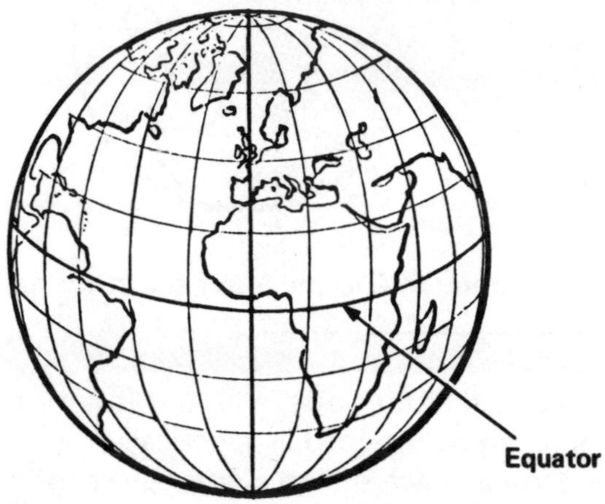

Positions on the globe are defined by their distances from two axes on the Earth's surface. Firstly, positions are expressed as north or south of the *Equator.* As it is a line which cuts the globe exactly in half, the Equator is an example of a ______ _______.

great circle

Secondly, positions are expressed as either east or west of the *Greenwich Meridian.* A *meridian* is an imaginary line on the Earth's surface joining the North Pole to the South Pole, and is perpendicular to the Equator. There are an infinite number of meridians, and by international agreement the meridian passing through Greenwich in London has been chosen as the prime meridian.

Which of these lines marked on the drawing are meridians?

A – A.
B – B.
C – C.
D – D.

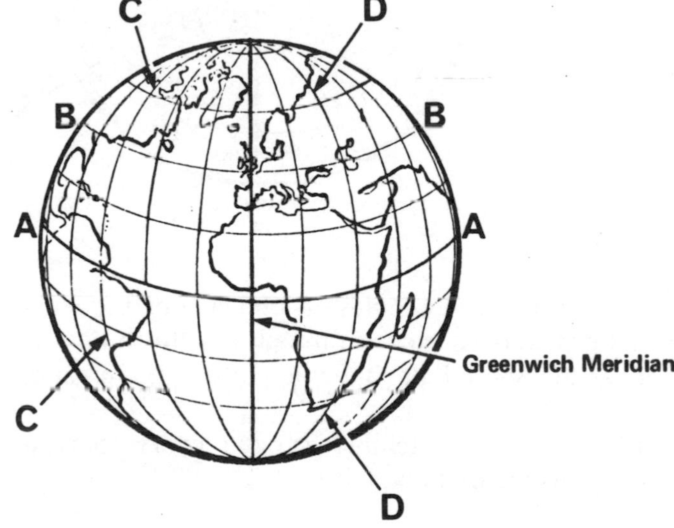

C – C }
D – D } are meridians

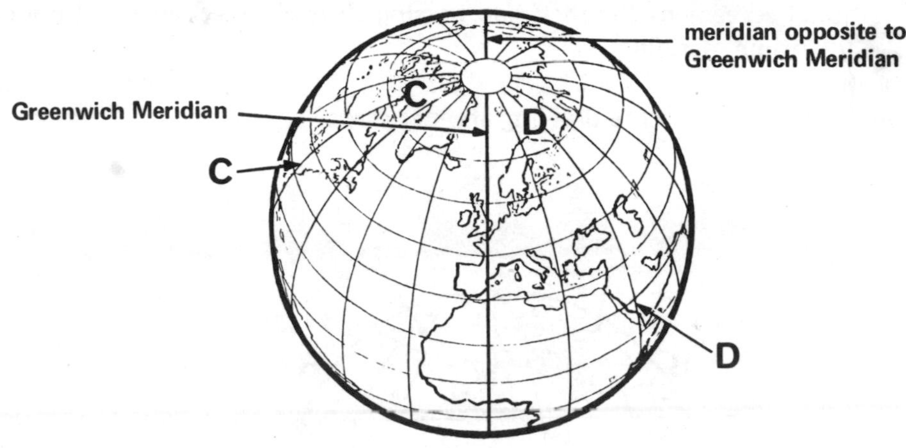

A meridian is a line joining the poles on <u>one</u> side of the globe. It is a semi-great circle. This means that if it were continued through the North Pole and across the other side of the globe as far as the South Pole, it would constitute a great circle.

We can define a meridian as a semi-great circle which joins the _______ , and which is _______________ to the Equator.

poles   perpendicular (at right angles)

Charts, maps and models of the globe are divided up by the lines of latitude and longitude.

Lines of latitude are parallel to the Equator. Are they:

great circles, semi-circles or small circles?

Small circles. (The Equator is the only line of latitude which is a great circle.)

Any point on the globe can be identified by its latitude and longitude e.g. the position of Dartmouth is 50° 21′N 003°36′W. As a start to understanding what these figures mean, let's consider a simpler example.

Look at the drawing below. The place F has a longitude of 045° East: the drawing shows how this angle of 045° is derived.

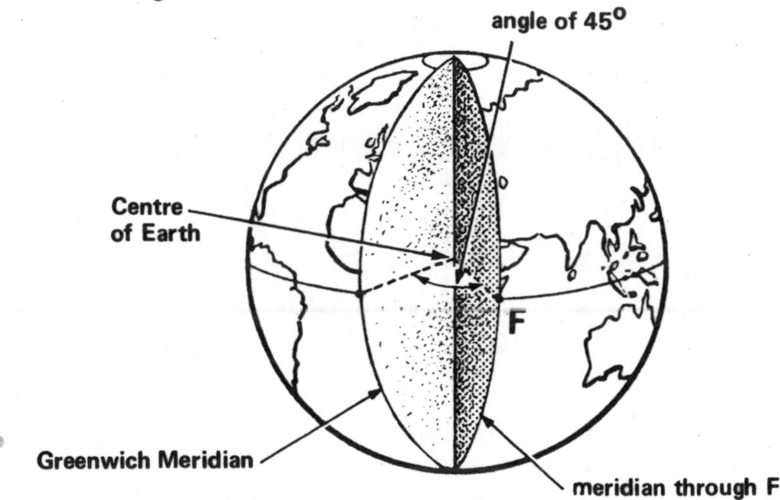

The next drawings show places G and H, which are further from the Greenwich Meridian. In fact the further the place is from the Greenwich Meridian, the larger the angle at the centre of the Earth becomes.

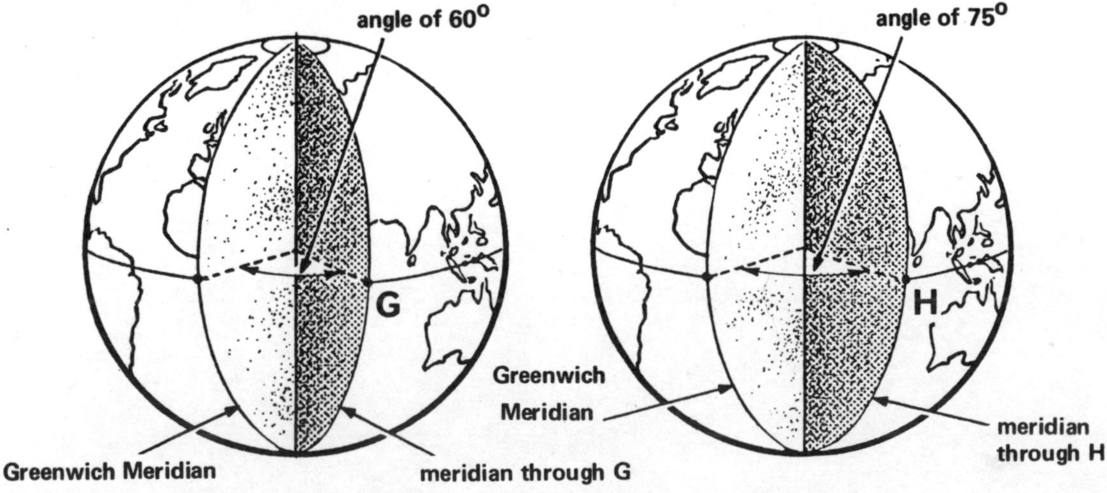

The distance of a place east or west from the Greenwich Meridian is given as an <u>angular distance</u>, i.e. the angle at the centre of the Earth. This is called the *longitude* of a place. What are the longitudes of G and H?

The longitude of G is 060° E and the longitude of H is 075° E.

The meridian through G is thus the 060° E line of longitude, and the meridian through H is the 075° E line of longitude.

Study this labelled diagram carefully. Note that the angle of longitude is measured at the centre of the Earth in the plane of the Equator.

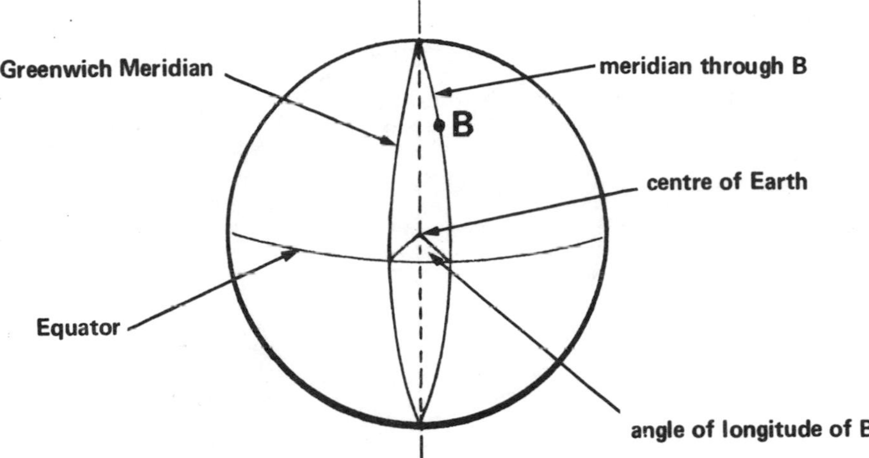

Longitude is expressed as East or West of the Greenwich Meridian. It cannot be greater than 180° East or West as there are only 360 degrees in a circle.

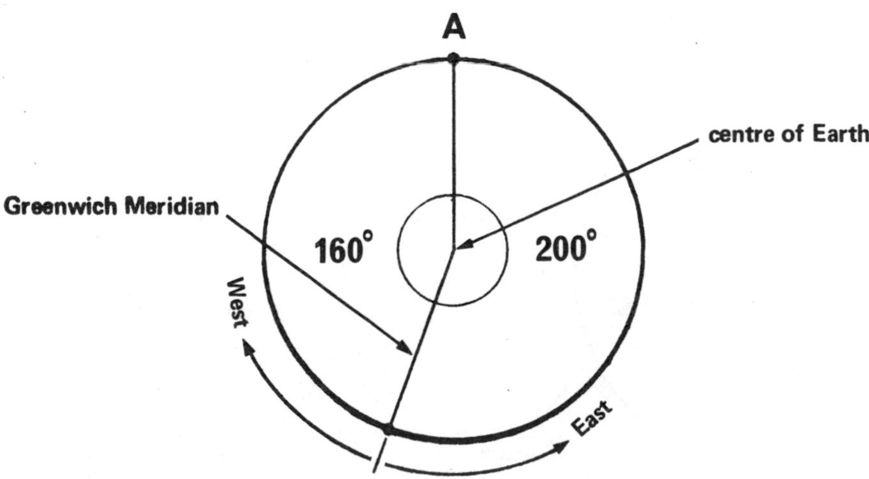

This diagram is a view of the Earth looking down from the North Pole. What is the longitude of place A on the Equator?

160° West.

You know that the longitude of B (in diagram below) represents the angular distance of B from the Greenwich Meridian, and you have seen how this is measured. A similar means is used for deriving the *latitude* of a place (i.e. the angular distance of that place north or south of the Equator).

This angle can never be more than 90°.

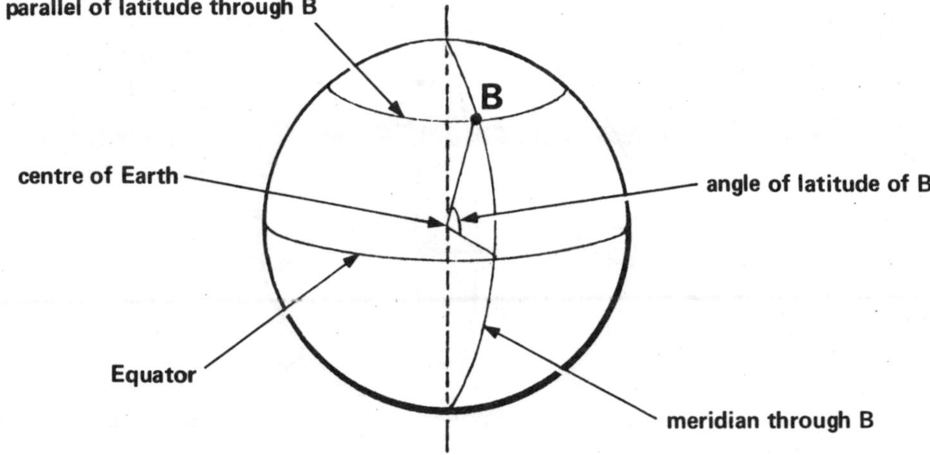

Study the diagrams below and then say how you would express the latitude and longtude of C.

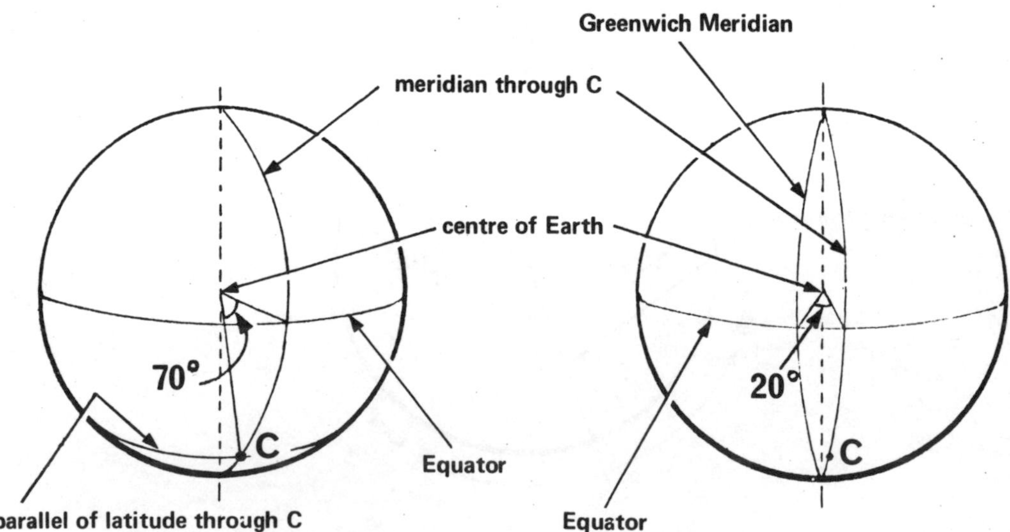

70° South 020° East.

The latitude and longitude would normally be written thus: 70° 00′S 020° 00′E. The symbol (°) stands for 'degree' and the symbol (′) stands for 'minute', (60 minutes = 1 degree). The correct order is *latitude before longitude, degrees before minutes.*

For accurate plotting, latitude and longitude are expressed to tenths of a minute. Let's say, for example, that your position is 50°01′ · 4N 004° 06′ · 9W.

Notice that the minute sign comes before the decimal point. This is the normal convention – it prevents any misreading of the decimal point.

On the chart below the position of point X is 50° 01′ · 4N 004° 06′ · 9W.
What is the position of point Y?

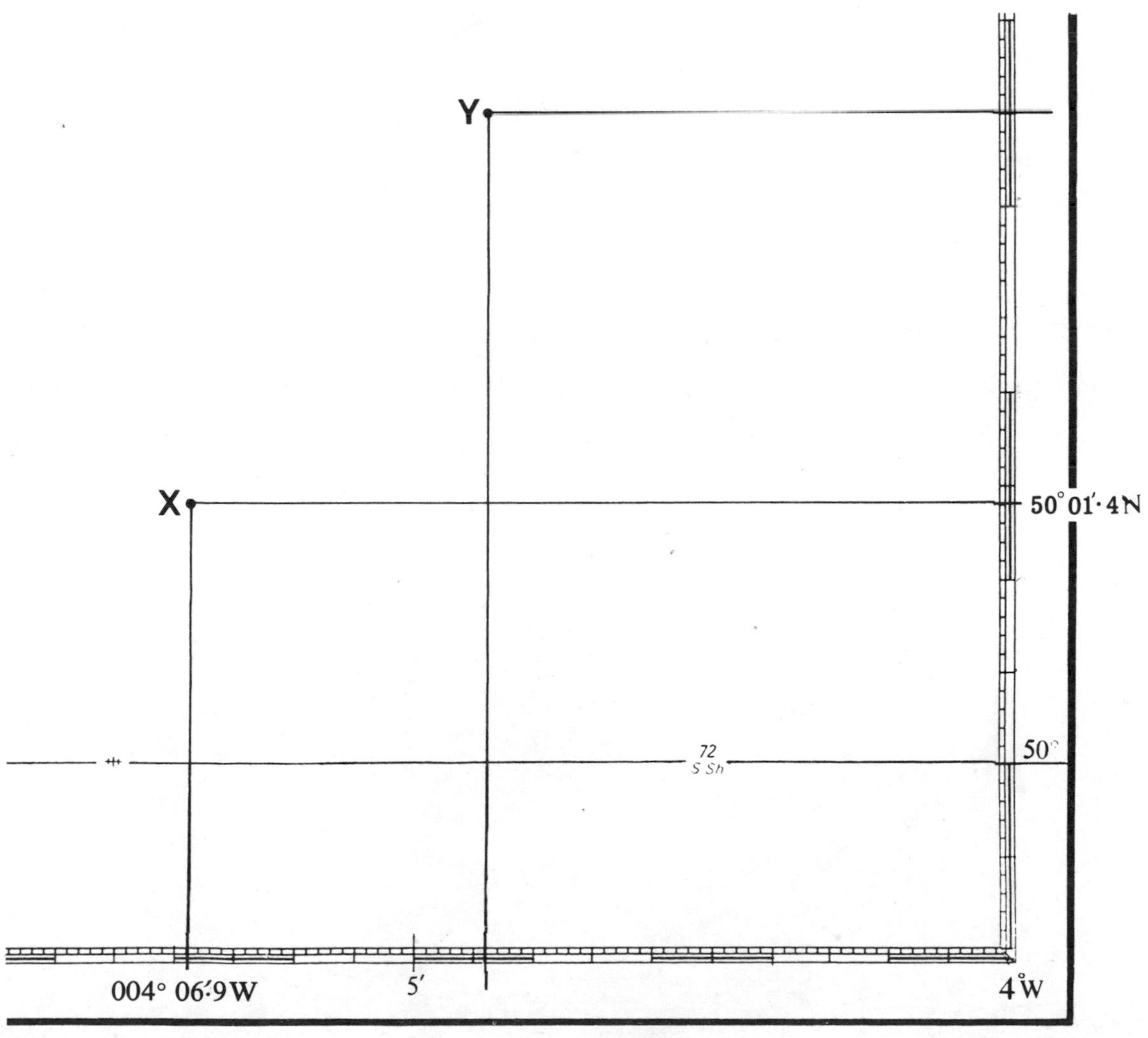

50° 03′·5N 004° 04′·4W

Various latitudes and longitudes are given below; some are correct and some are incorrect. Study them carefully and then say which are correctly written and which are incorrectly written or impossible, giving your reasons.

1. 60° 00′N 015° 00′E
2. 90° 17′2·N 192° 42′·7E
3. 56° 20·5′N 001° 16·9′W
4. 88° 33′·7S 108° 49′·1E

1. Correct (60° 00′ · 0N 015° 00′ · 0E is too cumbersome).
2. 90°17′·2N 192°42′·7E. Latitude cannot be greater than 90°, longitude cannot be greater than 180°.
3. 56° 20·5′N 001°16·9′W. The sign for minutes should be put before the decimal point.
4. Correct.

Section 1: Self-test

At the end of each section in this book there is a self-test on the essential points that have been covered. We would recommend you to write down your answers to all the questions in the test before turning to the answer page.

1. Which of these diagrams shows correctly the Earth's direction of rotation?

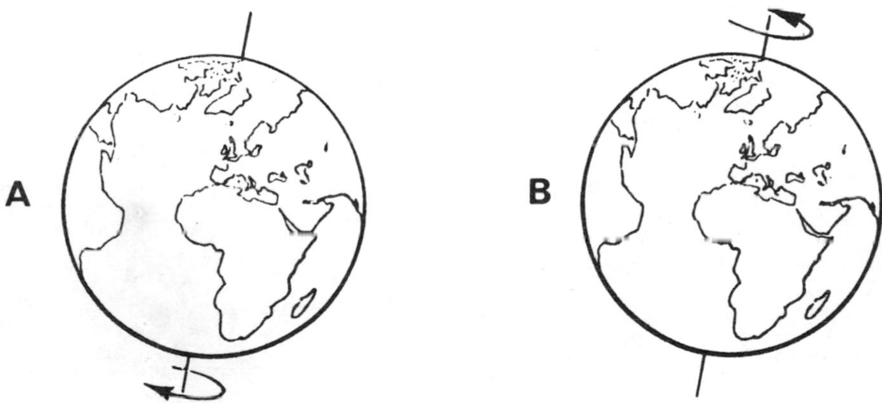

2. What are the extremities of the axis of rotation called?
3. Define 'meridian'.
4. How many minutes are there in a degree?
5. Latitude is expressed as north or south of the ____________ and longitude is expressed as east or west of the ________ ___________

6. What are the latitudes and longitudes of the positions, X and Y?

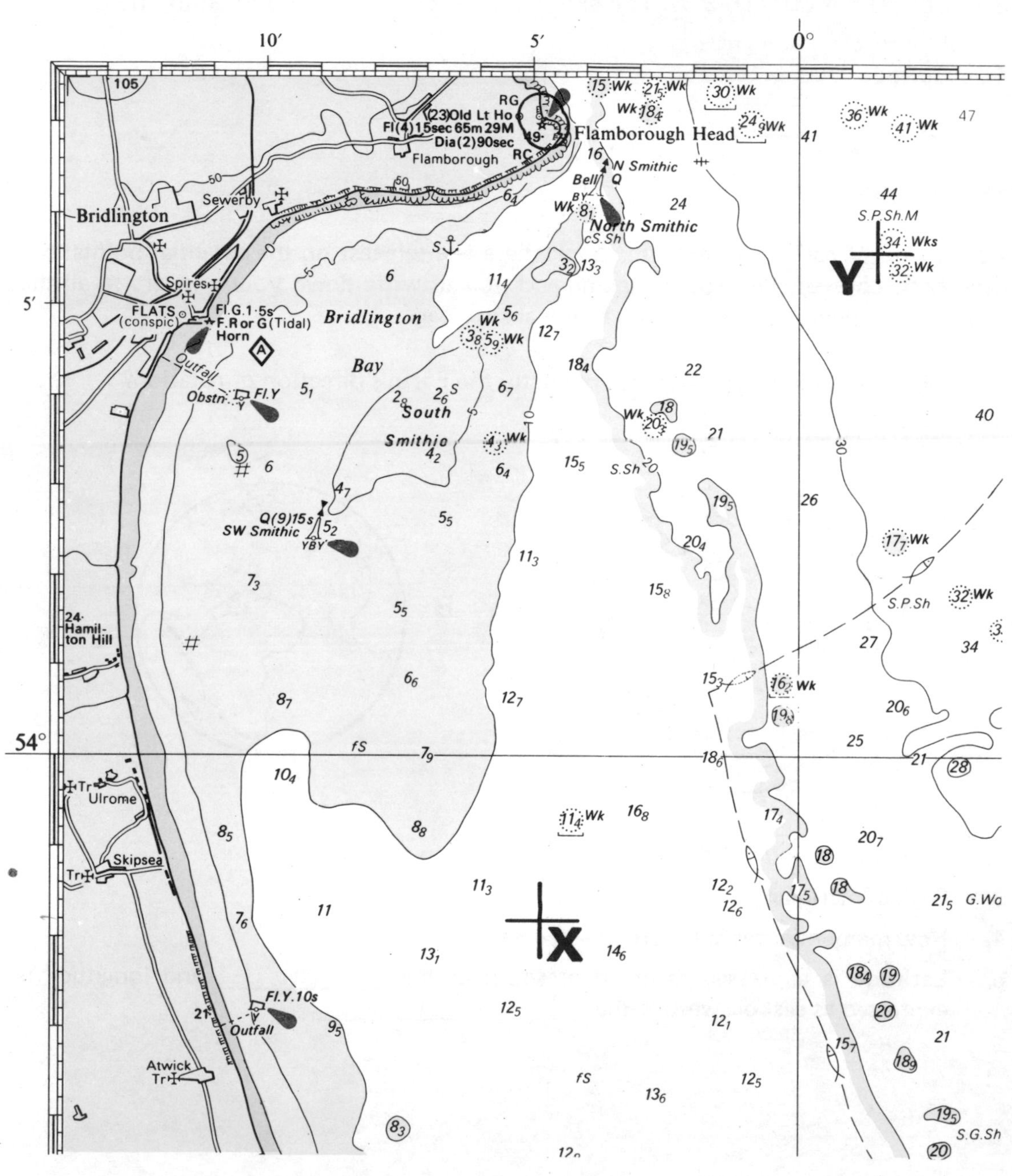

7. Define a 'great circle' and a 'small circle'.

8. Which of these is a great circle?

   The Greenwich Meridian.
   The South Pole.
   The Equator.

9. Which of the diagrams below shows a) the angle of latitude of a place F, and b) the angle of longitude of a place F?

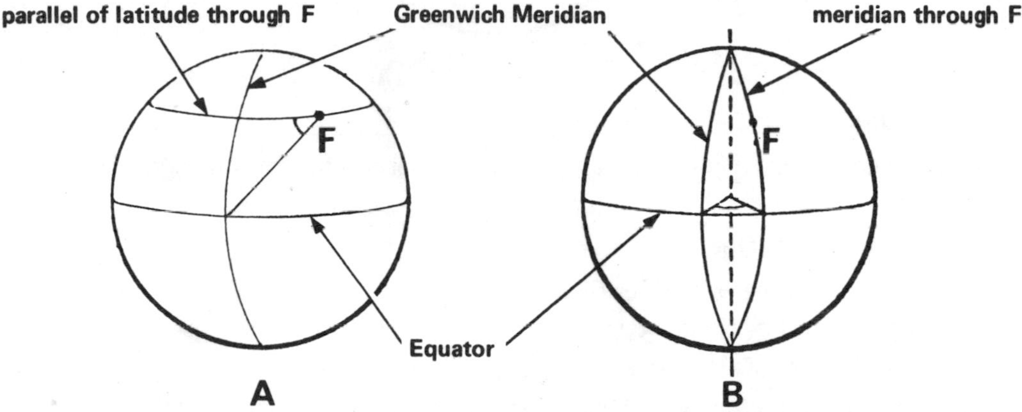

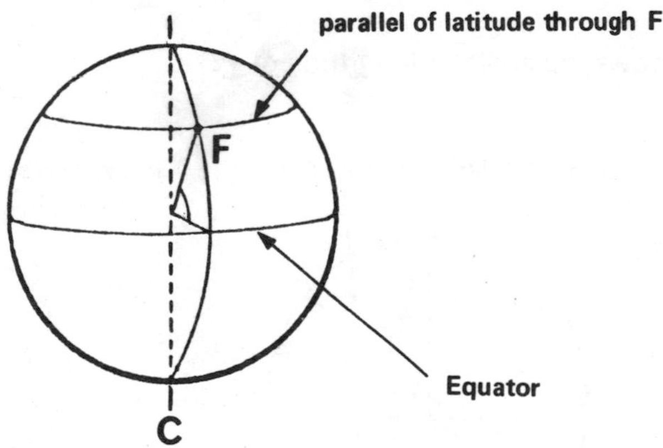

Now turn to page 16 for the answers.

Section 1: Answers to Self-test

1.

2. The poles.
3. A semi-great circle joining the poles, and perpendicular (at right-angles) to the Equator.
4. 60 minutes = 1 degree.
5. Equator Greenwich Meridian
6. X is 53°58′·2N 000°04′·8W
   Y is 54°05′·6N 000°01′·5E
7. A great circle is a circle which cuts the sphere (or the Earth) exactly in half. A small circle is a circle which does not cut the sphere (or the Earth) exactly in half.
8. The Equator. (The Greenwich Meridian is a semi-great circle.)
9. C shows the angle of latitude of F.
   B shows the angle of longitude of F.

parallel of latitude through F

F

Equator

C

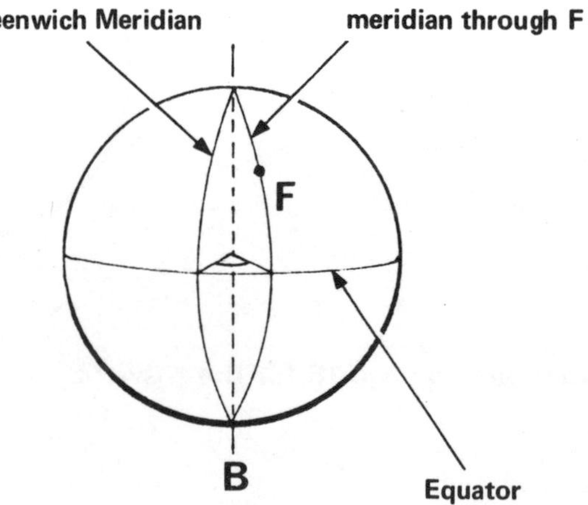

Section 2: Compass Bearings and Courses

In navigation the term 'mile' does not refer to the land mile – it refers either to the sea mile or nautical mile, (the symbol (′) is used for both,e.g. 3′).

The sea *mile* is the length of a minute of arc measured along the meridian in the latitude of the position. A minute of latitude in any place is subtended by an angle, not at the centre of the Earth, but at the centre of curvature at that place. The drawings of the Earth are exaggerated to make this point.

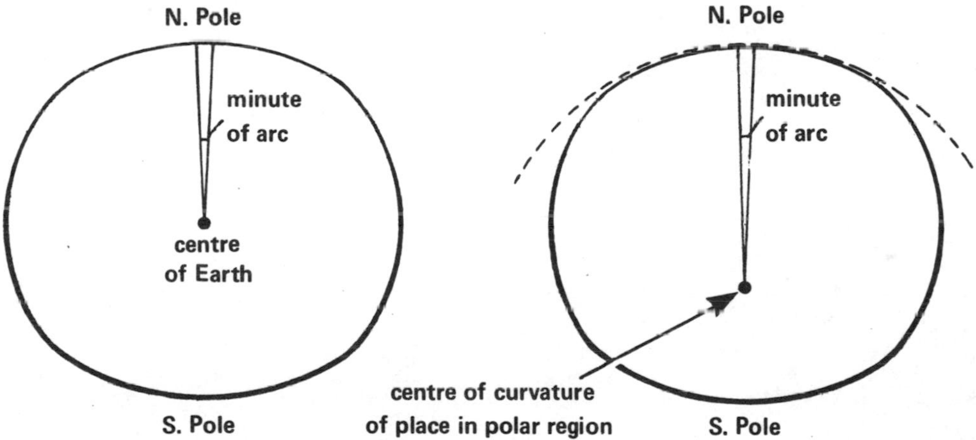

Due to the irregularity of the shape of the Earth, the length of a sea mile varies from 6046·1 feet at the Equator to 6108·3 at the poles. In order to avoid recalibrating ships' logs (the recorders of speed and distance) and radar sets in different latitudes a nautical mile of fixed length (6076 feet) is used for these instruments. This is the *International nautical mile,* and is rather longer than the land mile.

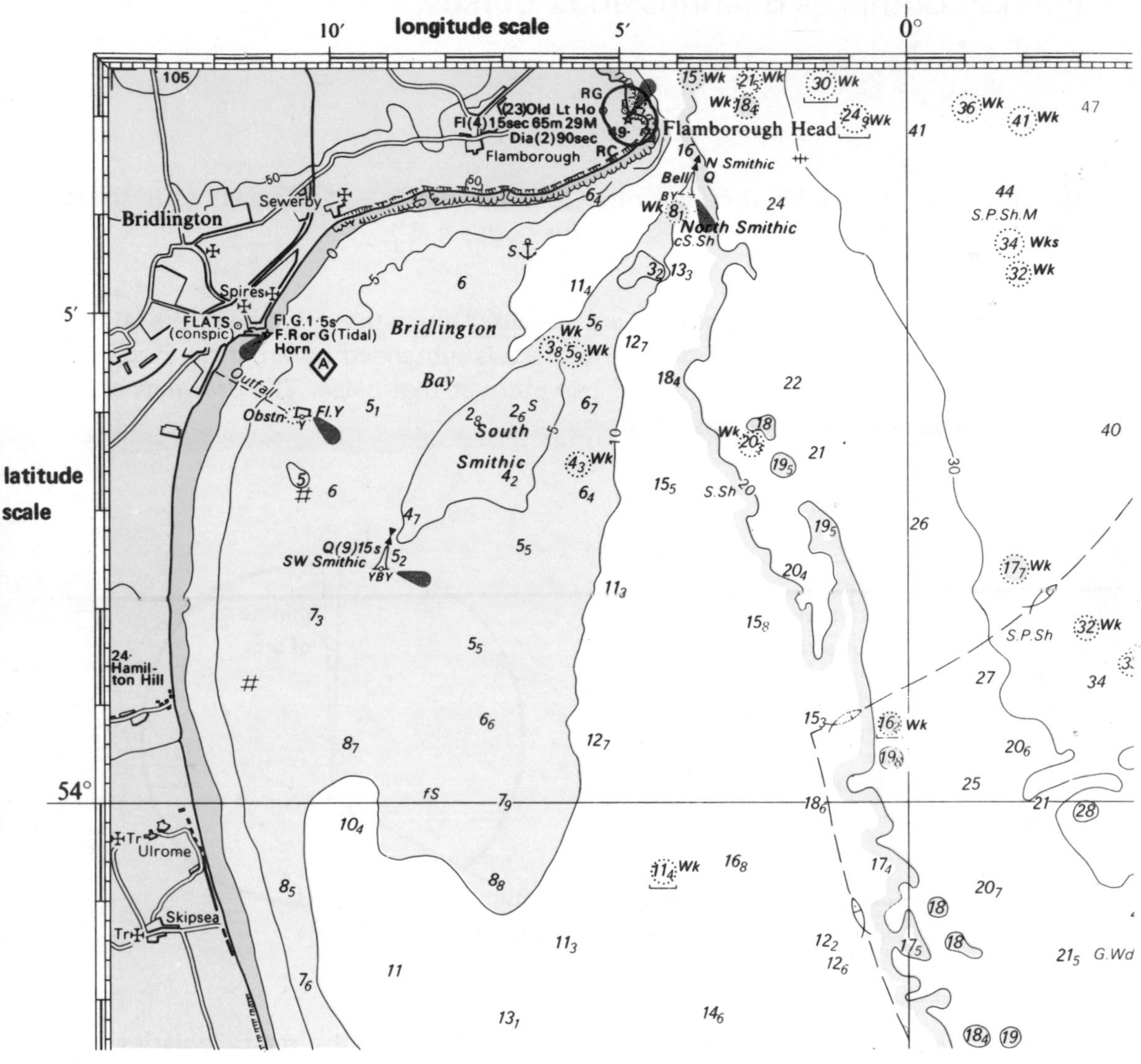

However, when you are using a chart you will be using sea miles; one sea mile is equivalent to one minute on the latitude scale.

The distance recorded by the ship's instruments is the International nautical mile. How many feet are there in a nautical mile (International)? Choose the correct answer.

5000 feet.

5280 feet.

5604 feet.

6076 feet.

8780 feet.

6076 feet.

The knot is the unit of speed used in navigation. One knot is one nautical mile per hour.

Another unit which you will meet in navigation is the cable. This is taken as roughly 200 yards, or alternatively as a tenth of a nautical mile. Coming into an anchorage, for instance, the distance to go is called out in cables.

To help familiarise yourself with these units, try the following questions:

1. Which is going faster – a ship with a speed of 20 knots or a car with a speed of 20 m.p.h.?

2. A ship is 1 nautical mile from you, whilst another ship is 12 cables away. Which ship is nearer?

1. The ship.
2. The ship that is 1 nautical mile away.

The instrument used to record the speed and distance covered by the ship is the *log.* Only a few words will be given here on the different types of log, and you should take the opportunity of looking at the actual instruments.

The *impeller log (Chernikeeff log)* measures the number of rotations of an underwater impeller fitted to the ship. The *Pitometer log* is operated by the variation in the pressure of the water underneath the ship, as detected by a rodmeter protruding below the ship's hull. A different sort of rodmeter is used by the *Electro-magnetic log.* This one is fitted with an iron-cored coil which is supplied with an alternating current. The voltage produced in the water is proportional to the speed of the ship, and this is recorded by the log. Most modern warships are fitted with an *Electro-magnetic log.*

1. How many feet are there in a nautical mile (International)?
2. How long is a cable?

1. 6076 feet.
2. 200 yards (approx.) or a tenth of a nautical mile.

The navigating officer needs to know at all times the precise direction in which the ship is heading, i.e. her *course.*

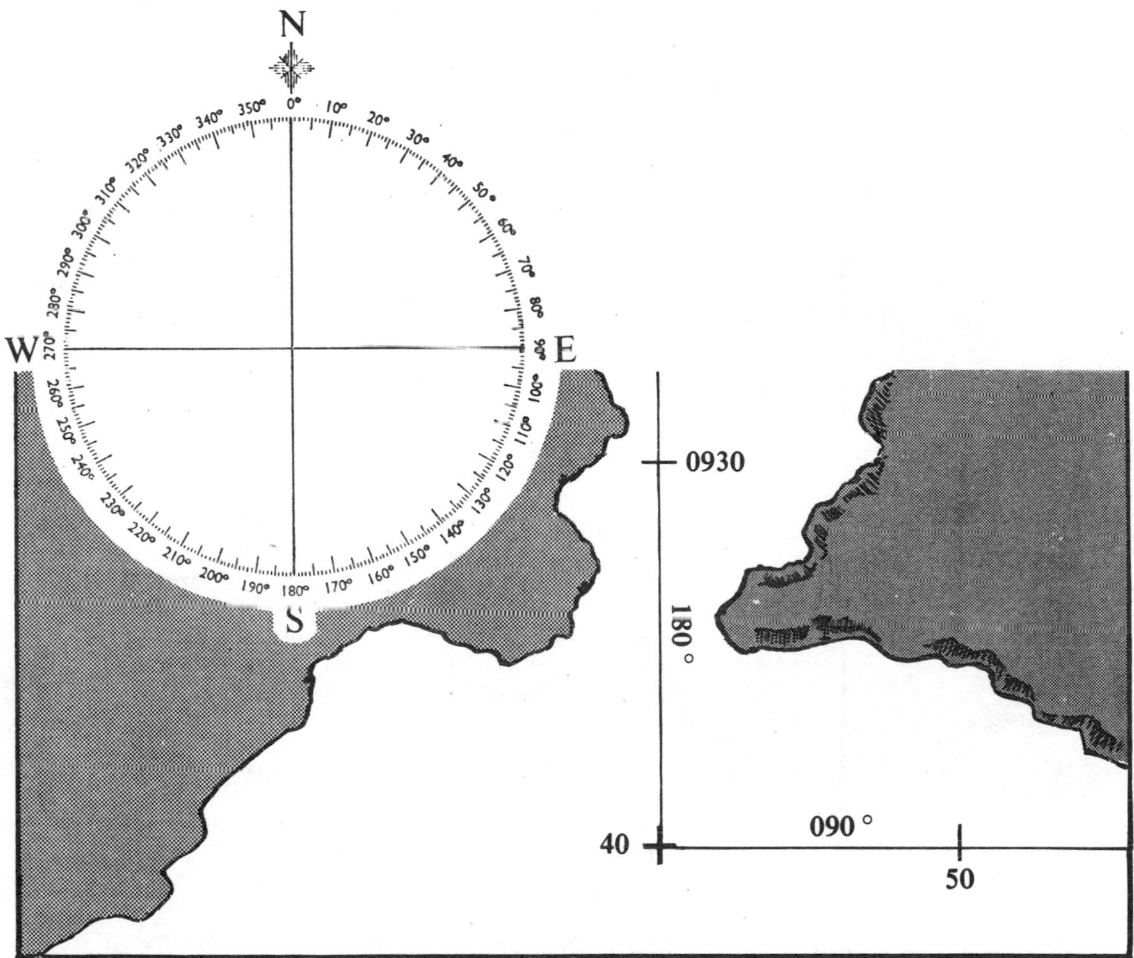

If a ship leaves harbour at 0930, and its course at that time is due south, the navigating officer would give his course as 180°. This is based on the division of the compass into 360 degrees, with due north being 000°, due east 090°, due south 180°, due west 270°. Note that a course is given as a three-figure number. A line representing the course is plotted on the chart, and the three-figure number written alongside it.

At 0940 the ship alters course. What is the new course (in degrees) which the navigator would write alongside the plotted course?

090°(not 90°).

The direction of one thing from another is referred to in navigational terms as the *bearing.* For instance, on the chart below, the navigating officer would express the fact that the lighthouse is north east of the ship by saying that the bearing of the lighthouse from the ship is 045° (or that the lighthouse bears 045° from the ship). When this bearing is given orally, it is given as "Zero— four – five degrees". Bearings, like courses are given as three-figure numbers, and they are important, as you will see later, for fixing the ship's position.

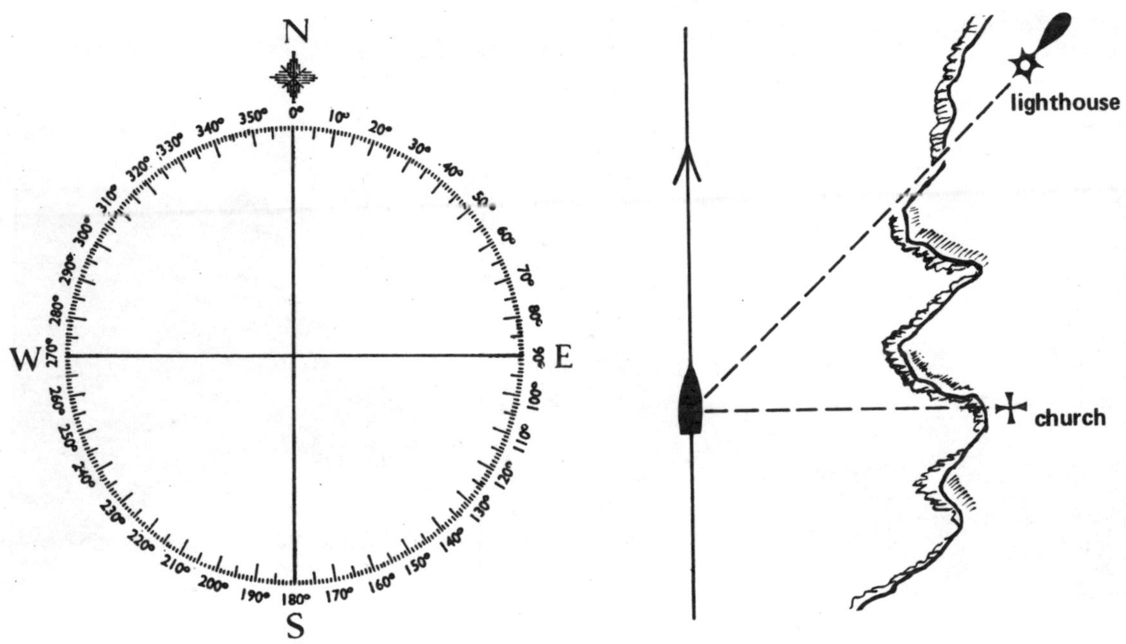

Look at the illustrations carefully and then answer the following questions.

1. How would you i) write this ship's course and ii) express it in words ?
2. What is the bearing of the church from the ship ?
3. What is the bearing of the ship from the church ?

1. i) 000° ii) Only "Zero - zero - zero" is acceptable as the way of expressing it orally.
2. 090°.
3. 270°.

So far we have been ignoring the fact that there are two 'norths': true north and magnetic north. *True north* is the direction towards the geographical North Pole. However, compasses which use a magnet for finding north do not point towards the Geographical North Pole — they point towards the Magnetic North Pole which is at present situated in the Hudson Bay area in Northern Canada.

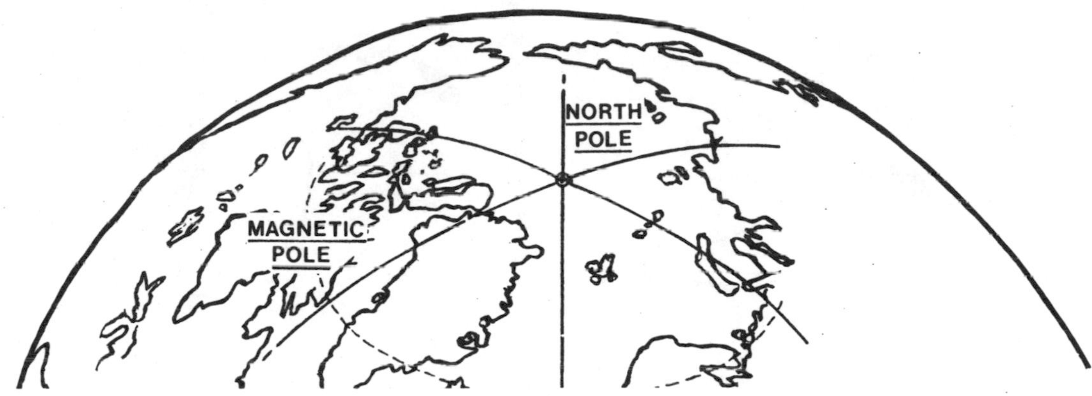

The direction towards the Geographical North Pole is true north; the direction towards the Magnetic Pole is *magnetic north.*

Thus a course can be either a *true course* (measured from true north) or a *magnetic course* (measured from magnetic north).

Every chart has what is known as a compass 'rose' printed on it. When there are two concentric rings, the outer ring represents the true compass, and the inner ring represents the magnetic compass.

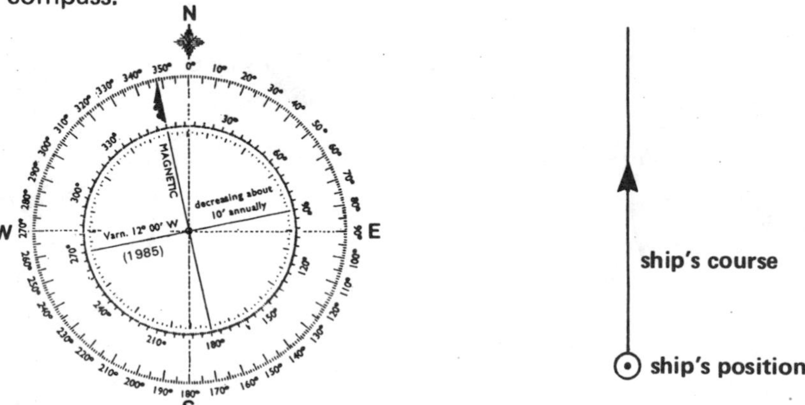

What is the ship's magnetic course, 000° or 012°?

012°

Which of these represents the magnetic bearing of ship A from ship B?

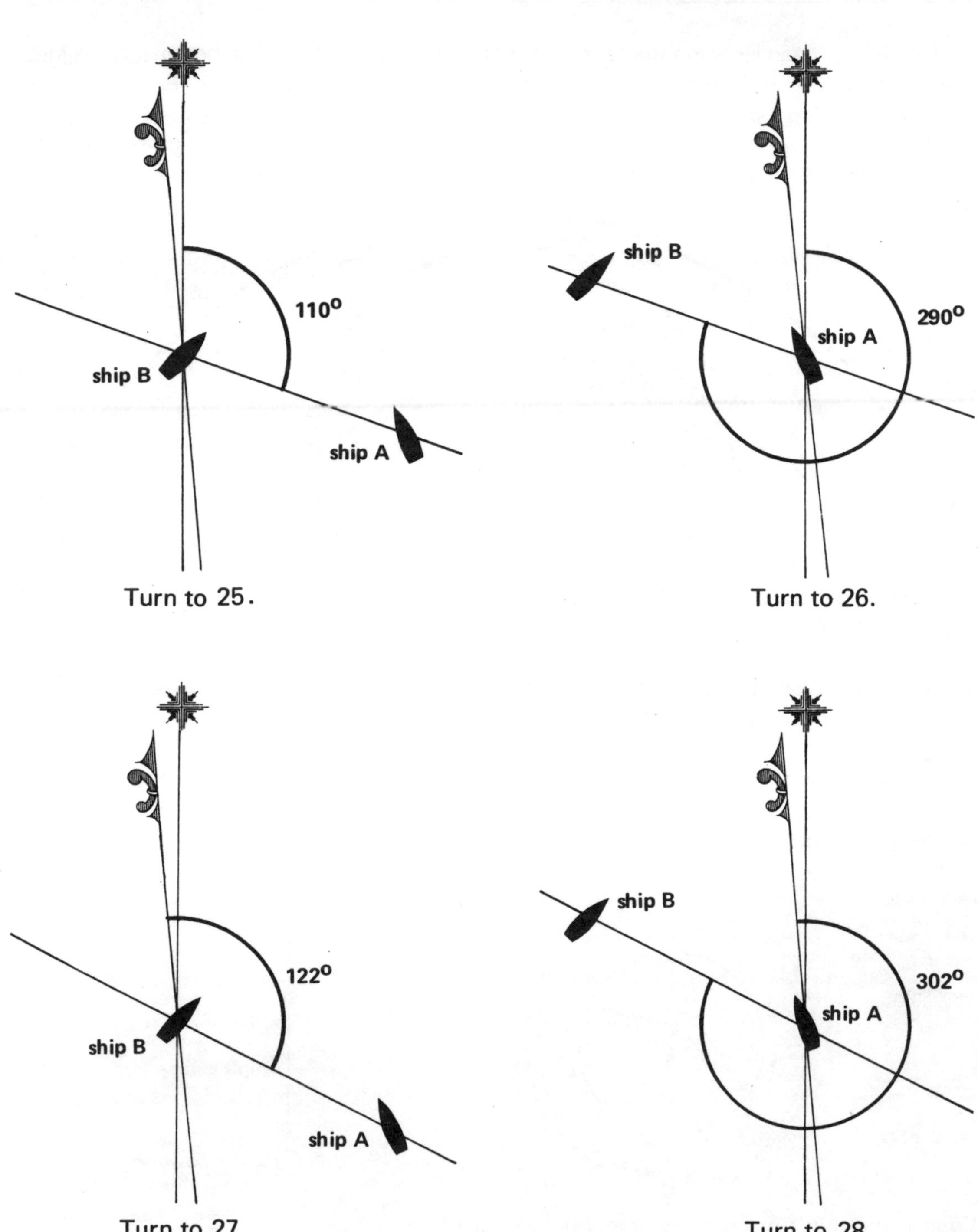

Turn to 25.

Turn to 26.

Turn to 27.

Turn to 28.

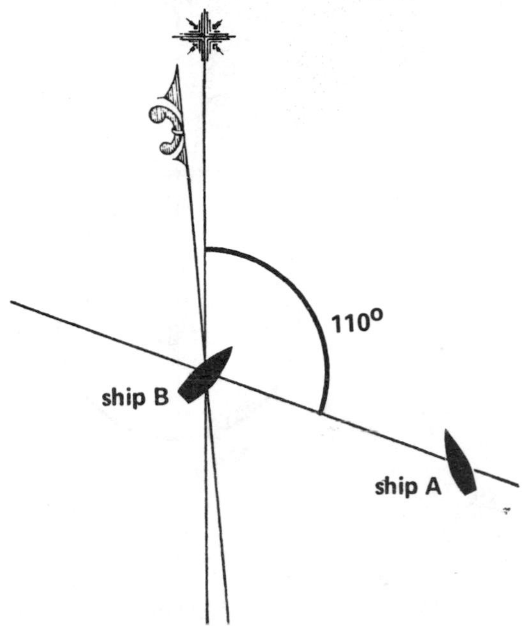

You say that this represents the magnetic bearing of Ship A from Ship B. The magnetic bearing is the angle between the object and magnetic north, not true north as shown in the drawing. So your answer was not correct.

Now which diagram represents the magnetic bearing of Ship A from Ship B?

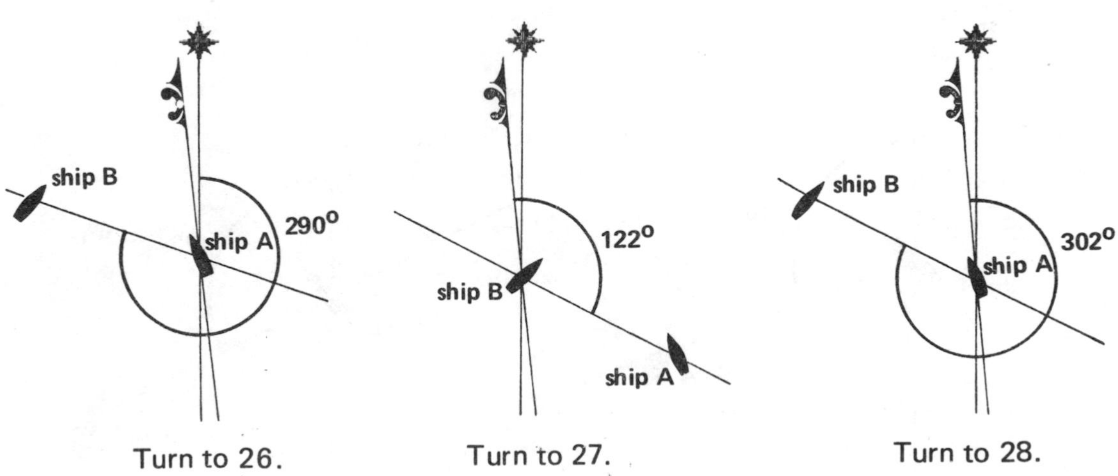

Turn to 26.

Turn to 27.

Turn to 28.

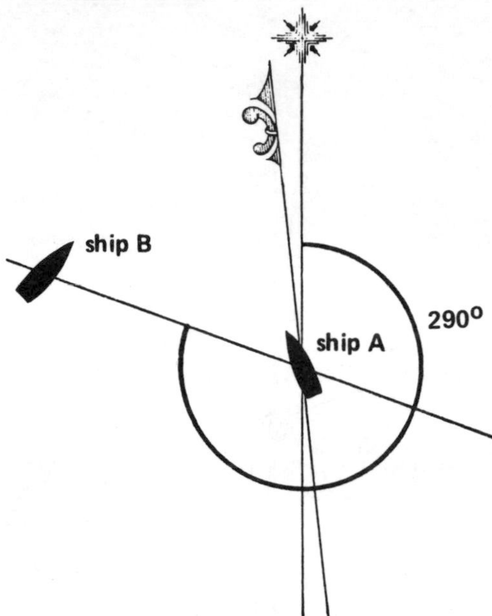

You say that this represents the magnetic bearing of Ship A from Ship B. No, you have made two mistakes here.

If you imagine yourself on Ship B then you would see Ship A to the east of you. The bearing of Ship A must, therefore, be in the region of 090°. Your answer was 290° which you can see is incorrect.

Which of these represents the magnetic bearing of Ship A from Ship B?

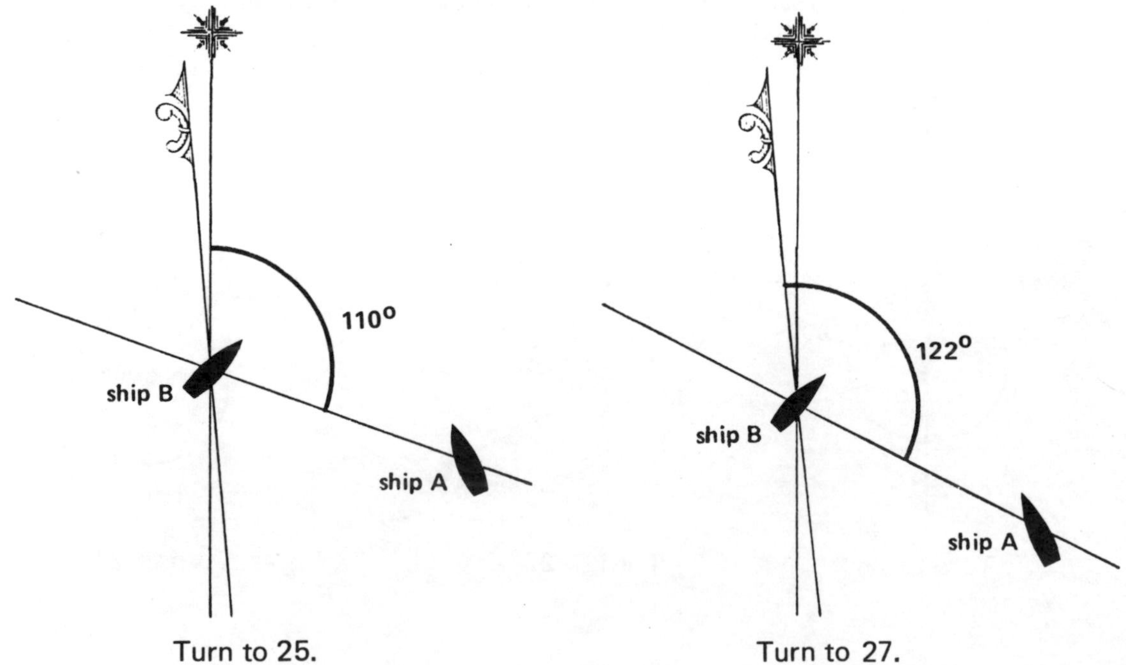

Turn to 25.

Turn to 27.

Good, 122° is the correct answer.

When plotting courses and bearings, you will be making use of a compass rose printed on the chart. On the compass rose to the right you can see the words Varn. 12°00'W. This gives the amount of *variation*, the difference in degrees between true and magnetic.

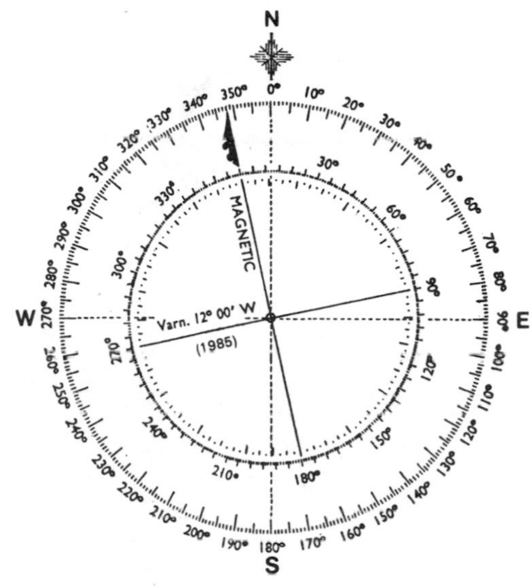

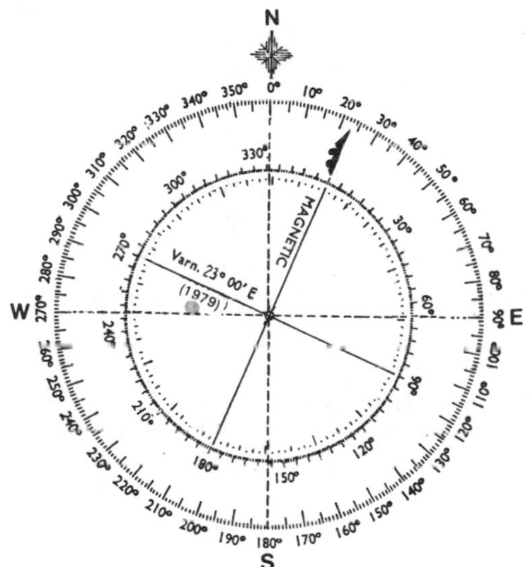

The variation is different in different parts of the world: if you bear in mind that the Magnetic Pole is situated in Northern Canada you can see that this must be so. To the left is a compass rose of Vancouver Island on the west coast of Canada. Here magnetic north lies to the east of true north and the variation is 23°E.

A ship's true course off the coast of Vancouver Island is 180°. What is its magnetic course?

Turn to 29.

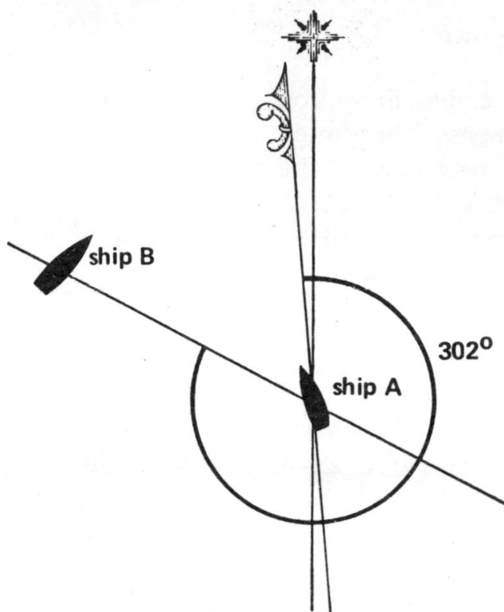

You say that this represents the magnetic bearing of Ship A from Ship B.

If you imagine yourself on Ship B then you would see Ship A to the east of you. The bearing of Ship A must, therefore, be in the region of 090°. Your answer was 302° which you can see is incorrect.

Which of these represents the magnetic bearing of Ship A from Ship B?

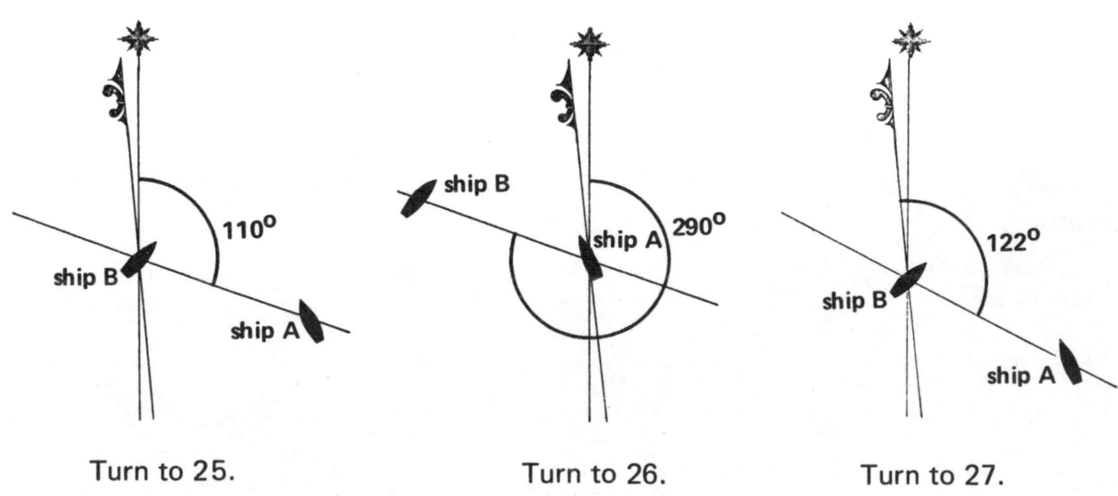

Turn to 25.

Turn to 26.

Turn to 27.

157°

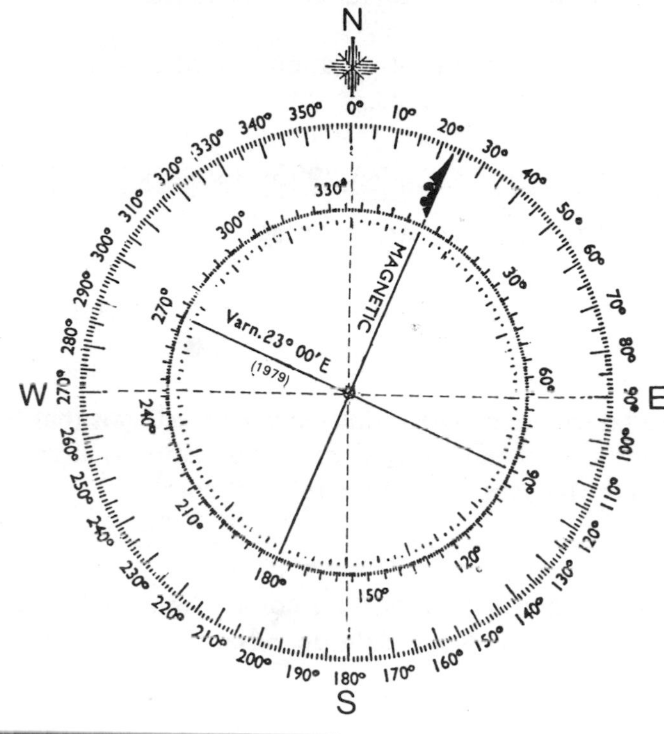

In this case you were able to make a direct reading from the compass rose. But, as you will see, there is more than one correction that has to be made when you are using a magnetic compass so it is best to start by learning a basic rule in these circumstances. For the next few pages let us consider the conversion of a magnetic course to a true course as this is less complicated and, indeed, is more commonly encountered.

As you have just seen, variation can be westerly or easterly.

With a variation of 10° west:

a magnetic course of 010° will be a true course of 000°.

a magnetic course of 290° will be a true course of 280°.

With a variation of 10° east:

a magnetic course of 010° will be a true course of 020°.

a magnetic course of 290° will be a true course of 300°.

What rules can you infer about the conversion of a magnetic course to a true course?

With an easterly variation, the amount of variation is added.

With a westerly variation, the amount of variation is subtracted.

There is a mnemonic (aid to memory) that you will probably find useful: "CADET".

COMPASS TO TRUE ADD EAST C AD E T

So when converting from a magnetic compass reading to a true reading you must add east.

Another factor to be taken into consideration when converting is that the Magnetic Pole is shifting over the years. The amount by which the variation is increasing or decreasing in any area is given on the compass rose of the relevant chart.

Try this problem. The magnetic bearing of a certain light from you is 154° (1985). What is its true bearing? (Use all the data on variation given on the compass rose below.)

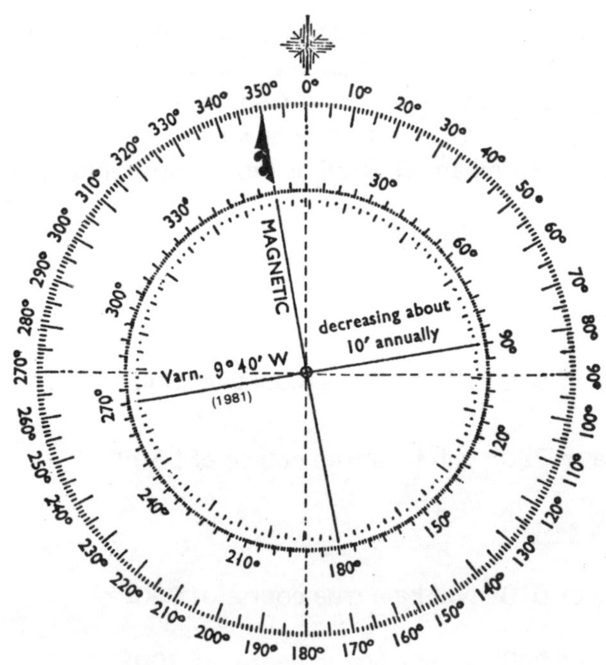

Amount of westerly variation in 1981		9° 40′
Decrease in variation in 4 years (4 x 10′)		0° 40′
Amount of westerly variation in 1985		9° 00′
Magnetic bearing in 1985	154°	
Amount of westerly variation in 1985	9°	
True bearing	145°	

The direction in which the compass needle points is called compass north, and a reading is followed by (C). With a ship's magnetic compass this will not be the same as magnetic north because the ship as a whole possesses a magnetic field: the magnetic compass is always carefully sited on the ship, but nevertheless it will be affected by the iron and steel of the ship's structure.

The difference between compass north and magnetic north is called the *deviation.* The deviation can be reduced to some extent by attaching counteracting magnets to the compass. But some deviation will still remain and has to be taken into account when converting compass readings.

In each of these drawings state which of the angles is the deviation. (State whether easterly or westerly.)

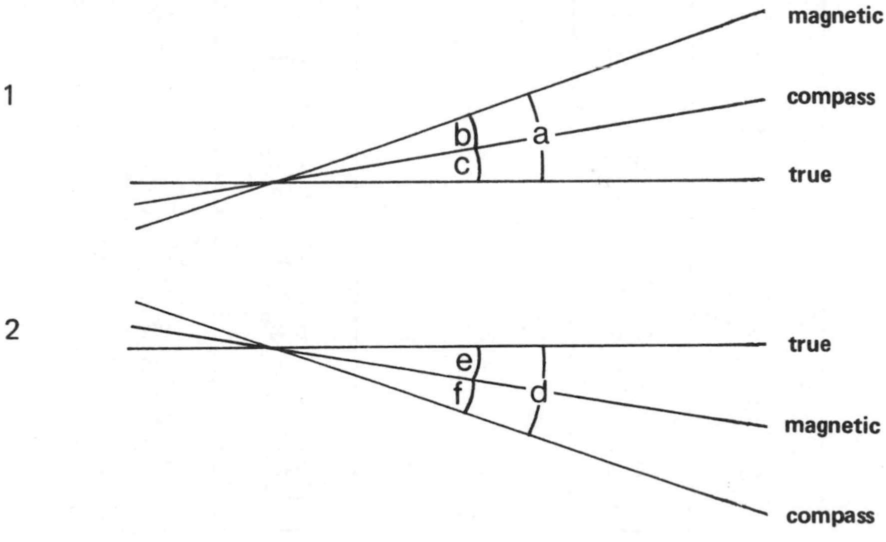

1. b) Easterly. 2. f) Easterly.

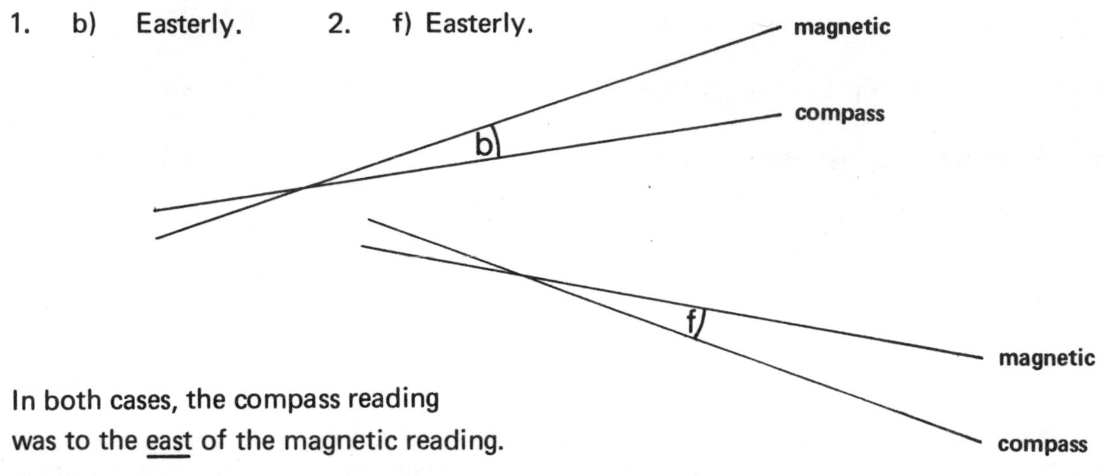

In both cases, the compass reading was to the east of the magnetic reading.

Because of the effect of the ship's magnetic field, the deviation will change for every change of course. Each magnetic compass has its own deviation table – such as the one below – and this shows the deviation for different headings of the ship. Note that the deviation table gives the deviation for the compass heading of the ship. In corrections for deviation the CADET rule also applies.

Ship's Head (Compass)	Deviation
000°	2°W
010°	4°W
020°	5°W
030°	7°W
040°	9°W
050°	11°W
060°	12°W
070°	13°W
080°	14°W
090°	13°W
100°	12°W
110°	11°W
120°	10°W
130°	9°W
140°	8°W
150°	7°W
160°	5°W
170°	3°W

Ship's Head (Compass)	Deviation
180°	0°
190°	3°E
200°	5°E
210°	7°E
220°	9°E
230°	11°E
240°	12°E
250°	13°E
260°	14°E
270°	13°E
280°	12°E
290°	11°E
300°	10°E
310°	9°E
320°	7°E
330°	5°E
340°	3°E
350°	1°E

The heading of the ship is 170°(C). The compass bearing of a distant church tower is 155°(C). What is its magnetic bearing? (Use the deviation table above.)

152°.

Bearings and courses are always true unless otherwise stated. For example,

102°	means 102° true.
102°(M)	means 102° magnetic.
102°(C)	means 102° compass.

For what two errors do you have to correct the compass course (or bearing) when converting to true?

Correction must be made for both variation and deviation.

In both these corrections the CADET rule applies:

COMPASS TO TRUE ADD EAST C AD E T

There is a useful way of combining both corrections in a single calculation. Draw up five columns in your notebook and head each column as shown below.

Compass course or bearing	Deviation	Magnetic course or bearing	Variation	True course or bearing
115°	2°E		9°W	
		117°		108°

The illustration shows you how to convert a compass bearing of 115° to true, given a deviation of 2°E and a variation of 9°W. The first step is to enter the figures in the appropriate columns. Working from left to right, you first apply the deviation in order to calculate the magnetic bearing, and then apply the variation to arrive at the true bearing.

Now try the following problems using this method.

1. Your compass course is 348°(C). What is your true course? (Variation 11°E. Deviation ½°E.)
2. The bearing of a distant church tower is 085°(C). What is the true bearing? (Variation 9°W. Deviation 1½°E.)

1. 359½°. 2. 077½°.

Check your working:

Compass	Deviation	Magnetic	Variation	True
348°	½°E		11°E	
		348½°		359½°
085°	1½°E		9°W	
		086½°		077½°

Now for some more complicated examples. Remember to use the <u>compass</u> heading of the ship to find the deviation. Note also that the <u>total</u> variation must be calculated.

1. The heading of the ship is 120° (C). According to your compass the bearing of an object is 323°(C). What is the true bearing? (Variation is 10°W (1979) decreasing 10′ annually. The year is 1985).

2. The heading of the ship is 195°(C). What is the true course? (Variation is 18°E (1975) increasing 5′ annually. The year is 1985.)

Ship's Head (Compass)	Deviation
000°	2°W
010°	4°W
020°	5°W
030°	7°W
040°	9°W
050°	11°W
060°	12°W
070°	13°W
080°	14°W
090°	13°W
100°	12°W
110°	11°W
120°	10°W
130°	9°W
140°	8°W
150°	7°W
160°	5°W
170°	3°W

Ship's Head (Compass)	Deviation
180°	0°
190°	3°E
200°	5°E
210°	7°E
220°	9°E
230°	11°E
240°	12°E
250°	13°E
260°	14°E
270°	13°E
280°	12°E
290°	11°E
300°	10°E
310°	9°E
320°	7°E
330°	5°E
340°	3°E
350°	1°E

1. 304°   2. 218° (or, more precisely, 217°50′).

Check your working:

Compass	Deviation	Magnetic	Variation	True
323°	10°W		9°W	
		313°		304°
195°	4°E		18°50′E	
		199°		217°50′

So far you have been converting compass courses and compass bearings to true. For converting from true to compass the opposite of the CADET rule applies; it also means that you must work from right to left in making your calculation.

1. According to your chart the bearing of one mark from another is 077°. If the variation is 8°W and the deviation is 1°W, what is the compass bearing?

2. If the true bearing of an object is 055° what is the compass bearing? (Deviation 1°E. Variation 11°W.)

1. 086°. 2. 065°.

Check your working:

Compass	Deviation	Magnetic	Variation	True
	1°W		8°W	077°
086°		085°		
	1°E		11°W	055°
065°		066°		

(Remember that the opposite of the CADET rule applies here.)

The method of setting out your working that we have advised you to use is helpful when you are learning how to do compass conversions. However, the navigator should be able to make rapid conversions, and so this method can be discarded once you are fully conversant with the principles behind conversions.

The last examples required you to convert true bearings to compass bearings. Converting a true course to a compass course is not so straightforward. To see why, let us consider how we obtain our figures.

1. Where would you look for the figure for the variation?

2. Where would you look for the figure for the deviation?

3. What item of information must you know before obtaining the figure for the deviation?

1. On a chart – or more precisely, from a compass rose on a chart.
2. On a deviation table.
3. The compass heading of the ship.

In converting from true course to compass course we have a problem. We cannot obtain the figure for the deviation without knowing the compass heading of the ship – but this is in fact what we are wanting to calculate!

Ship's Head (Compass)	Deviation
000°	2°W
010°	4°W
020°	5°W
030°	7°W
040°	9°W
050°	11°W
060°	12°W
070°	13°W
080°	14°W
090°	13°W
100°	12°W
110°	11°W
120°	10°W
130°	9°W
140°	8°W
150°	7°W
160°	5°W
170°	3°W

Ship's Head (Compass)	Deviation
180°	0°
190°	3°E
200°	5°E
210°	7°E
220°	9°E
230°	11°E
240°	12°E
250°	13°E
260°	14°E
270°	13°E
280°	12°E
290°	11°E
300°	10°E
310°	9°E
320°	7°E
330°	5°E
340°	3°E
350°	1°E

If we could read off the correct deviation in some other way our problem would be solved. To see how, consider what happens when we add or subtract the appropriate deviation to or from the ship's head (C). What do we get?

The magnetic course.

The problem is consequently overcome by using a deviation table in which deviations are given for the ship's magnetic course. This has been done in the third column of the deviation table below. (You may find that deviation cards in use at sea have not yet been converted to have a third column.)

Ship's Head (Compass)	Deviation	Ship's Head (Magnetic)
000°	2°W	358°
010°	4°W	006°
020°	5°W	015°
030°	7°W	023°
040°	9°W	031°
050°	11°W	039°
060°	12°W	048°
070°	13°W	057°
080°	14°W	066°
090°	13°W	077°
100°	12°W	088°
110°	11°W	099°
120°	10°W	110°
130°	9°W	121°
140°	8°W	132°
150°	7°W	143°
160°	5°W	155°
170°	3°W	167°

Ship's Head (Compass)	Deviation	Ship's Head (Magnetic)
180°	0°	180°
190°	3°E	193°
200°	5°E	205°
210°	7°E	217°
220°	9°E	229°
230°	11°E	241°
240°	12°E	252°
250°	13°E	263°
260°	14°E	274°
270°	13°E	283°
280°	12°E	292°
290°	11°E	301°
300°	10°E	310°
310°	9°E	319°
320°	7°E	327°
330°	5°E	335°
340°	3°E	343°
350°	1°E	351°

If your course is 325° and variation is 8°W what is your compass course?

327½° (C). (Ship's head (M) is 325° + 8° = 333°. Deviation is 5½°E.)

Remember that you do not need this system when converting from ship's head (C) to ship's head (T), because you can read off the correct deviation straightaway against ship's head (C).

If you think that you are quite competent at making compass reading conversions, turn to page 41 now.

If you feel that you need more practice, try the following questions. (Use the deviation table below where necessary.)

1. Convert a compass course of 105°(C) to true, given a variation of 14°E.
2. Convert a true course of 300° to compass, given a variation of 10°W.
3. Convert a compass bearing of 120°(C) to true, given a variation of 9°W and a compass course of 180°(C).
4. Convert a true bearing of 333° to compass, given a variation of 15°W (1972) increasing 10′ annually. The year is 1985 and the compass course if 090°.

Ship's Head (Compass)	Deviation	Ship's Head (Magnetic)
000°	2°W	358°
010°	4°W	006°
020°	5°W	015°
030°	7°W	023°
040°	9°W	031°
050°	11°W	039°
060°	12°W	048°
070°	13°W	057°
080°	14°W	066°
090°	13°W	077°
100°	12°W	088°
110°	11°W	099°
120°	10°W	110°
130°	9°W	121°
140°	8°W	132°
150°	7°W	143°
160°	5°W	155°
170°	3°W	167°

Ship's Head (Compass)	Deviation	Ship's Head (Magnetic)
180°	0°	180°
190°	3°E	193°
200°	5°E	205°
210°	7°E	217°
220°	9°E	229°
230°	11°E	241°
240°	12°E	252°
250°	13°E	263°
260°	14°E	274°
270°	13°E	283°
280°	12°E	292°
290°	11°E	301°
300°	10°E	310°
310°	9°E	319°
320°	7°E	327°
330°	5°E	335°
340°	3°E	343°
350°	1°E	351°

1. 107½°.
2. 300°(C).
3. 111°.
4. 003°(C) (or more precisely 003°10′ (C)).

Answers from page 40.

The only compass you are likely to have met is The Magnetic Compass that consists of a freely suspended magnetic needle mounted on a compass card. This type of compass, with the needle floating in liquid to give it stability, is still found in modern ships (as a secondary compass) and in ships' boats. Its disadvantage is that the needle oscillates while the ship is turning.

The *gyro-magnetic compass* works on the same principle as the magnetic compass, but in addition it uses a gyroscope for damping the oscillation. The magnetic compass and the Admiralty gyro-magnetic compass (AGMC) both point to magnetic north.

Do you have to make a correction for deviation with a gyro-magnetic compass?

Yes, because it is a form of magnetic compass. (The corrections are achieved by means of the datec unit.)

The main compass used by ships today, the *gyro-compass*, works on a different principle altogether from the other two. It uses a free gyroscope, but for a different purpose than in a gyro-magnetic compass.

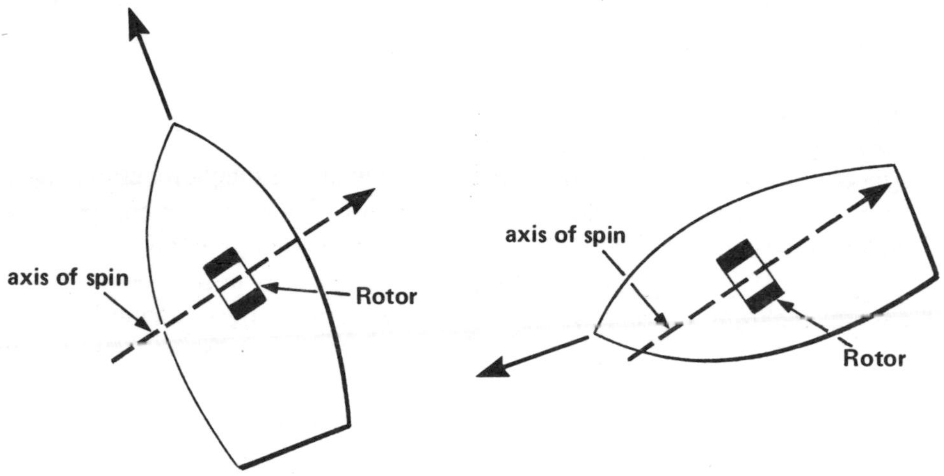

The axis of spin of a free gyroscope will maintain the same direction in space when the rotor is spun at a sufficiently high speed. The supporting frame may be turned this way and that – but the axis of spin will stay pointing in the same direction.

This special property of a free gyroscope is known as 'stability in space'. It can be utilized in a compass if a suitable settling position is found for the axis of the rotor. What position would you suggest?

It should be aligned with a point on the horizon which lies in the direction of true north.

The magnetic compass points to magnetic north.

The gyro-magnetic compass points to magnetic north.

The gyro-compass points to true north.

The last statement may not always be strictly true. The gyro-compass is a complex instrument, and there are a number of reasons why it may not point exactly to true north. If the compass does not point exactly to true north, then it is said to be reading either 'high' or 'low'.

The diagrams below show both situations. In one case the gyro-compass north lies to the west of true north; in the other it lies to the east.

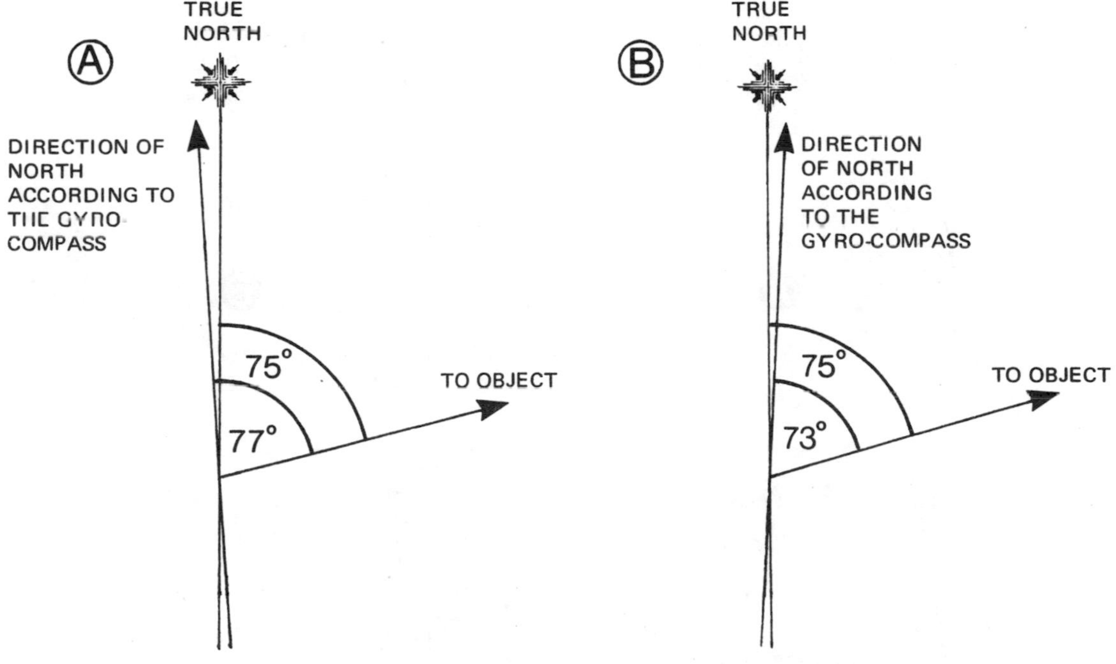

Bearing of object by gyro	= 077°	Bearing of object by gyro	= 073°
True bearing	= 075°	True bearing	= 075°

In which case is the gyro-reading high, and in which case is it low?

A – Error = 2° high.

B – Error = 2° low.

This section has not dealt with the actual workings of these compasses. Chapters VIII and IX of *Admiralty Manual of Navigation, Volume I* provide full information on the subject.

Section 2 : Self-test

1. How many feet are there in a nautical mile (International)?
2. How long is a cable?
3. What is meant by 'true north' and 'magnetic north' ?
4. What is the true bearing of the church tower from your present position?

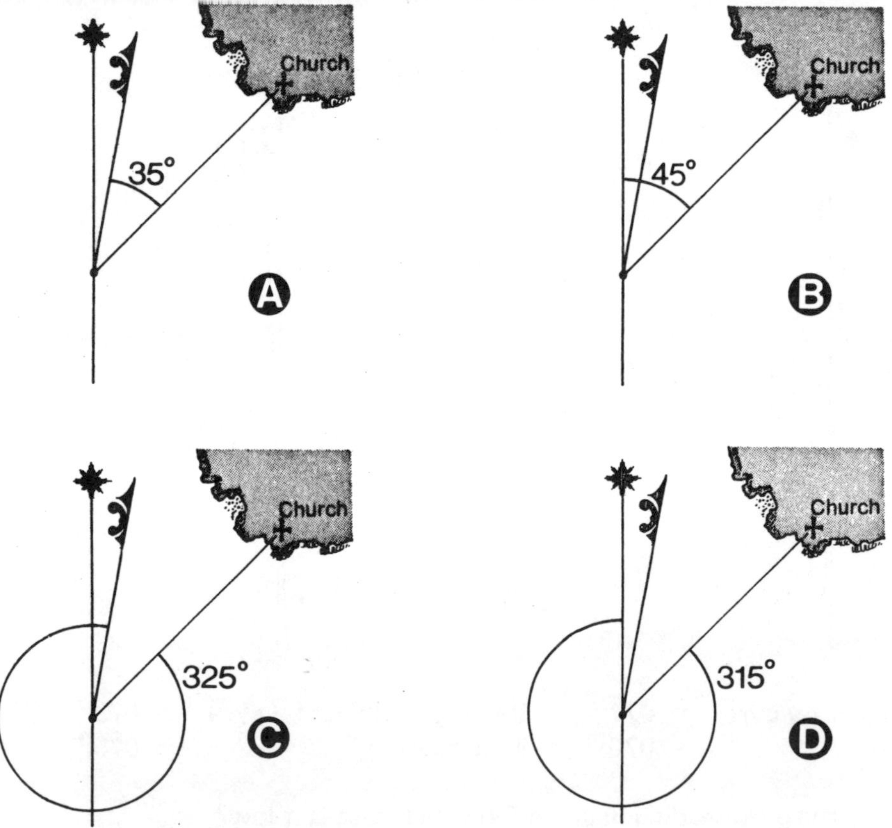

5. What two corrections must be made to a reading from a magnetic compass to convert it to a true reading?

6. Define variation and deviation.
7. To what is deviation attributable?
8. Where does one obtain i) the variation ii) the deviation?
9.

i) The ship's true course is 125°. Work out the compass course, given a variation of 4° E.

ii) The compass bearing (1985) of a distant object is 087° (C). What is the true bearing? Variation is 12° 00′W(1980) decreasing 8′ annually. The heading of the ship is 110° (C).

Ship's Head (Compass)	Deviation	Ship's Head (Magnetic)
000°	2°W	358°
010°	4°W	006°
020°	5°W	015°
030°	7°W	023°
040°	9°W	031°
050°	11°W	039°
060°	12°W	048°
070°	13°W	057°
080°	14°W	066°
090°	13°W	077°
100°	12°W	088°
110°	11°W	099°
120°	10°W	110°
130°	9°W	121°
140°	8°W	132°
150°	7°W	143°
160°	5°W	155°
170°	3°W	167°

Ship's Head (Compass)	Deviation	Ship's Head (Magnetic)
180°	0°	180°
190°	3°E	193°
200°	5°E	205°
210°	7°E	217°
220°	9°E	229°
230°	11°E	241°
240°	12°E	252°
250°	13°E	263°
260°	14°E	274°
270°	13°E	283°
280°	12°E	292°
290°	11°E	301°
300°	10°E	310°
310°	9°E	319°
320°	7°E	327°
330°	5°E	335°
340°	3°E	343°
350°	1°E	351°

Now turn to page 46 for the answers.

Section 2 : Answers to Self-test

1. 6076 feet.
2. 200 yards (approximately), or a tenth of a nautical (or sea) mile.
3. True north is the direction towards the Geographical North Pole. Magnetic north is the direction towards the Magnetic North Pole.
4. 045°.
5. Corrections for variation and deviation.
6. Variation is the difference (in degrees) between the true meridian and magnetic meridian. Deviation is the difference (in degrees) between a compass reading and magnetic meridian.
7. Deviation is caused by the presence of various magnetic fields (iron and steel) in the ship.
8. i) Variation is obtained from the chart.
   ii) Deviation is obtained from the deviation table.
9. i) 130^{o}(C).
   ii) 064° 30′ (or more precisely 064°40′).

Section 3: Mercator and Gnomonic Projections

The navigating officer's task is to plan a safe passage for the ship and ensure that this plan is followed. To do this he has to plot the position, course and speed of the ship on the chart.

The ship's true course is the angle between the direction of true north and the ship's fore-and-aft line. When it is plotted on the chart it cuts all meridians at the same angle, and in addition it cuts parallels of latitude at the same angle (drawing 1). A line that does this is called a *rhumb line.*

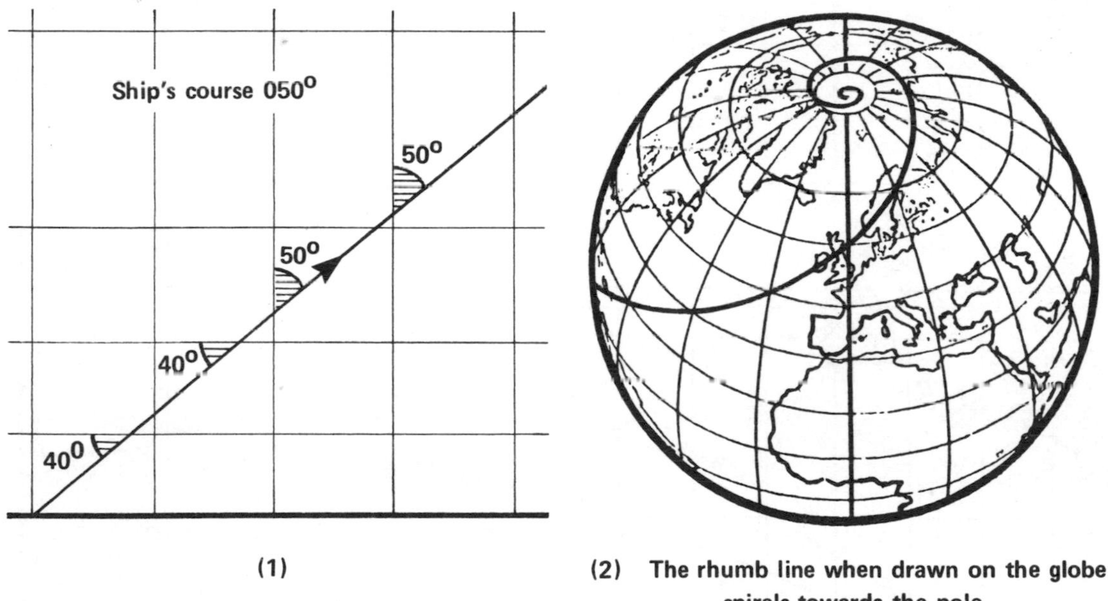

(1)

(2) **The rhumb line when drawn on the globe spirals towards the pole.**

If drawn on a globe a rhumb line would appear as a curved line spiralling towards the pole (drawing 2).

What will be the most convenient type of chart for navigational use?

A chart where a rhumb line is represented as a straight line.

A chart where a rhumb line is represented as a curve.

It doesn't matter.

Choose the correct answer.

A chart where a rhumb line is represented as a straight line.

This is convenient for the navigator because it enables him to show the track of his ship by drawing straight lines between starting point, turning points and destination, and then measure the courses he must steer. There are certain projections where the rhumb line would not be represented as a straight line, and any chart based on one of these projections would not be suitable for plotting courses.

Unfortunately the rhumb line does not represent the shortest distance between two points on the Earth's surface. The shortest track between two points on a sphere is the great circle. The difference between the distances along a great circle and a rhumb line is considerable across a large stretch of ocean.

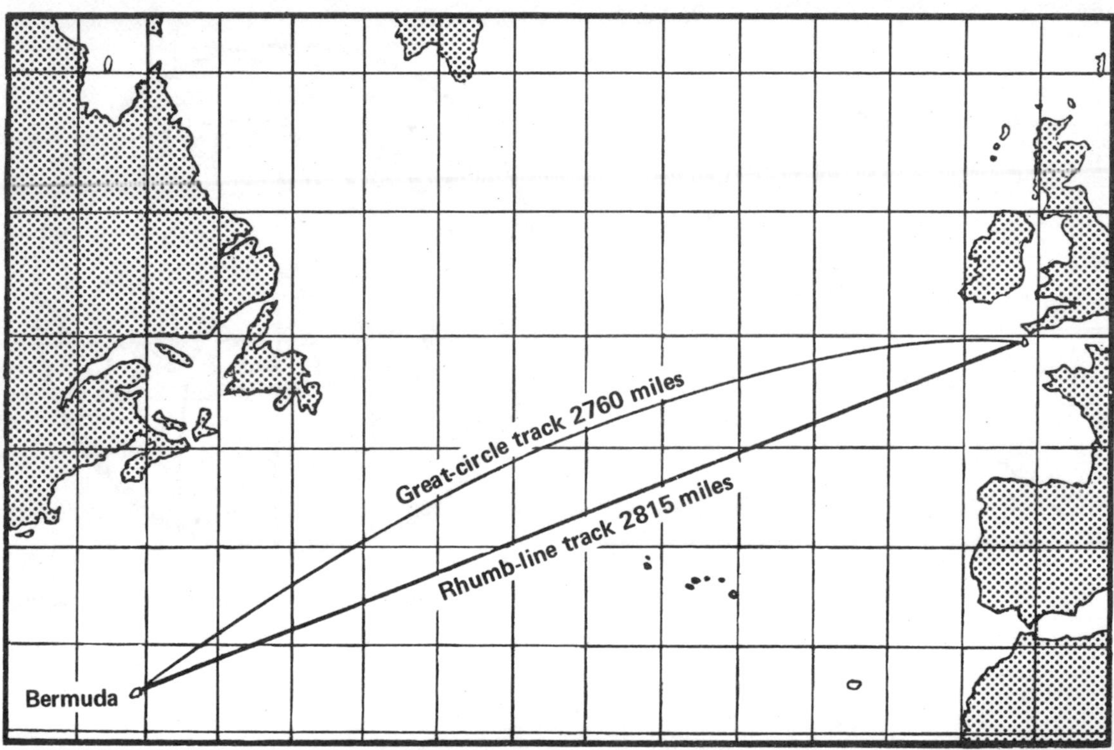

Example of Mercator projection

Would the heading of a ship vary or remain constant when following:

a) A rhumb-line track?

b) A great-circle track?

Along (a) it would remain constant; along (b) it would vary.

Since a great circle joining two places on the Earth's surface is the shortest distance between them, this track is used not only by navigators but also by airline pilots. The great circle is, incidentally, also the path travelled by radio waves.

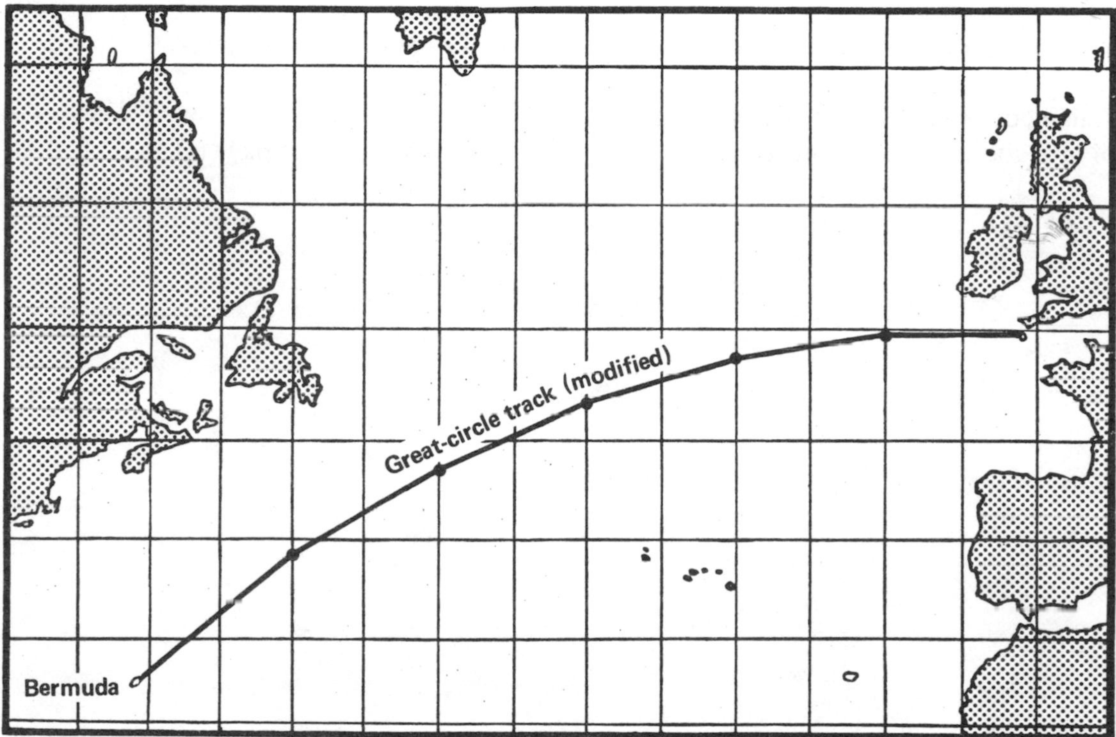

The ship's track is never plotted as a curve, so in practice the ship follows a modified great-circle track. Thus the great-circle track is divided into suitable lengths, successive points on the great circle being joined to form a sucession of ______ ______.

rhumb lines

What is the best definition of a rhumb line?

A straight line between two points. → Turn to page 51.

The shortest distance between two points. → Turn to page 52.

A line cutting meridians and parallels of latitude at the same angle. → Turn to page 53.

You say that a rhumb line is a straight line between two points. This is how it is represented on a Mercator projection but not on all projections.

There is a better definition of a rhumb line. Turn back to page 50 and choose the definition that you think is more exact.

No, a rhumb line is not the shortest distance between two points – this is the great circle joining them. Though it may be difficult to picture, a ship taking the shortest possible track between two places would have to take a slightly curved track.

Turn back to page 50 and choose another answer.

Yes, a rhumb line is a line cutting all meridians at the same angle, and all parallels of latitude at the same angle. (It is a straight line on some, but not all, projections.)

Navigational charts also need to show lines of latitude and longitude: these provide a grid on which the navigator can identify the ship's position.

In addition, the latitude scale is important to the navigator for another reason. Can you remember what it is?

The latitude scale on a chart is used for measuring distance. (1 minute of latitude = 1 sea mile.)

____

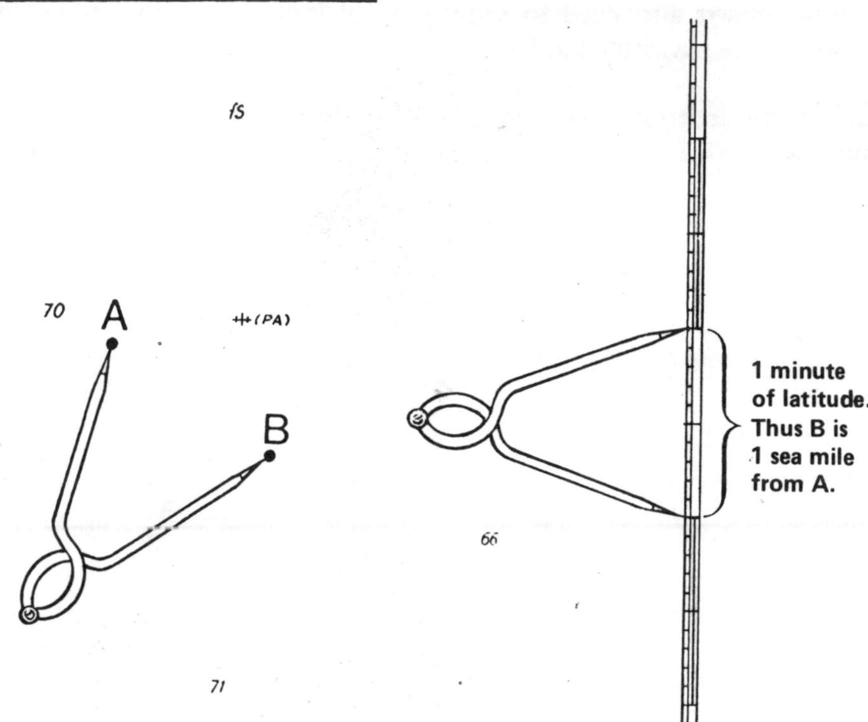

It is done in this way. Let's say you want to measure the distance between A and B on a chart. Using a pair of dividers, you find how far apart they are and then transfer the dividers to the latitude scale to find what distance this represents.

To be suitable for navigational purposes, the chart must be based on a projection that allows bearings to be accurately measured. The navigator needs to take it for granted that he can represent a visual bearing of, say 355°, by a line on a chart drawn at an angle of 355°.

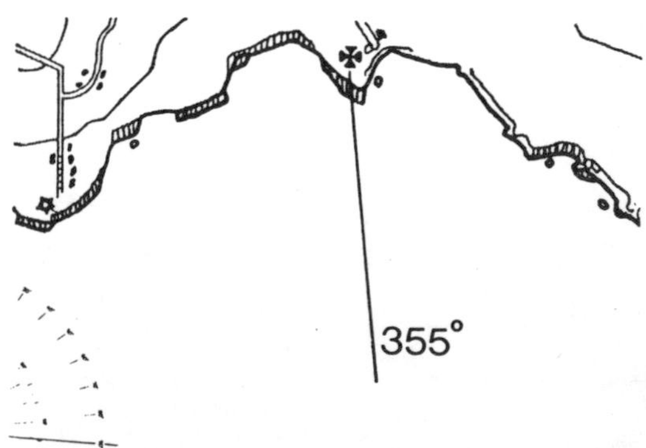

So another requirement of a chart is that it must enable __________ to be accurately measured.

The most commonly used charts are those based on the Mercator projection, which we will now examine. The Mercator projection, like all projections, is one particular solution to the problem of representing a spherical surface on a two-dimensional piece of paper. To see how the Mercator chart copes with this problem, compare it with the drawing of the globe.

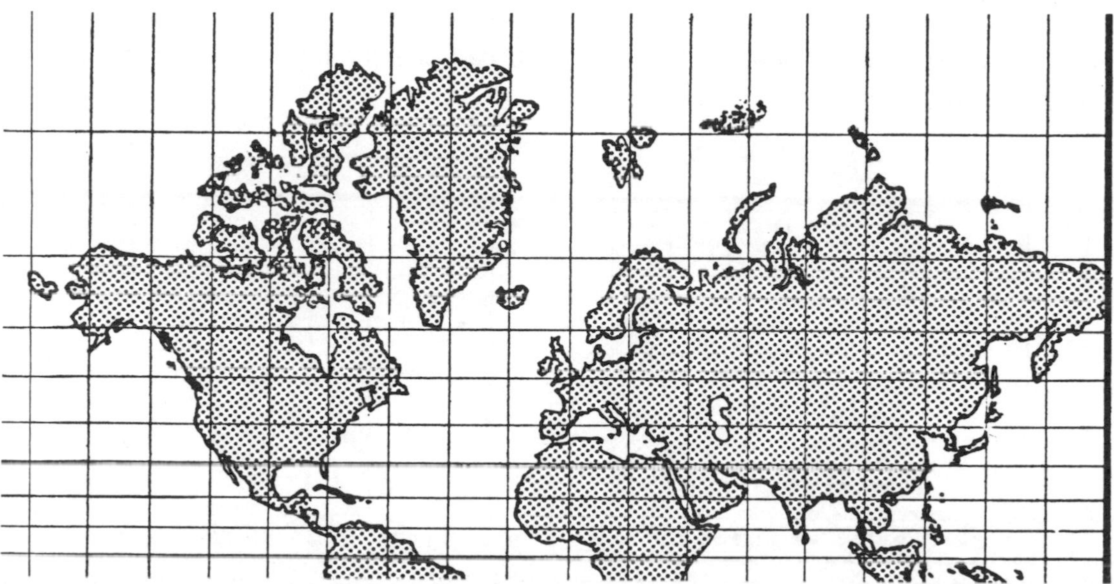

Mercator projection

1. How are the parallels of latitude and the meridians represented by the Mercator projection?

2. What do you notice on the Mercator projection about the spacing of:

   a) the meridians?

   b) the parallels of latitude?

1. The meridians and parallels of latitude are represented as straight lines.
2. a) The meridians are spaced equally.
   b) The parallels of latitude are spaced at increasing intervals towards the poles.

On the globe the meridians converge towards the poles. On a Mercator chart, however, they are represented as being parallel to each other. This means that the further north or south of the Equator a land mass is situated, the more it is distorted in an east-west direction. Ultimately, the pole (which is a point) is shown as the whole width of the chart, while Greenland becomes three times as broad as it should be, and appears almost as large as Africa.

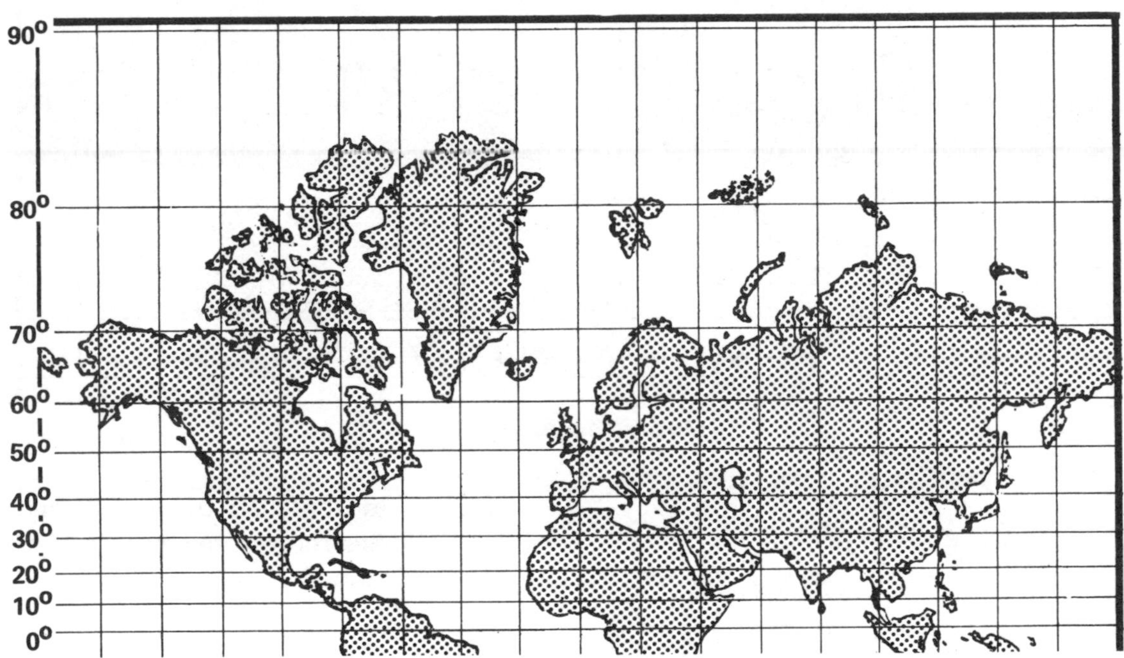

A Mercator projection has the parallels of latitude spaced at increasing intervals towards the poles. This has the effect of reducing the distortion of land masses in shape and size.

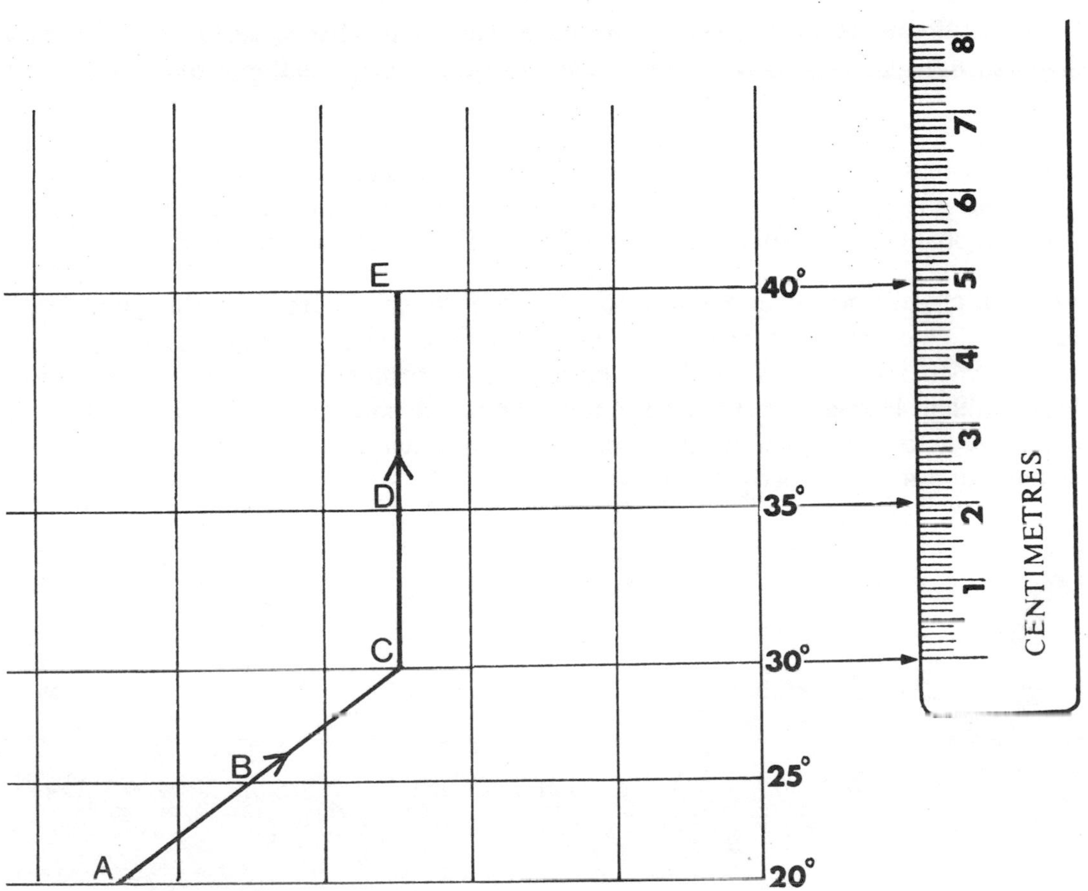

The latitude scale on the Mercator chart is used for measuring distance. But some qualification should be made to this statement. The drawing above represents a Mercator projection and shows the parallels of latitude spaced at increasing intervals towards the poles. As you can see, the actual distances from C to D and from D to E are the same: 300′ (i.e. 5° x 60). But the ruler measures 2 cm from C to D, and 2·8cm from D to E. This is because of the spacing of the lines of latitude on a Mercator chart.

Thus one can say that the latitude scale on a Mercator chart does give the correct distances between places, as long as one proviso is made. What is this proviso?

On a Mercator chart the latitude scale measures correct distances <u>only for places in that latitude.</u>

All the requirements mentioned so far for navigational charts could be adequately satisfied by a blank chart! But of course there are certain obvious things that charts must show.

Charts are maps of the sea, and you will naturally expect very full information from them about the sea itself. Of prime importance are the navigational hazards. Rocks, wrecks, mudbanks, sandbanks etc. must be included on a navigational chart.

On coastal charts you will also expect to see part of the land portrayed, though not in as much detail as on an Ordnance Survey map. From the navigator's point of view, coastal features which are conspicuous from the sea are important. For instance on the chart below, Gullane House is marked <u>conspic</u> (meaning conspicuous) indicating that it is a suitable mark for taking a visual bearing. On the other hand Gullane village is not shown in detail, nor are all the roads and tracks.

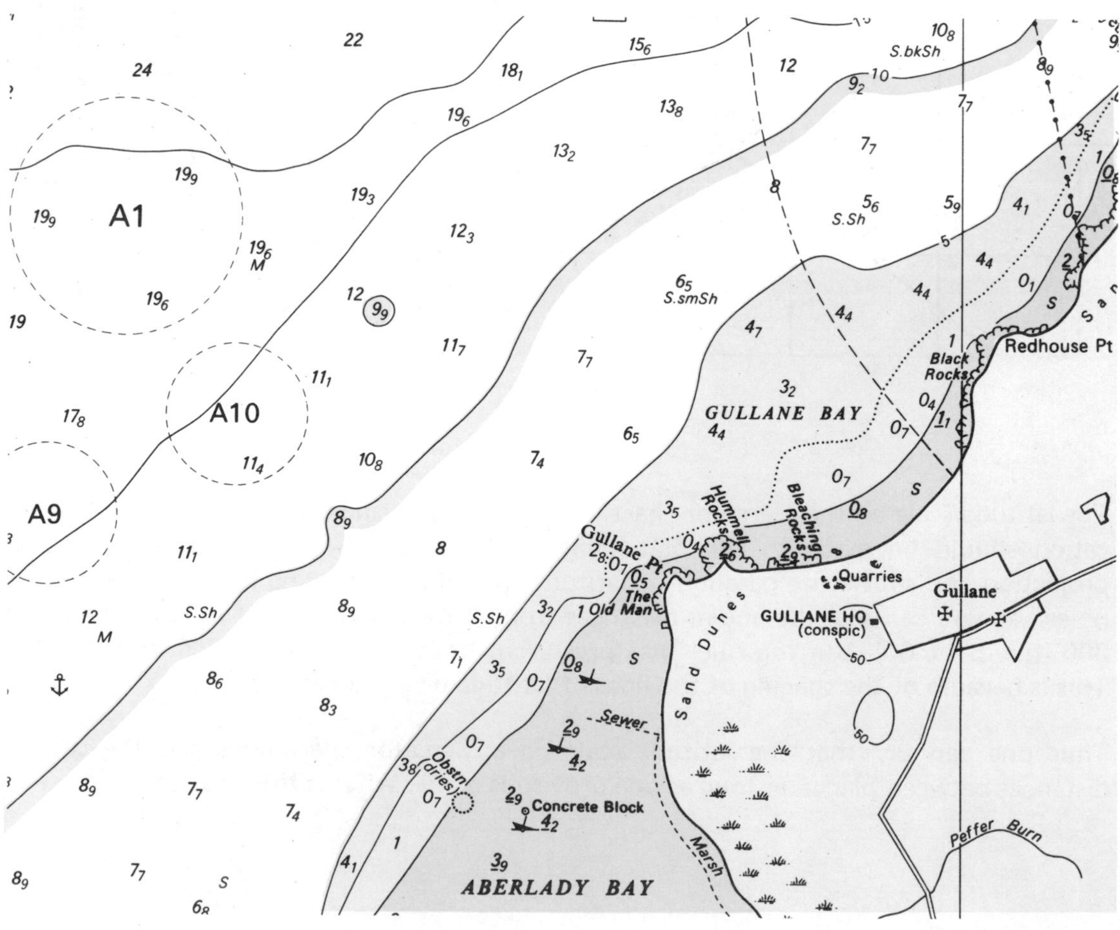

If we summarise what is required of a chart for it to be suitable for navigational purposes, we find that the Mercator projection meets all these requirements.

So you should be able to complete the following characteristics of a chart drawn on the Mercator projection.

1. The ________ ________ appear as straight lines. (For representing the ship's course).

2. It shows ____________ and _________. (For providing a grid on which the ship's position can be identified.)

3. It has a distance scale.

4. It enables __________ to be measured. (For fixing the ship's position.)

5. It shows features of land visible from the sea.

6. It shows all navigational hazards.

The full list is:

1. The rhumb lines appear as straight lines.
2. It shows latitude and longitude.
3. It has a distance scale.
4. It enables bearings to be measured.
5. It shows features of land visible from the sea.
6. It shows all navigational hazards.

How are the following represented on a Mercator chart?

a) lines of latitude.

b) lines of longitude.

c) rhumb lines.

d) great circles.

a) straight lines.

b) straight lines.

c) straight lines.

d) curved lines.

Though the Mercator chart is suitable for most navigational purposes, there are some cases where another projection, the *Gnomonic* (pronounced nom-on-ic) projection, is required. For instance, in order to assist the navigator in finding the great-circle track between two places, there are specially constructed Gnomonic charts where any straight line drawn on them represents a great circle. Rhumb lines are not straight and angles are distorted, and it is, therefore, impossible to take courses and distances from a Gnomonic chart. A great-circle track obtained from one of these charts must be transferred to a Mercator chart for navigational use. (For more information on these two projections refer to *Admiralty Manual of Navigation, Volume I*).

Mercator charts cannot accurately represent the Polar regions, as you remember, and so Polar charts are drawn on the Gnomonic projection with the pole as the tangent point.

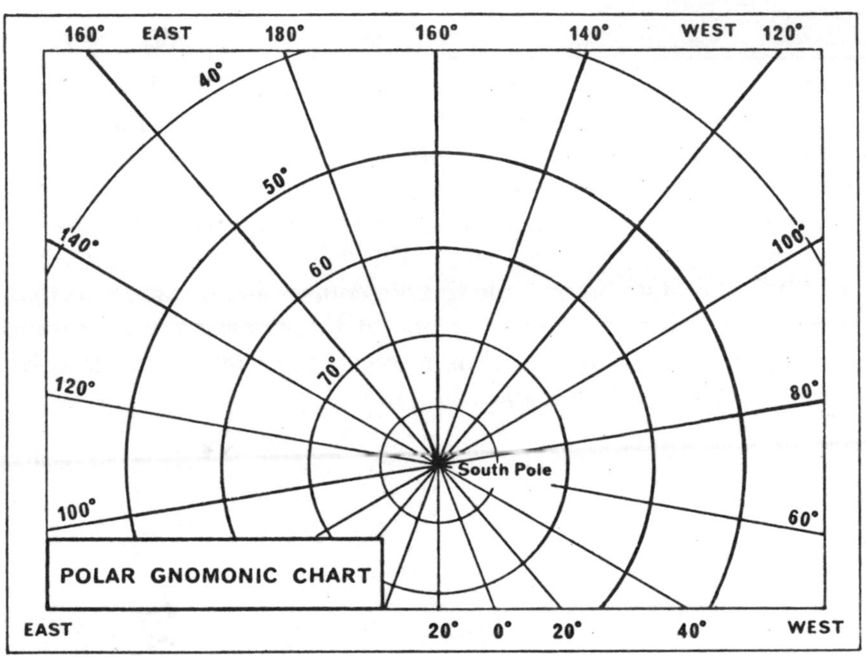

1. Taking the chart above as an example of a Gnomonic chart:
   i) how are lines of latitude represented?
   ii) how are lines of longitude represented?

2. i) How are great-circle tracks represented on a Gnomonic chart?
   ii) How are rhumb lines represented on a Gnomonic chart?

1. i) Lines of latitude – as curves (circles).
   ii) Lines of longitude – as straight lines converging to the poles.

2. i) Great-circle tracks – as straight lines.
   ii) Rhumb lines – as curves.

(The properties of a Gnomonic chart listed above are all different from those of a Mercator chart – in most cases they are the exact opposite.)

Another use of the Gnomonic projection is for charts with a natural scale larger than 1/50,000. These charts are normally Harbour Plans, which though not strictly Gnomonic charts are closely akin to them. They cover a very small area of the Earth and treat that area as if it were flat. It is possible to take courses and distances from these charts.

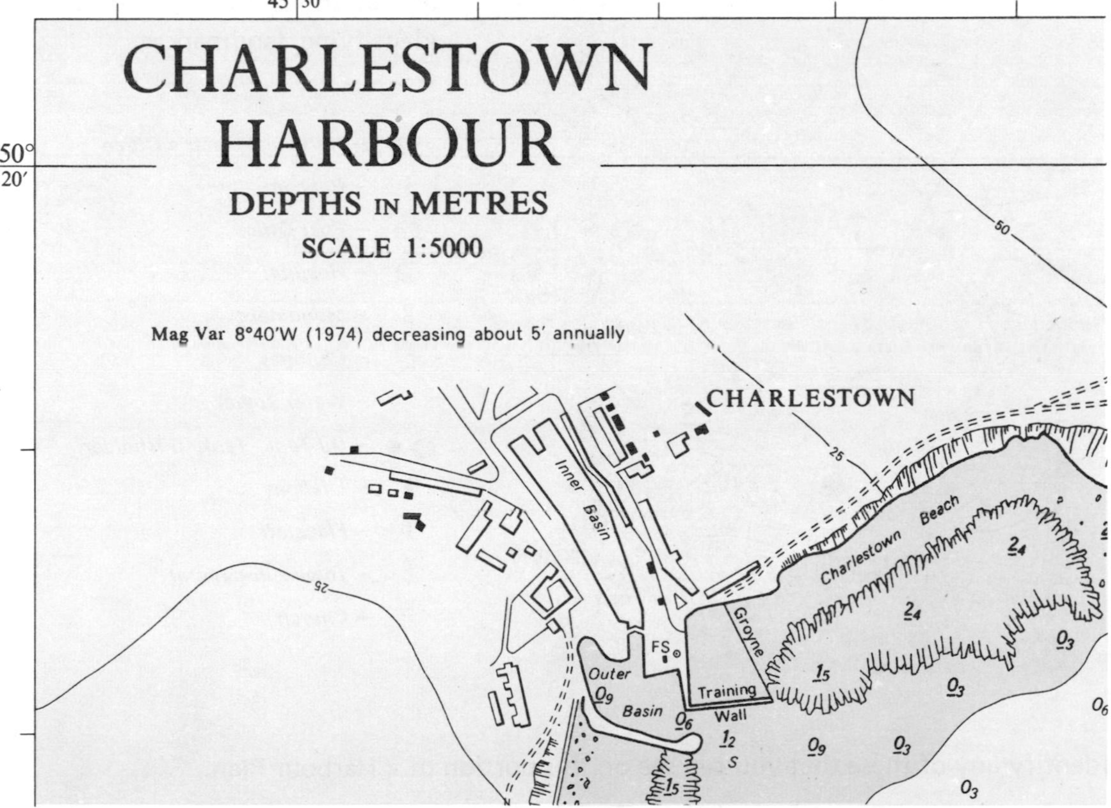

This projection gives a constant scale in all directions, and hence accurate measurement is possible on large scales where the navigator needs to plan to 50 yards or less.

It should be noted that a large-scale chart is one which covers a small area, and an example of a scale larger than 1/50,000 would be 1/40,000.

In this example of a Harbour Plan, which of the two properties of the Gnomonic chart, shown in answers 1 (i) and (ii) above, do not appear to apply?

"Lines of latitude are curves" — this property of Gnomonic charts is not discernible on Harbour Plans. (This is because such a small area is covered by a Harbour Plan that the lines of latitude appear as straight lines.)

As you have learnt, if a chart is to be of any use to the navigator it must show features of land visible from the sea and all navigational hazards. It follows from this that the navigator has an equal responsibility in being able to interpret the chart correctly. The reference book which is an absolute 'must' for this is *Symbols and Abbreviations used on Admiralty Charts (Chart 5011).*

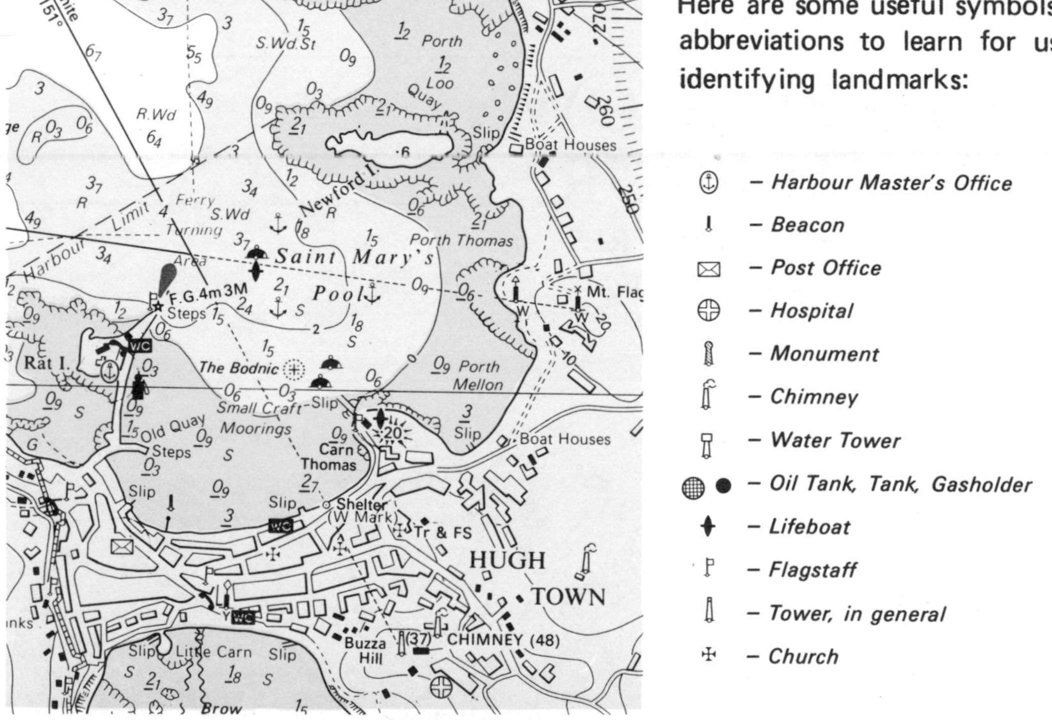

Here are some useful symbols and abbreviations to learn for use in identifying landmarks:

- *Harbour Master's Office*
- *Beacon*
- *Post Office*
- *Hospital*
- *Monument*
- *Chimney*
- *Water Tower*
- *Oil Tank, Tank, Gasholder*
- *Lifeboat*
- *Flagstaff*
- *Tower, in general*
- *Church*

Identify any of these that you can see on this portion of a Harbour Plan.

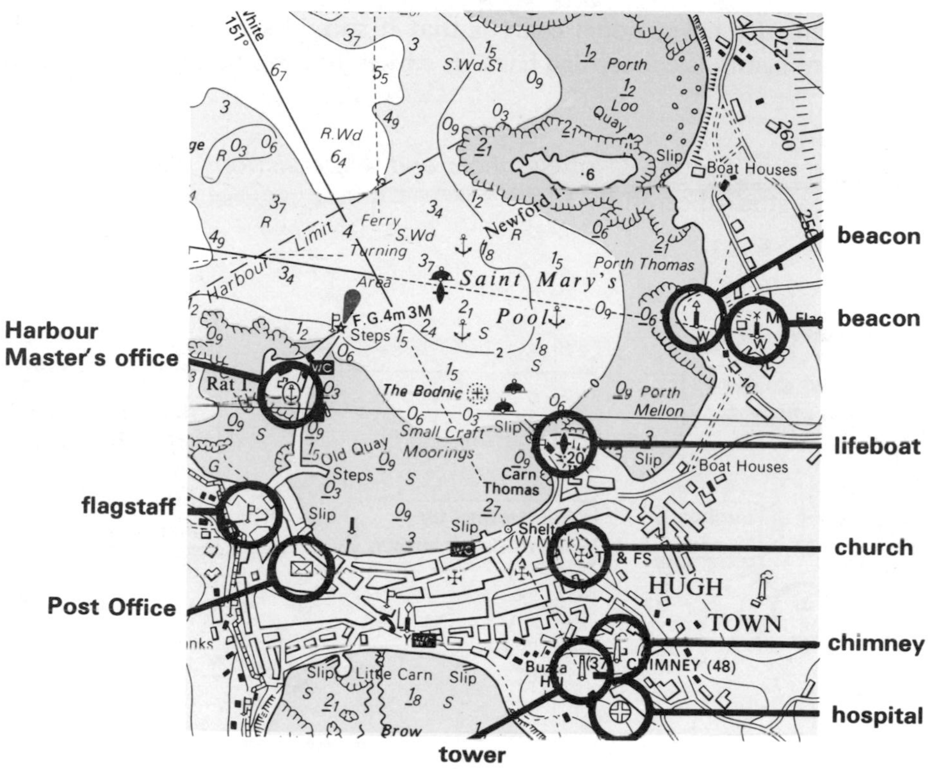

Symbols of interest to small craft are shown on the harbour plan in magenta. Some of these symbols are shown here.

The complete list is shown in Chart 5011 – symbols and abbreviations used on Admiralty Charts.

- Visitors' mooring
- Visitors Berth
- Yacht Marina
- Public Landing
- Slipway for small craft
- Water Tap
- Fuel
- Public Telephone
- Public House or Inn
- Restaurant
- Yacht or Sailing Club
- Toilets
- Public Car Park
- Parking for boats/trailers
- Laundrette
- Caravan Site
- Camping Site

Another requirement of a navigational chart is that it should show all navigational hazards. Some important symbols concerning hazards which you should know are illustrated on these charts.

(The full list is given in Section O of *Symbols and Abbreviations used on Admiralty Charts* and should be studied carefully.)

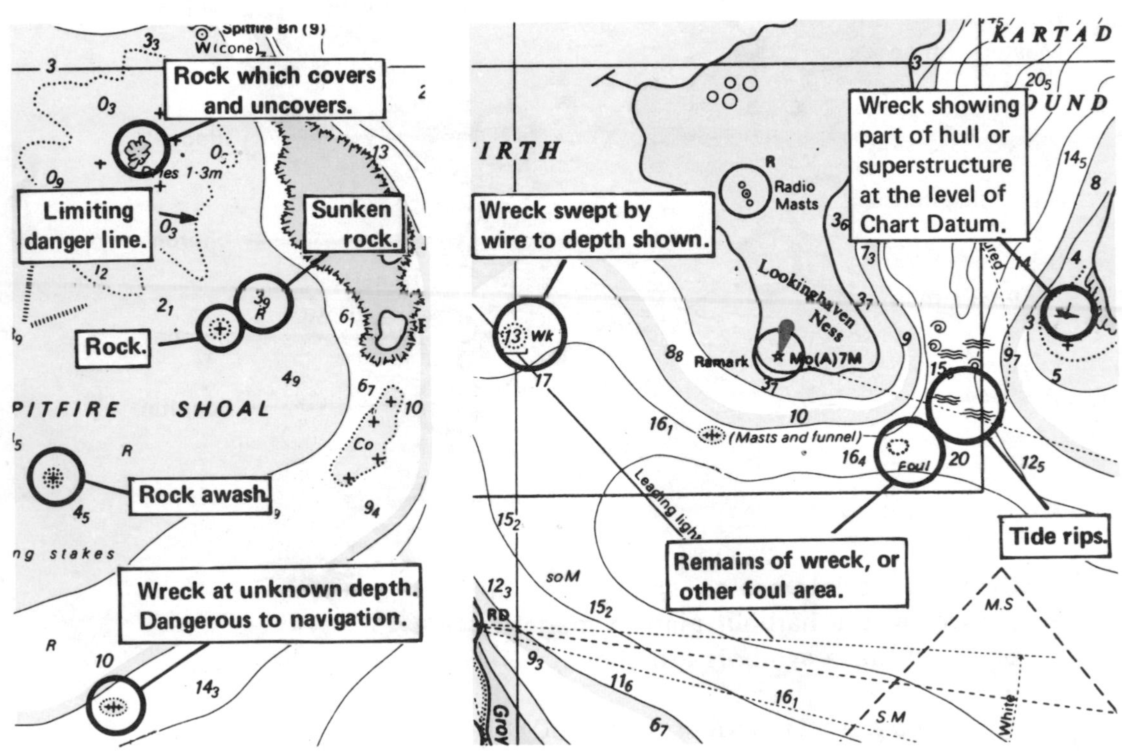

(PA) – Position approximate. (PD) – Position doubtful. (ED) – Existence doubtful.

When you think you have learnt this selection of symbols and abbreviations, turn to page 67 to test your knowledge.

What is the meaning of the symbols and/or abbreviations indicated on this portion of chart 777?

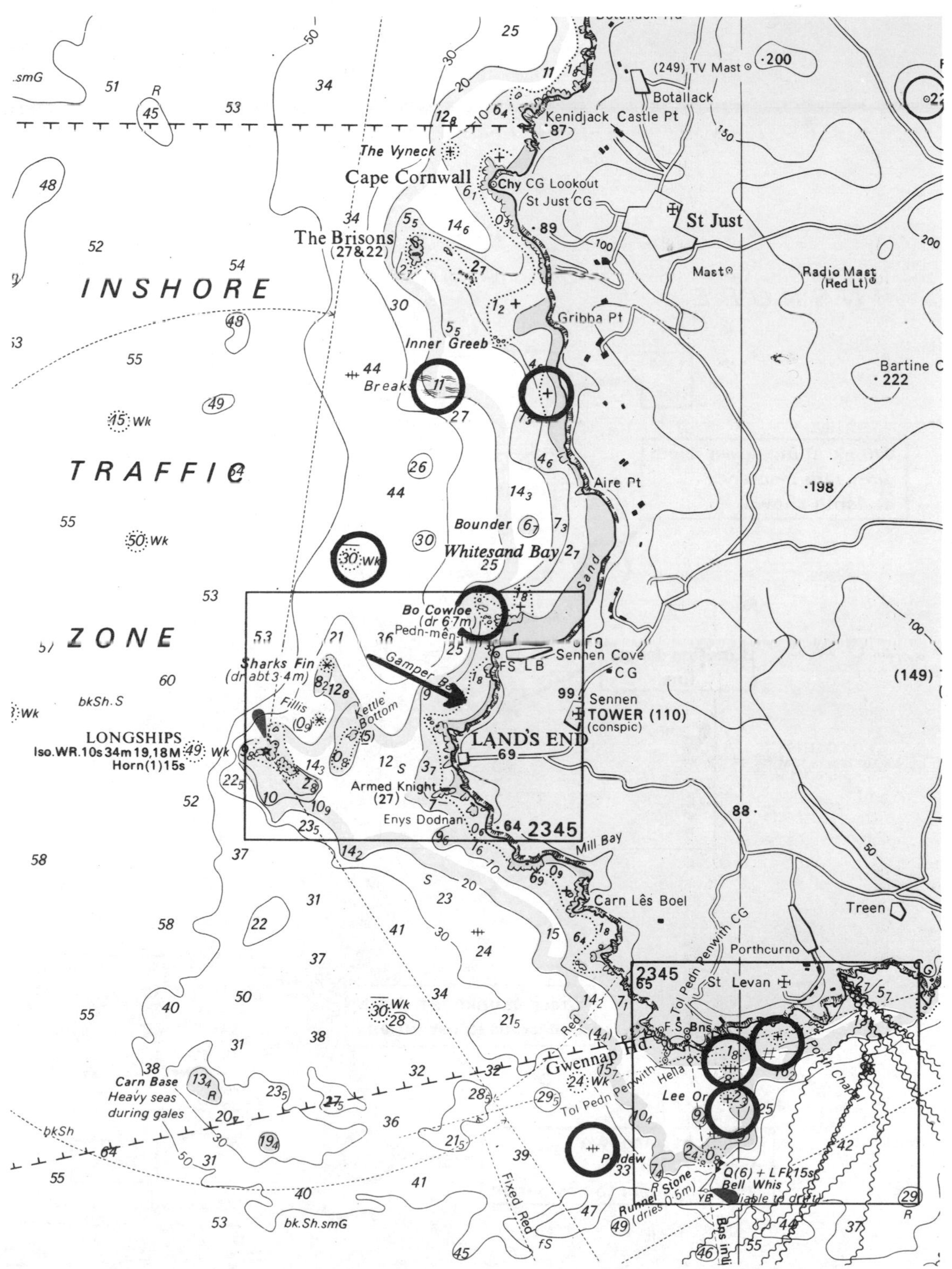

Check your answers:

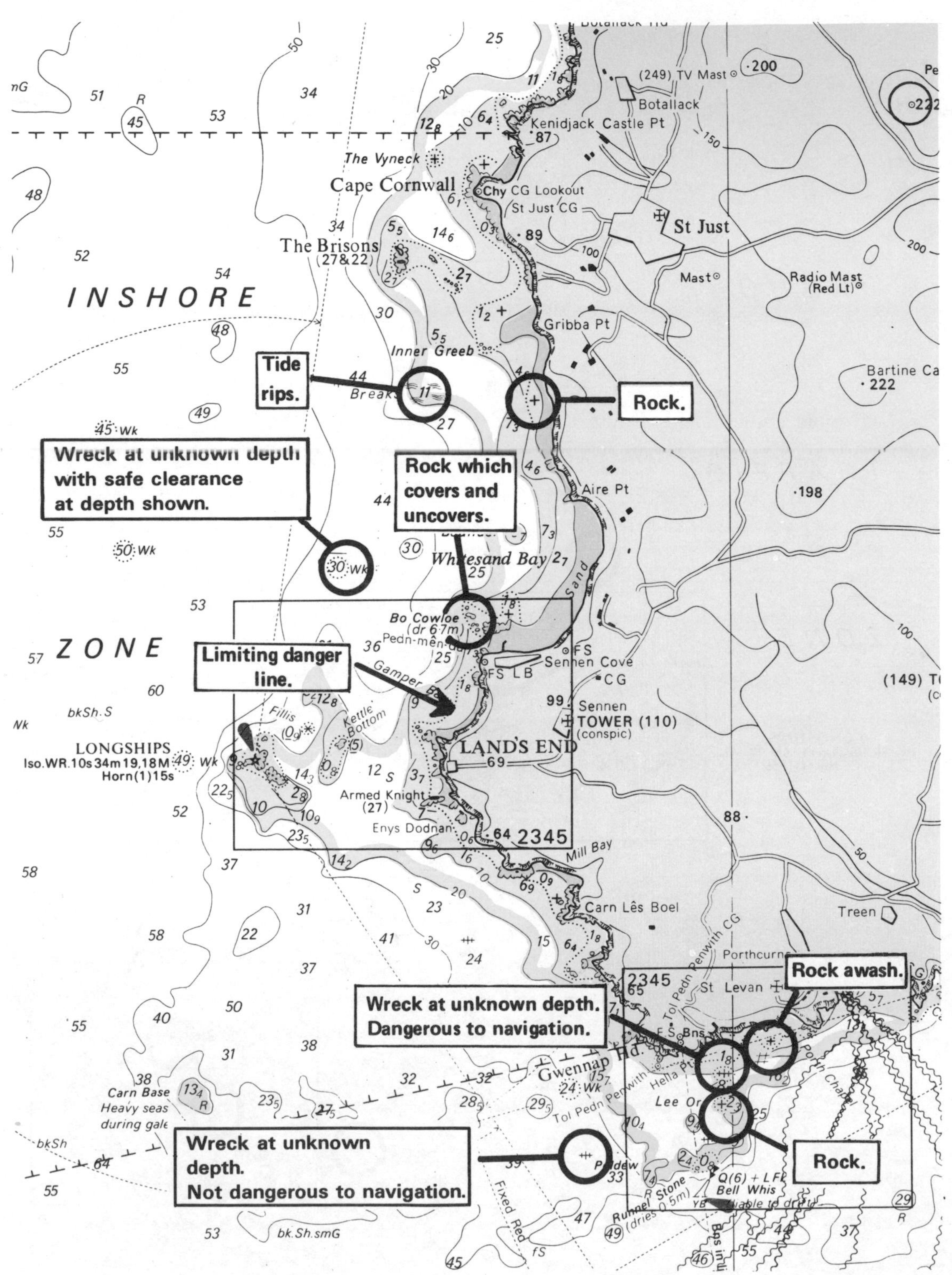

Section 3 : Self-test

1. How are the following represented on:

   i) a Mercator chart?

   ii) a Gnomonic chart?

   Rhumb lines.

   Great circles.

   Lines of latitude.

   Lines of longitude.

2. What qualification should be made to the statement that distances can be correctly measured on a Mercator chart using the latitude scale?

3. What three uses of the Gnomonic projection are there?

4. Give at least four requirements that a chart has to fulfil to enable it to be suitable for navigational purposes.

5. What is the shortest track between two places on the globe?

6. Define a 'rhumb line'.

Now turn to page 70 for answers.

Section 3 : Answers to Self-test

1. Rhumb lines — i) as straight lines, ii) as curves.

   Great circles — i) as curves, ii) as straight lines.

   Lines of latitude — i) as straight lines, ii) as curves.

   Lines of longitude — i) as straight lines, ii) as straight lines (converging to the poles).

2. It measures distances correctly only for places in that latitude.

3. Great circle sailing charts.

   Polar charts.

   Charts with a scale larger than 1/50,000.

4. Any four of these:

   The rhumb lines must appear as straight lines.

   It must show latitude and longitude.

   It must have a distance scale (e.g. latitude scale).

   It must enable bearings to be measured.

   It must show features of land visible from the sea.

   It must show all navigational hazards.

5. The great-circle track.

6. A line which cuts meridians and parallels of latitude at the same angle.

Section 4 : Tides and Tidal Streams

To the navigator, tides are important because they affect both the depth of the water and generate horizontal water movements. A rise and fall in water-level attributable to tidal factors can be expected in all seaports. In almost all ports high and low water occur at roughly six-hour intervals, producing a succession of two high tides and two low tides in a period of just over 24 hours.

The reason for this is that tides are caused by the gravitational pull of the Moon (and, to a lesser extent, of the Sun). The gravitational pull of the Moon produces a 'heaping up' of

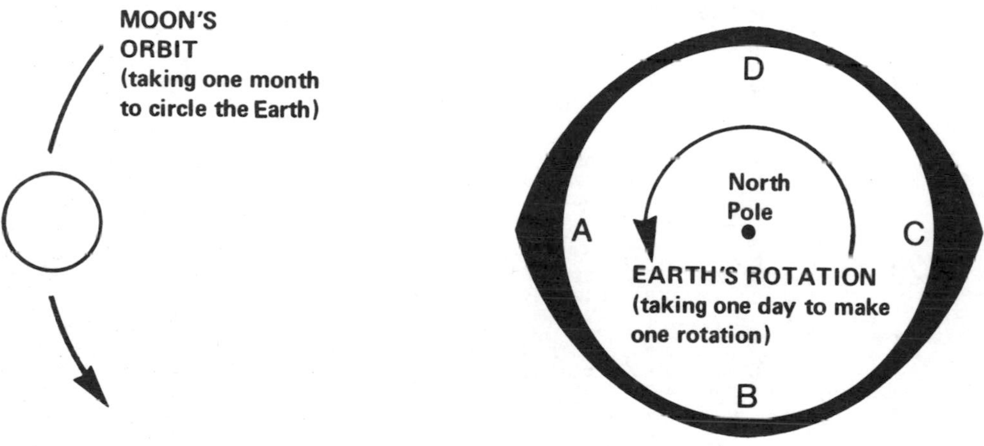

the water on the side of the Earth facing it (A). At the same time there is a similar heaping up on the far side (C). This is due to the resultant of centripetal force over attractive force, but tide generating forces are a complex question and outside the scope of this book. At points B and D the water-level falls. As the Earth rotates it exposes a different side to the Moon, so that, for instance, in just over 6 hours time, point A will have moved round to position B and will be experiencing [high tide/low tide]. Choose the correct answer and then turn to page 72.

low tide

The times and heights of high and low water on any day of the year are contained in the *Admiralty Tide Tables*. These day-by-day tidal predictions relate to a set of Standard Ports and they are set out like this *:

ENGLAND, EAST COAST - MARGATE

LAT 51°24′N LONG 1°23′E

TIME ZONE GMT — TIMES AND HEIGHTS OF HIGH AND LOW WATERS — YEAR 1985

JANUARY

Day	TIME	M	Day	TIME	M
1 TU	0041 0653 1333 1948	1.7 3.9 1.3 3.9	16 W	0052 0700 1351 1958	1.4 4.3 0.8 4.1
2 W	0149 0758 1430 2047	1.6 3.9 1.2 4.0	17 TH	0212 0812 1458 2105	1.3 4.2 0.9 4.2
3 TH	0250 0857 1521 2139	1.5 4.0 1.2 4.2	18 F	0324 0927 1600 2210	1.2 4.2 0.9 4.2
4 F	0343 0952 1607 2227	1.3 4.1 1.1 4.3	19 SA	0430 1038 1657 2306	1.0 4.3 1.0 4.3
5 SA	0433 1041 1652 2312	1.2 4.3 1.0 4.5	20 SU	0527 1137 1744 2353	0.8 4.4 1.0 4.4
6 SU	0520 1127 1737 2354	1.0 4.4 0.9 4.6	21 M ●	0617 1225 1825	0.7 4.5 0.9
7 M ○	0607 1212 1821	0.9 4.5 0.9	22 TU	0034 0659 1309 1903	4.5 0.6 4.6 0.9
8 TU	0035 0652 1255 1903	4.7 0.7 4.7 0.9	23 W	0112 0740 1348 1940	4.6 0.5 4.6 0.9
9 W	0116 0737 1338 [illegible]	4.7 0.6 4.7 [illegible]	24	[illegible]	[illegible]

FEBRUARY

Day	TIME	M	Day	TIME	M
1 F	0155 0806 1429 2051	1.6 3.7 1.4 3.9	16 SA	0315 0928 1549 2159	1.2 4.1 1.2 4.1
2 SA	0303 0917 1529 2153	1.5 3.8 1.3 4.1	17 SU	0433 1044 1654 2259	1.0 4.2 1.1 4.2
3 SU	0406 1019 1628 2247	1.3 4.1 1.2 4.3	18 M	0530 1139 1742 2344	0.7 4.3 1.1 4.3
4 M	0504 1112 1722 2334	1.0 4.3 1.0 4.5	19 TU ●	0615 1222 1818	0.6 4.4 1.0
5 TU ○	0556 1200 1808	0.8 4.6 0.8	20 W	0022 0650 1259 1848	4.4 0.5 4.5 0.9
6 W	0019 0642 1245 1852	4.7 0.5 4.7 0.7	21 TH	0055 0723 1330 1919	4.5 0.5 4.5 0.9
7 TH	0100 0726 1330 1934	4.8 0.4 4.8 0.7	22 F	0126 0752 1359 1948	4.6 0.6 4.5 0.9
8 F	0141 0809 1413 2015	4.9 0.3 4.8 0.7	23 SA	0157 0822 1427 2019	4.6 0.6 4.4 0.9
9	0220 0851 [illegible]	4.9 0.3 4.7	24	0226 [illegible]	[illegible]

MARCH

Day	TIME	M	Day	TIME	M
1 F	0553 1221 1839	3.7 1.6 3.7	16 SA	0131 0744 1413 2016	1.3 3.9 1.5 3.8
2 SA	0103 0713 1341 2005	1.7 3.6 1.6 3.7	17 SU	0307 0925 1538 2142	1.1 4.0 1.4 4.0
3 SU	0223 0844 1456 2121	1.6 3.7 1.5 3.9	18 M	0423 1034 1644 2242	0.8 4.3 1.2 4.2
4 M	0339 0955 1604 2220	1.3 4.0 1.3 4.2	19 TU	0518 1125 1729 2327	0.6 4.4 1.1 4.3
5 TU	0442 1052 1702 2309	0.9 4.4 1.0 4.5	20 W	0558 1205 1800	0.6 4.5 1.0
6 W	0534 1142 1749 2354	0.6 4.7 0.8 4.7	21 TH ●	0001 0629 1236 1825	4.4 0.6 4.5 0.9
7 TH ○	0621 1227 1831	0.3 4.8 0.6	22 F	0029 0655 1303 1850	4.5 0.6 4.5 0.9
8 F	0035 0703 1310 1912	4.9 0.2 4.9 0.6	23 SA	0057 0720 1327 1919	4.6 0.6 4.5 0.8
9	0116 [illegible]	5.0 0.1	24 SU	0126 0745 1351 [illegible]	4.6 0.7 [illegible]

APRIL

Day	TIME	M	Day	TIME	M
1 M	0152 0815 1426 2046	1.5 3.8 1.6 3.9	16 TU	0356 1010 1616 2212	0.8 4.3 1.3 4.2
2 TU	0311 0928 1538 2146	1.2 4.2 1.3 4.2	17 W	0449 1058 1659 2255	0.6 4.4 1.1 4.3
3 W	0416 1026 1634 2237	0.8 4.5 1.0 4.5	18 TH	0527 1134 1729 2329	0.6 4.5 1.0 4.4
4 TH	0506 1115 1720 2320	0.5 4.8 0.8 4.8	19 F	0556 1204 1754 2357	0.7 4.5 0.9 4.5
5 F ○	0551 1201 1803	0.2 4.9 0.6	20 SA ●	0619 1229 1819	0.7 4.5 0.9
6 SA	0003 0635 1245 1845	4.9 0.1 5.0 0.5	21 SU	0027 0645 1253 1849	4.6 0.7 4.5 0.8
7 SU	0046 0717 1327 1927	5.0 0.1 4.9 0.5	22 M	0056 0712 1317 1921	4.6 0.8 4.5 0.8
8 M	0130 0759 1409 2009	5.1 0.2 4.8 0.6	23 TU	0126 0738 1342 1952	4.6 0.9 4.5 0.9
9	0215 0842 1450	5.0 0.5 4.6 0.7	24 W	0157 0808 [illegible]	4.5 [illegible]

The difference in levels between successive high and low water is called the *range* of the tide. For instance, the range between the first two tides at Margate on January 1 st 1985 is 2·2m.

The time for a succession of two high tides and two low tides varies but a useful guide is that it makes a lunar day of __________________________.
(Complete the sentence.)

just over twenty four hours

The Sun also exerts a gravitational attraction, but although the Sun is so much larger than the Moon, it is very much further away from the Earth and so the resulting displacement of the water is less than half that caused by the Moon. The different phases of the Moon are associated with the Sun and you will find it useful to remind yourself of the sequence of the Moon's phases before continuing:

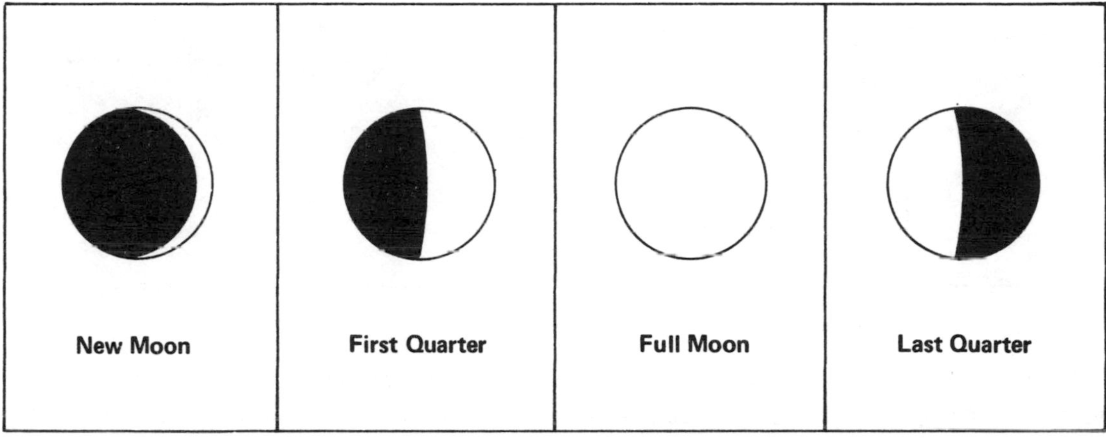

As looked at from the Earth.

The Sun's gravitational attraction plays its part in this way. When the Sun, Earth and Moon are in the same straight line (at new Moon and full Moon) the Sun and Moon 'pull together', and then the high tides are particularly high and the low tides are particularly low. These are known as *spring tides.*

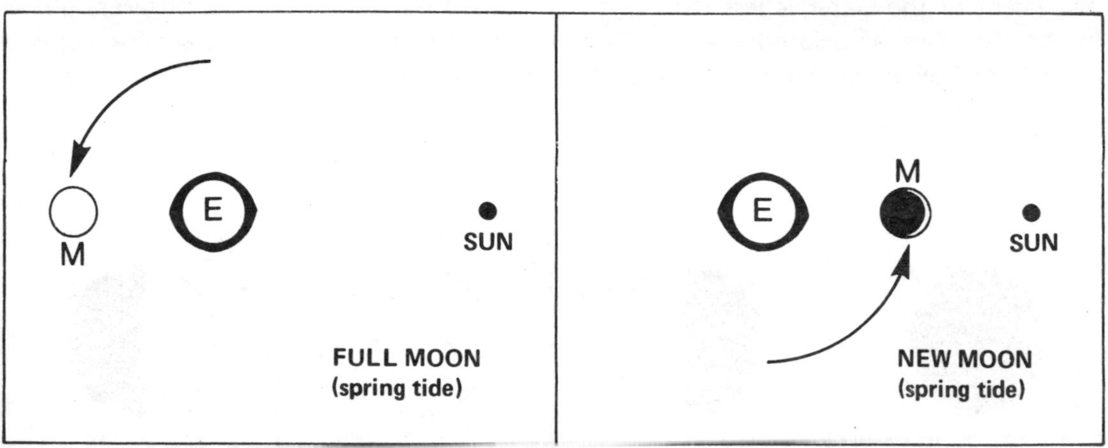

At other times they are not 'pulling' together, and the range is less. At half Moon (i.e. at the first and last quarter) the Sun and Moon are 'pulling' at right angles to each other and the *neap tides* that are produced have a small range.

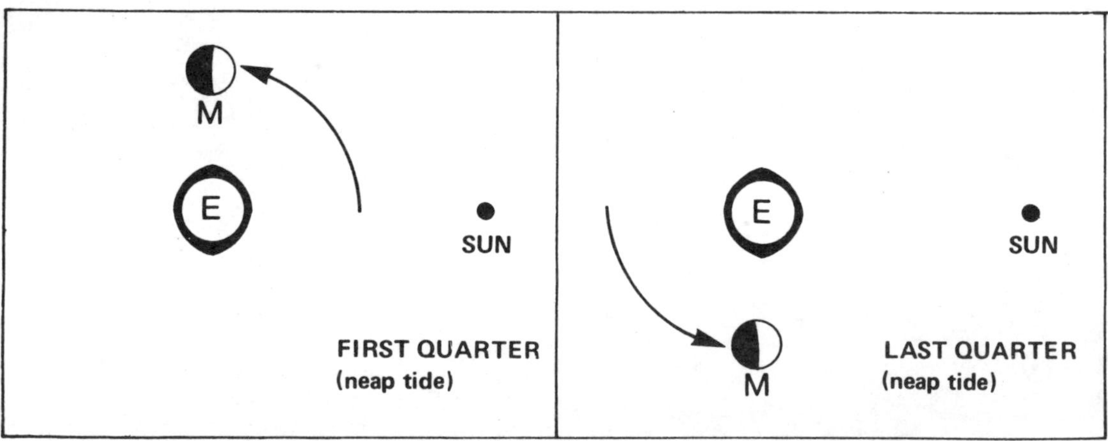

Which of the following statements most accurately describe spring tides ?

Spring tides are those that occur early in the year and are likely to be high.
Spring tides are tides which are particularly high.
Spring tides are those where the range is large.

Spring tides are those where the range is large (i.e. when the high tides are particularly high and the low tides are particularly low).

CHAN

TIME ZONE **GMT** | TIME

SEPTEMBER | OC

	TIME	M		TIME	M		TIME	M
1	0205	1.4	**16**	0138	0.6	**1**	0159	1
	0738	10.6		0714	11.8		0734	1
SU	1416	1.7	M	1354	0.7	TU	1409	
	1951	10.9		1930	12.0		1948	
2	0233	1.5	**17**	0218	0.5	**2**	0225	
	0806	10.5		0752	11.9		0801	1
M	1443	1.8	TU	1434	0.7	W	1436	1
	2020	10.7		2008	12.0		2016	10.
3	0258	1.7	**18**	0257	0.7	**3**	0250	2.
	0833	10.4		0830	11.7		0826	10.4
TU	1507	2.0	W	1514	1.0	TH	1501	2.2
	2047	10.4		2046	11.5		2042	10.1
4	0322	2.0	**19**	0335	1.3	**4**	0314	2.
	0900	10.1		0907	11.1		0851	10.
W	1531	2.3	TH	1552	1.7	F	1528	2
	2115	10.0		2125	10.7		2100	9
5	0346	2.4	**20**	0413	2.1	**5**	0341	
	0927	9.8		0948	10.2		0919	9
TH	1556	2.7	F	1633	2.5	SA	1556	3
	2142	9.5		2209	9.7		2136	8.
6	0413	3.0	**21**	0457	3.1	**6**	0410	3.7
	0956	9.2		1033	9.2		0952	8.8
F	1627	3.3	SA	1723	3.4	**SU**	1631	4.0
	2214	8.8		2302	8.7		2213	8.2
7	0445	3.6	**22**	0556	4.0	**7**	0451	4.
	1030	8.6		1139	8.2		1035	8
SA	1706	3.9	**SU**	1839	4.2	M	1727	
	2254	8.1					2313	
8	0532	4.3	**23**	0034	7.8	**8**	0603	
	1119	8.0		0733	4.6		1205	
SU	1810	4.5	M	1341	7.8	TU	1903	
				2026	4.3			
9	0001	7.5	**24**	0246	7.8	**9**	0138	
	0649	4.7		0924	4.4		0755	
M	1256	7.5	TU	1521	8.2	W	1418	
	1945	4.7		2200	3.8		2050	4
10	0215	7.3	**25**	0402	8.5	**10**	0308	8.
	0832	4.7		1037	3.7		0925	4.
TU	1454	7.8	W	1620	9.0	TH	1527	8.7
	2122	4.3		2302	3.0		2202	3.5
11	0341	8.0	**26**	0451	9.2	**11**	0400	9.
	0953	4.1		1126	3.0		1024	3.
W	1559	8.6	TH	1705	9.7	F	1616	9.
	2231	3.6		2347	2.3		2254	2
12	0433	8.8	**27**	0530	9.8	**12**	0444	1
	1054	3.3		1205	2.4		1113	
TH	1648	9.5	F	1743	10.3	SA	1659	1
	2325	2.7					2340	
13	0516	9.8	**28**	0025	1.8	**13**	0526	1
	1144	2.4		0604	10.3		1200	1
F	1730	10.4	SA	1241	1.9	**SU**	1742	11
				1818	10.7			
14	0012	1.8	**29**	0100	1.5	**14**	0025	0.
	0557	10.7		0636	10.6		0607	11.
SA	1229	1.6	**SU**	1313	1.7	M	1245	0.8
●	1811	11.2	○	1849	10.9	●	1824	12.0

1. On the left is an excerpt from the *Admiralty Tide Tables.* What do you notice about the tides on the 9th September compared with those on the other days, and what are they called?

2. With which two phases of the Moon do you associate the tides you have just mentioned?

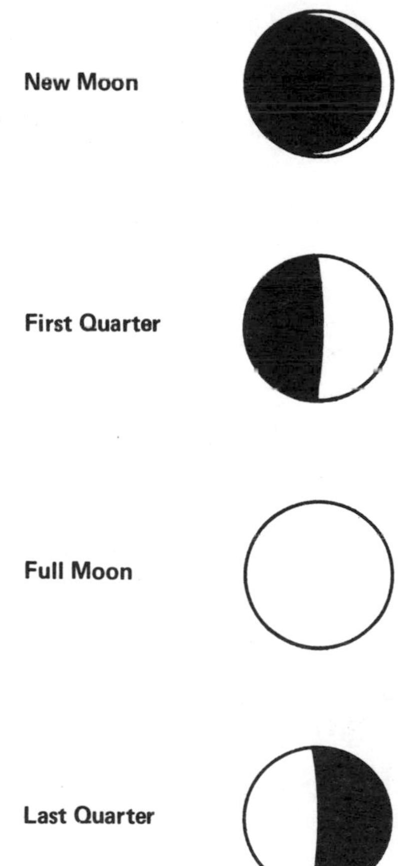

As looked at from the Earth.

1. They have the smallest range. Neap tides.

2. First quarter and last quarter.

The *Admiralty Tide Tables* give daily predictions of the times and heights of high and low water for a selected number of *Standard Ports.* For all other ports, called *Secondary Ports,* sufficient information is given at the back of the *Tide Tables* to enable the times and heights of tides to be calculated. The computed predictions for Standard Ports are based on the analysis of one year's observations at least, and can be taken as correct for all occasions except for some abnormal weather conditions.

The time used in the *Admiralty Tide Tables* is always local time. The amount that you have to add or subtract to get Greenwich Mean Time is always shown against 'Time Zone' on the top left-hand corner of each page. Use local time in all the examples employed in this book.

ENGLAND, EAST COAST - LOWESTOFT

LAT 52°28'N **LONG 1°45'E**

TIME ZONE **GMT** TIMES AND HEIGHTS OF HIGH AND LOW WATERS YEAR **1985**

MAY						JUNE						JULY						AUGUST					
	TIME	M		TIME	M		TIME	M		TIME	M		TIME	M		TIME	M		TIME	M		TIME	M
1	0634	2.2	**16**	0103	0.5	**1**	0120	0.3	**16**	0149	0.6	**1**	0151	0.5	**16**	0157	0.8	**1**	0319	0.8	**16**	0303	0.8
	1231	0.9		0741	2.2		0748	2.3		0819	2.2		0813	2.3		0819	2.3		0929	2.5		0908	2.4
W	1811	2.1	TH	1319	1.0	SA	1341	0.7	**SU**	1406	0.9	M	1413	0.7	TU	1423	0.9	TH	1549	0.4	F	1531	0.5
				1920	2.2		1947	2.4		2011	2.2		2034	2.4		2036	2.2		2217	2.4	●	2155	2.4
2	0055	0.4	**17**	0147	0.5	**2**	0212	0.3	**17**	0225	0.7	**2**	0243	0.6	**17**	0236	0.9	**2**	0400	0.9	**17**	0343	0.7
	0730	2.3		0819	2.2		0836	2.3		0851	2.3		0901	2.4		0853	2.3		1007	2.5		0950	2.5
TH	1323	0.7	F	1359	0.9	**SU**	1430	0.6	M	1443	0.9	TU	1505	0.6	W	1505	0.8	F	1631	0.4	SA	1612	0.3
	1917	2.3		2004	2.2		2044	2.5		2054	2.2	O	2132	2.5	●	2124	2.2		2258	2.4		2235	2.4
3	0149	0.2	**18**	0225	0.4	**3**	0300	0.3	**18**	0300	0.7	**3**	0329	0.7	**18**	0317	0.8	**3**	0437	0.9	**18**	0423	0.6
	0818	2.4		0853	2.2		0921	2.4		0922	2.3		0945	2.4		0929	2.4		1041	2.5		1031	2.6
F	1411	0.6	SA	1434	0.8	M	1517	0.5	TU	1519	0.8	W	1556	0.5	TH	1546	0.7	SA	1709	0.3	**SU**	1652	0.2
	2015	2.4		2042	2.3	O	2139	2.5	●	2135	2.2		2226	2.5		2209	2.3		2336	2.3		2316	2.4
4	0237	0.1	**19**	0257	0.5	**4**	0345	0.4	**19**	0334	0.8	**4**	0414	0.8	**19**	0357	0.8	**4**	0512	0.9	**19**	0502	0.6
	0903	2.4		0924	2.3		1003	2.4		0952	2.4		1024	2.5		1006	2.4		1112	2.5		1113	2.6
SA	1454	0.5	**SU**	1508	0.7	TU	1603	0.4	W	1557	0.7	TH	1642	0.4	F	1628	0.5	**SU**	1746	0.4	M	1733	0.2
O	2105	2.5	●	2118	2.3		2230	2.5		2217	2.2		2313	2.4		2252	2.3					2357	2.4
5	0322	0.1	**20**	0328	0.5	**5**	0428	0.6	**20**	0409	0.8	**5**	0455	0.9	**20**	0438	0.8	**5**	0011	2.3	**20**	0540	0.6
	0946	2.4		0952	2.3		1044	2.5		1023	2.4		1101	2.5		1045	2.5		0544	0.9		1154	2.7
SU	1536	0.4	M	1541	0.7	W	1649	0.4	TH	1637	0.7	F	1727	0.4	SA	1709	0.4	M	1140	2.5	TU	1814	0.2
	2155	2.6		2155	2.3		2322	2.5		2301	2.2		2358	2.3		2336	2.3		1821	0.4			
6	0406	0.1	**21**	0357	0.6	**6**	0509	0.8	[illegible]	0447	0.9	[illegible]	[illegible]	1.0	**21**	0519	0.8	**6**	0046	2.2	**21**	0039	2.3
	1027	2.4		[illegible]	[illegible]		1122	[illegible]		[illegible]						1126	2.5					0619	0.6
M	1619	[illegible]				TH										1751	[illegible]					[illegible]	2.6

Using the excerpt above, answer these questions.

1. What is the time and height of high water at Lowestoft on the morning of May 16th 1985.
2. What is the time and height of the next low water?
3. What is the range?

1. High water is at 0741. Height 2·2 m.
2. Low water follows at 1319. Height 1·0 m.
3. The range is 1·2 m.

In the next few examples you will need a copy of *Admiralty Tide Tables, Volume 1.*

Let's say you want to find out the height of the tide at 0941 on the same day (i.e. two hours after high water). You could make a rough estimate by inspection, but if greater accuracy is required, you have to use the diagram showing the mean tidal curves at both springs and neaps, and this diagram is given in the *Admiralty Tide Tables.* (The diagram for Lowestoft is reproduced below.)

The following steps must be carried out:

1. On Standard Curve diagram, plot heights of H.W. and L.W. occurring either side of required time and join by sloping line.
2. Enter H.W. time and sufficient others to embrace required time.
3. From required time, proceed vertically to curves, using heights plotted in 1 to assist interpolation between Springs and Neaps. Do NOT extrapolate.
4. Proceed horizontally to sloping line, thence vertically to Height scale.
5. Read off height.

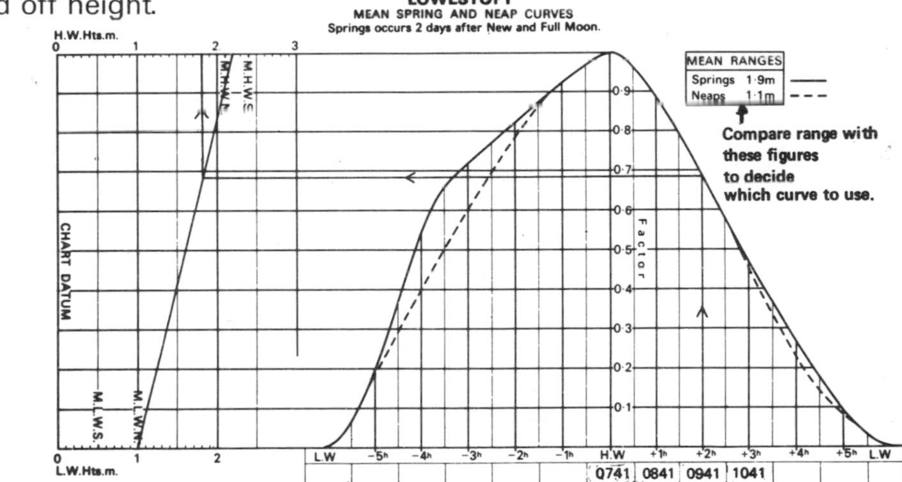

In this case mark on 2·2 m as the height of H.W. and 1·0 m as the height of L.W. on the appropriate scales to the left of the curve and join them with a sloping line.
Mark the times in the boxes beneath the curve. Then starting from the appropriate time, 0941 (2 hours after H.W.), proceed vertically until you reach the neaps curve (this is used as it is a neap tide, range 1·2 m), then proceed horizontally to the sloping line and then vertically to the H.W. scale.
Read off the height, in this case 1·8 m.

Carrying out the same steps as above and using the extract from the Tide Table on the previous page, calculate the height of the tide at 1618 on the same day.

Check your working:

LW 1319 1·0m HW 1920 2·2m Range 1·2m

1. Plot the heights of H.W. and L.W. and join them with a sloping line.
2. Enter time of H.W. (1920) and the time required in the boxes under the curve.
3. Proceed vertically from the time required (–0302h) to the neaps curve (range 1·2m), then horizontally to the sloping line, then vertically to the H.W. scale.
4. Read off the height, in this case 1·7m.

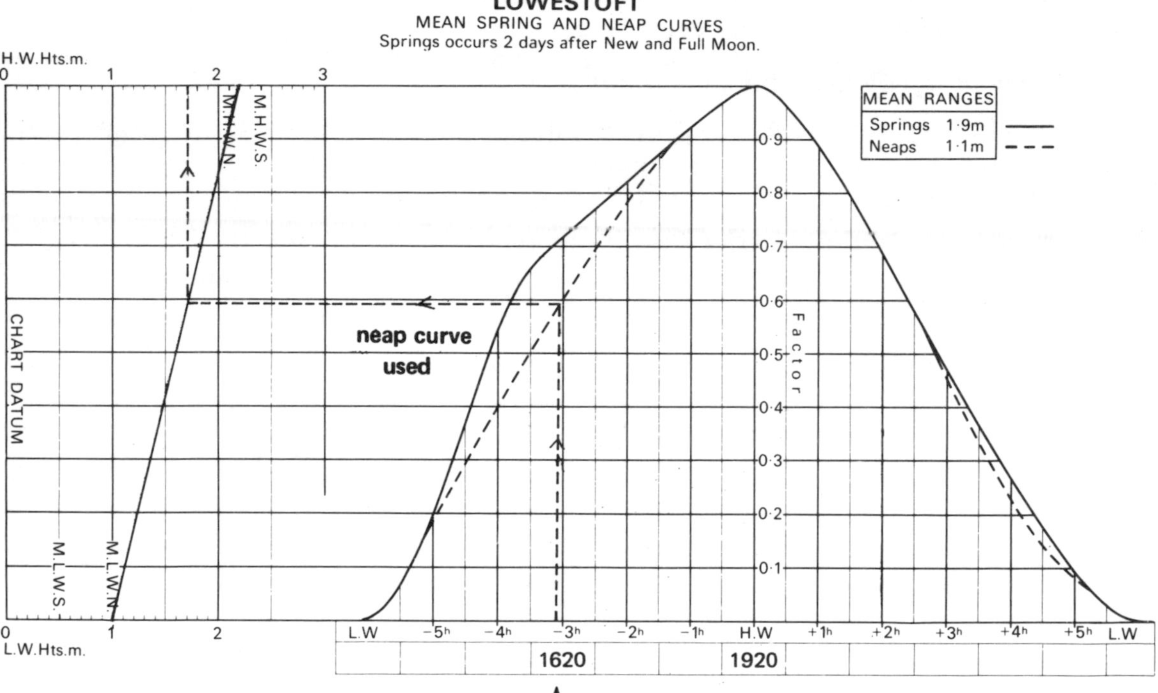

Springs occurs 2 days after New and Full Moon.

The mean neap range for Lowestoft is 1·1 m, so for calculations where the range is close to or less than 1·1 m the neap curve is used. The spring curve is used for the remainder of occasions. (Strictly speaking, where the range lies between the mean spring and neap range it is advisable to work out the answer on both curves and then interpolate, but for many practical occasions it is sufficient to use only the spring curve in these conditions.)

For further practice here are some more problems. You will find the appropriate excerpts from the *Admiralty Tide Tables* on the next two pages.

1. Find the height of tide at Immingham at 0400 on Thursday 10th January 1985.
2. Find the height of tide at Immingham at 0700 on Thursday 3rd January 1985.
3. Find the height of tide at Immingham at 0200 on Thursday 7th March 1985.
4. Find the height of tide at Immingham at 0900 on Wednesday 6th February 1985.

To give you a start, the working of the first problem is shown below.

LW 0213 1·0m HW 0809 7·0m Range 6·0 m

1. Plot the heights of H.W. and L.W. and join them with a sloping line.
2. Enter the time of H.W. (0809) and the time required in the boxes under the curve.
3. Proceed vertically from the time required (–0409 h) to the springs curve (range 6·0 m is very close to the spring range of 6·4 m), then horizontally to the sloping line, then vertically to the H.W. scale.
4. Read off the height. In this case 2·4 m.

IMMINGHAM

MEAN SPRING AND NEAP CURVES

Springs occurs 2 days after New and Full Moon.

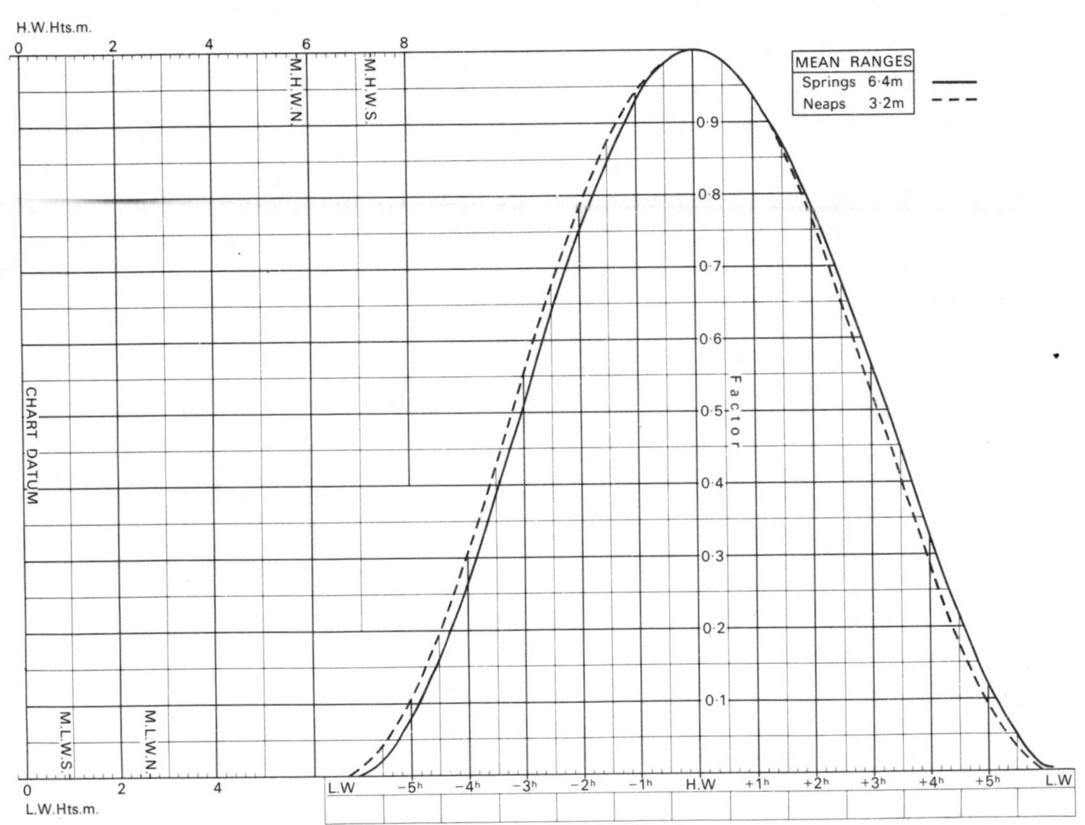

ENGLAND, EAST COAST - IMMINGHAM

LAT 53°38'N LONG 0°11'W

TIME ZONE **GMT** — TIMES AND HEIGHTS OF HIGH AND LOW WATERS — YEAR **1985**

JANUARY

Date	Day	Time	M	Time	M	Time	M	Time	M
1	TU	0031	5.9	0712	2.6	1337	5.5	1930	3.0
2	W	0145	5.9	0815	2.5	1439	5.7	2036	2.7
3	TH	0249	6.0	0911	2.4	1531	6.0	2135	2.4
4	F	0343	6.2	1002	2.1	1616	6.2	2228	2.1
5	SA	0431	6.4	1049	1.9	1657	6.5	2318	1.8
6	SU	0516	6.5	1136	1.7	1736	6.6		
7	M ○	0004	1.6	0600	6.7	1218	1.6	1815	6.8
8	TU	0049	1.3	0643	6.8	1300	1.5	1853	6.9
9	W	0131	1.1	0726	6.9	1341	1.4	1933	7.0
10	TH	0213	1.0	0809	7.0	1422	1.4	2012	7.1
11	F	0256	1.0	0853	6.9	1503	1.6	2054	7.0
12	SA	0338	1.1	0938	6.7	1543	1.8	2138	6.9
13	SU	0423	1.3	1027	6.5	1628	2.1	2228	6.7
14	M	0512	1.5	1126	6.2	1720	2.3	2330	6.5
15	TU	0614	1.7	1234	6.1	1827	2.5		
16	W	0043	6.4	0726	1.9	1344	6.1	1949	2.5
17	TH	0158	6.4	0837	1.9	1453	6.2	2107	2.2
18	F	0315	6.4	0943	1.8	1557	6.4	2216	1.9
19	SA	0427	6.5	1042	1.7	1652	6.6	2316	1.7
20	SU	0525	6.6	1136	1.6	1737	6.8		
21	M ●	0010	1.4	0612	6.7	1221	1.6	1818	6.9
22	TU	0056	1.3	0655	6.6	1302	1.6	1855	7.0
23	W	0135	1.3	0731	6.6	1337	1.6	1930	7.1
24	TH	0211	1.3	0805	6.5	1409	1.7	2002	7.1
25	F	0242	1.4	0837	6.4	1439	1.8	2036	7.1
26	SA	0311	1.6	0910	6.3	1510	1.9	2110	6.9
27	SU	0341	1.8	0942	6.2	1542	2.1	2148	6.7
28	M	0414	2.0	1020	5.9	1620	2.4	2230	6.3
29	TU	0457	2.4	1105	5.7	1709	2.7	2323	5.9
30	W	0553	2.7	1207	5.5	1817	2.9		
31	TH	0036	5.7	0704	2.8	1328	5.4	1938	2.9

FEBRUARY

Date	Day	Time	M	Time	M	Time	M	Time	M
1	F	0158	5.6	0818	2.7	1442	5.6	2054	2.6
2	SA	0310	5.8	0925	2.5	1542	5.9	2202	2.3
3	SU	0410	6.1	1026	2.2	1633	6.2	2301	1.8
4	M	0501	6.4	1118	1.8	1718	6.5	2350	1.4
5	TU ○	0547	6.7	1204	1.5	1758	6.9		
6	W	0036	1.0	0631	7.0	1248	1.2	1838	7.2
7	TH	0119	0.7	0713	7.2	1328	1.0	1917	7.4
8	F	0201	0.5	0754	7.3	1408	1.0	1957	7.6
9	SA	0240	0.4	0836	7.2	1447	1.1	2036	7.5
10	SU	0321	0.6	0917	7.0	1525	1.4	2119	7.3
11	M	0400	1.0	1002	6.7	1606	1.7	2206	7.0
12	TU	0444	1.4	1051	6.4	1651	2.1	2305	6.6
13	W	0539	1.9	1154	6.1	1753	2.4		
14	TH	0018	6.2	0653	2.2	1309	5.9	1926	2.6
15	F	0145	6.0	0815	2.3	1430	5.9	2056	2.4
16	SA	0321	6.0	0929	2.2	1546	6.2	2214	2.0
17	SU	0431	6.2	1034	2.0	1642	6.4	2315	1.7
18	M	0525	6.4	1126	1.8	1726	6.7		
19	TU ●	0003	1.4	0605	6.5	1208	1.6	1803	6.9
20	W	0042	1.3	0639	6.6	1245	1.5	1836	7.1
21	TH	0116	1.2	0710	6.7	1317	1.4	1907	7.2
22	F	0147	1.2	0740	6.7	1347	1.4	1938	7.3
23	SA	0215	1.2	0808	6.7	1416	1.5	2009	7.2
24	SU	0242	1.3	0836	6.6	1444	1.6	2040	7.1
25	M	0308	1.6	0904	6.5	1512	1.9	2111	6.8
26	TU	0335	1.9	0935	6.2	1543	2.1	2148	6.4
27	W	0407	2.2	1010	5.9	1623	2.4	2231	6.0
28	TH	0451	2.6	1058	5.6	1718	2.7	2334	5.6

MARCH

Date	Day	Time	M	Time	M	Time	M	Time	M
1	F	0556	2.9	1212	5.3	1839	2.8		
2	SA	0110	5.4	0723	3.0	1352	5.4	2013	2.7
3	SU	0242	5.6	0850	2.7	1510	5.7	2136	2.2
4	M	0350	6.0	1006	2.3	1607	6.1	2241	1.7
5	TU	0445	6.4	1101	1.8	1655	6.6	2332	1.2
6	W	0530	6.8	1147	1.4	1736	7.0		
7	TH ○	0017	0.7	0612	7.2	1229	1.0	1815	7.4
8	F	0059	0.3	0652	7.4	1310	0.8	1855	7.7
9	SA	0140	0.1	0733	7.6	1349	0.7	1935	7.9
10	SU	0219	0.2	0812	7.5	1427	0.8	2018	7.8
11	M	0258	0.5	0853	7.2	1505	1.1	2101	7.5
12	TU	0336	1.0	0935	6.8	1545	1.5	2149	7.0
13	W	0417	1.5	1023	6.4	1628	1.9	2248	6.4
14	TH	0508	2.2	1120	6.0	1730	2.4		
15	F	0004	5.9	0625	2.6	1238	5.7	1917	2.6
16	SA	0149	5.6	0758	2.8	1413	5.7	2054	2.4
17	SU	0325	5.7	0919	2.6	1532	6.0	2210	2.0
18	M	0427	6.0	1023	2.3	1626	6.3	2302	1.7
19	TU	0512	6.3	1109	1.9	1706	6.6	2343	1.4
20	W	0547	6.4	1147	1.6	1739	6.9		
21	TH ●	0017	1.3	0615	6.6	1219	1.4	1811	7.1
22	F	0048	1.1	0643	6.8	1250	1.3	1842	7.3
23	SA	0116	1.1	0710	6.9	1321	1.2	1913	7.3
24	SU	0144	1.1	0737	6.9	1351	1.3	1942	7.2
25	M	0212	1.3	0804	6.8	1419	1.5	2012	7.0
26	TU	0237	1.6	0829	6.6	1446	1.7	2042	6.7
27	W	0303	1.9	0856	6.3	1514	1.9	2115	6.3
28	TH	0331	2.2	0927	6.0	1549	2.2	2157	5.9
29	F	0410	2.5	1010	5.7	1641	2.4	2259	5.6
30	SA	0511	2.9	1119	5.4	1757	2.6		
31	SU	0035	5.4	0636	3.0	1306	5.3	1937	2.5

APRIL

Date	Day	Time	M	Time	M	Time	M	Time	M
1	M	0213	5.6	0815	2.8	1433	5.6	2107	2.0
2	TU	0325	6.0	0938	2.4	1535	6.1	2213	1.5
3	W	0421	6.5	1035	1.8	1624	6.6	2305	1.0
4	TH	0508	6.9	1123	1.4	1708	7.1	2350	0.5
5	F ○	0549	7.3	1205	1.0	1749	7.5		
6	SA	0034	0.2	0628	7.5	1248	0.7	1831	7.8
7	SU	0114	0.1	0707	7.6	1327	0.6	1914	7.9
8	M	0155	0.2	0748	7.5	1408	0.7	1959	7.7
9	TU	0234	0.6	0829	7.2	1447	1.0	2047	7.3
10	W	0314	1.2	0911	6.8	1528	1.4	2139	6.7
11	TH	0353	1.8	0957	6.4	1614	1.9	2238	6.1
12	F	0442	2.4	1054	6.0	1722	2.3	2357	5.6
13	SA	0557	2.9	1207	5.7	1910	2.5		
14	SU	0147	5.4	0733	3.0	1344	5.6	2037	2.3
15	M	0308	5.6	0853	2.8	1503	5.9	2146	2.0
16	TU	0404	5.9	0955	2.4	1556	6.2	2234	1.8
17	W	0444	6.1	1040	2.1	1635	6.5	2309	1.6
18	TH	0516	6.4	1115	1.7	1709	6.8	2342	1.4
19	F	0544	6.6	1149	1.5	1742	7.0		
20	SA ●	0012	1.2	0611	6.8	1222	1.3	1814	7.1
21	SU	0043	1.2	0639	6.9	1255	1.3	1846	7.1
22	M	0114	1.2	0707	6.9	1327	1.4	1919	7.0
23	TU	0142	1.4	0734	6.7	1357	1.6	1949	6.7
24	W	0211	1.7	0801	6.5	1426	1.7	2020	6.5
25	TH	0237	1.9	0827	6.3	1456	1.8	2057	6.2
26	F	0308	2.2	0901	6.1	1534	2.0	2143	5.9
27	SA	0350	2.4	0946	5.8	1624	2.2	2245	5.7
28	SU	0448	2.7	1052	5.6	1734	2.3		
29	M	0012	5.6	0605	2.9	1227	5.5	1904	2.2
30	TU	0142	5.8	0737	2.7	1354	5.8	2030	1.8

1. <u>2·4m</u> (Worked example.)

2. <u>3·3m</u>

HW 0249	6·0m	LW 0911	2·4m	Range 3·6m
Time interval from H.W.				+0411h
Height of Tide				3·3m

3. <u>2·2m</u>

LW 0017	0·7m	HW 0612	7·2m	Range 6·5m
Time interval from H.W.				–0412h
Height of Tide				2·2m

4. <u>5·1m</u>

HW 0631	7·0m	LW 1248	1·2m	Range 5·8m
Time interval from H.W.				+ 0229h
Height of Tide				5·1m

If you study any page of the *Admiralty Tide Tables,* you will see how there is a constant swing from spring tides to neap tides. This, as you know, is in response to the changing phases of the Moon.

What tides would you expect at the following phases of the Moon?

i) New Moon ii) First quarter iii) Full Moon iv) Last quarter.

i) New Moon — spring tides.
ii) First quarter — neap tides.
iii) Full Moon — spring tides.
iv) Last quarter — neap tides.

All predicted tidal heights for any port (Standard or Secondary) are heights above Chart Datum at that port. *Chart Datum* is an arbitrarily fixed level devised so that it is below low-tide level (except for very low tides). It varies from port to port. (Table III in the *Admiralty Tide Tables* gives the height of Chart Datum relative to Ordnance Datum – the plane to which heights of features on land maps are referred – for most British ports.)

The predicted high water at a particular port is 12·0m. Which of these diagrams represents the height of 12 metres?

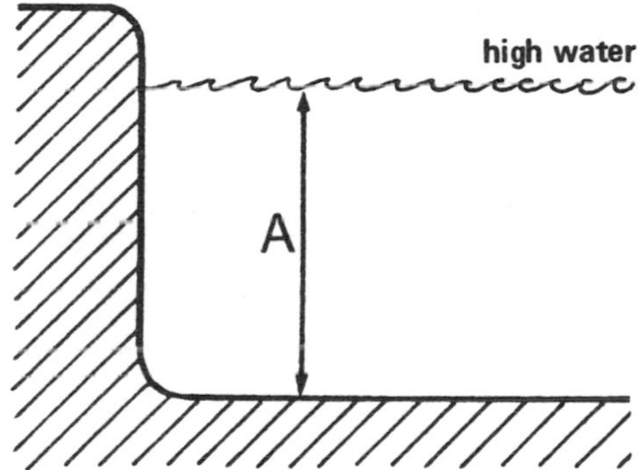

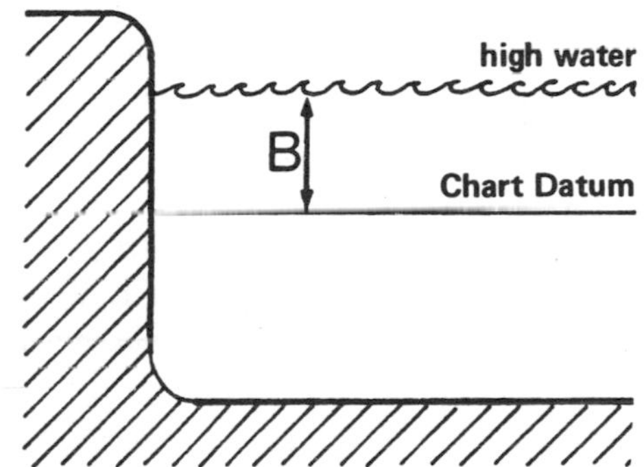

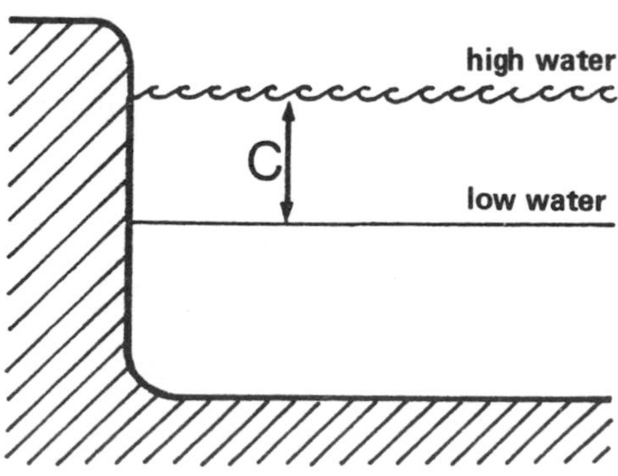

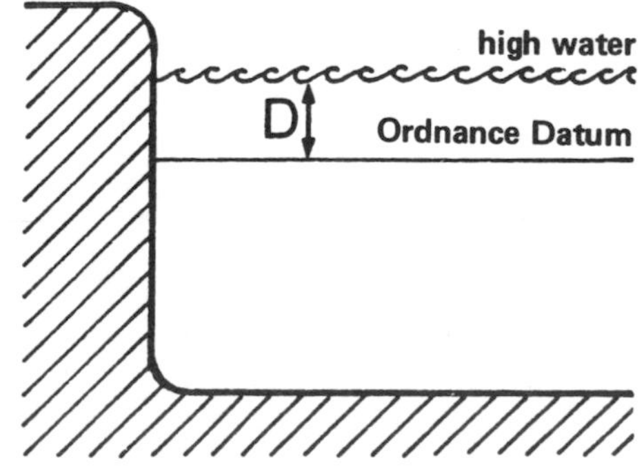

This diagram represents the height of 12·0 metres.

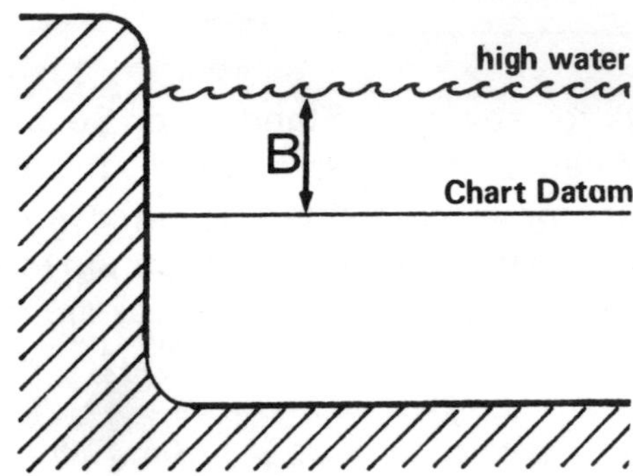

Chart Datum is also used as the datum for charted depths of water. For instance, if the chart tells you that the depth of water at a certain point is 13m, this means 13 metres below Chart Datum. The actual depth of water experienced at any particular time is almost always greater than the charted depth. Why is this?

Because Chart Datum is an arbitrarily fixed level, devised so that it is <u>below low-tide level</u> (except for very low tides which occur rarely, if ever).

It is 0345 on December 4th 1985 at Swansea and the height of tide according to the *Admiralty Tide Tables* is 2·7 m. You consult your chart and find that the depth at a particular point is given as 17 m. What is the total depth of water at that point?

19·7 metres.

The rise and fall of the water-level at ports sets up a horizontal movement of water. The word *tide* refers to the vertical movement of the water, and *tidal stream* refers to the horizontal movement.

The incoming tidal stream occurs when the tide is rising and is called the *flood stream.* Conversely the *ebb stream* occurs with a falling tide. In the British Isles the movement of the tidal streams is closely related to the tides in the vicinity, but this is not so in all parts of the world.

WALES - SWANSEA

LAT 51°37′N LONG 3°55′W

TIME ZONE **GMT** TIMES AND HEIGHTS OF HIGH AND LOW WATERS YEAR **1985**

JANUARY

	TIME	M		TIME	M
1	0106	7.0	16	0133	7.6
	0724	3.4		0744	2.7
TU	1341	7.3	W	1405	7.8
	1955	3.2		2029	2.7
2	0216	7.2	17	0250	7.8
	0829	3.3		0900	2.6
W	1446	7.5	TH	1521	8.0
	2057	3.0		2141	2.5
3	0317	7.6	18	0357	8.2
	0925	3.0		1004	2.3
TH	1542	7.8	F	1626	8.3
	2152	2.7		2240	2.2
4	0409	8.0	19	0455	8.6
	1016	2.7		1102	2.0
F	1631	8.2	SA	1723	8.6
	2238	2.4		2332	2.0
5	0454	8.4	20	0546	9.0
	1101	2.3		1154	1.8
SA	1718	8.5	SU	1811	8.8
	2323	2.1			
6	0537	8.8	21	0017	1.8
	1146	2.0		0631	9.1
SU	1803	8.8	M	1239	1.6
			●	1855	8.9
7	0005	1.7	22	0056	1.6
	0619	9.1		071[illegible]	[illegible]
M	1228	1.6	[illegible]		
○	184[illegible]				

FEBRUARY

	TIME	M		TIME	M
1	0218	7.1	16	0345	7.7
	0836	3.4		0957	2.8
F	1454	7.2	SA	1621	7.8
	2111	3.2		2235	2.7
2	0329	7.5	17	0448	8.2
	0943	3.0		1059	2.4
SA	1602	7.7	SU	1719	8.2
	2212	2.7		2327	2.2
3	0427	8.0	18	0539	8.7
	1040	2.5		1149	1.9
SU	1658	8.2	M	1804	8.6
	2304	2.1			
4	0518	8.6	19	0008	1.8
	1130	1.9		0621	9.0
M	1747	8.7	TU	1229	1.6
	2350	1.6	●	1843	8.9
5	0604	9.1	20	0043	1.5
	1217	1.3		0659	9.2
TU	1832	9.2	W	1303	1.4
○				1916	9.0
6	0034	1.1	21	0114	1.4
	0649	9.5		0731	9.3
W	1259	0.8	TH	1333	1.3
	1914	9.5		1945	9.0
7	0113	0.7	22	0142	1.3
	0731	9.8		0802	[illegible] 2
	[illegible]	[illegible] 6	F	1[illegible]	

MARCH

	TIME	M		TIME	M
1	0607	3.6	16	0202	7.1
	1234	6.9		0825	3.4
F	1856	3.7	SA	1451	7.0
				2117	3.4
2	0120	6.9	17	0331	7.4
	0748	3.7		0948	3.0
SA	1409	6.9	SU	1612	7.5
	2034	3.5		2224	2.8
3	0251	7.2	18	0434	8.0
	0912	3.2		1047	2.4
SU	1534	7.4	M	1705	8.1
	2146	2.9		2311	2.3
4	0402	7.8	19	0520	8.5
	1017	2.4		1130	1.9
M	1637	8.1	TU	1746	8.5
	2242	2.1		2349	1.8
5	0457	8.6	20	0600	8.9
	1109	1.6		1207	1.6
TU	1727	8.8	W	1819	8.9
	2330	1.3			
6	0544	9.3	21	0021	1.5
	1157	0.9		0635	9.2
W	1812	9.5	TH	1238	1.3
			●	1850	9.1
7	0014	0.7	22	0049	1.3
	0629	9.8		0706	9.3
[illegible]	1239	0.4	F	1306	1[illegible]
		[illegible] 9		19[illegible]	

APRIL

	TIME	M		TIME	M
1	0218	7.2	16	0404	7.9
	0843	3.0		1014	2.5
M	1504	7.4	TU	1635	7.9
	2117	2.8		2238	2.3
2	0332	7.9	17	0451	8.4
	0949	2.2		1057	2.0
TU	1610	8.2	W	1713	8.4
	2214	1.9		2315	1.9
3	0430	8.7	18	0527	8.8
	1042	1.4		1132	1.7
W	1701	9.0	TH	1747	8.8
	2304	1.1		2347	1.6
4	0519	9.4	19	0603	9.0
	1130	0.7		1204	1.5
TH	1747	9.7	F	1818	9.0
	2347	0.5			
5	0605	10.0	20	0018	1.5
	1214	0.3		0634	9.2
F	1829	10.1	SA	1234	1.4
○			●	1846	9.2
6	0029	0.2	21	0046	1.5
	0649	10.3		0703	9.2
SA	1255	0.1	SU	1302	1.4
	1910	10.3		1914	9.2
7	0110	0.1	22	0114	1.6
	[illegible]	10.4		0733	9
			[illegible]	1328	

The extract above is from the *Admiralty Tide Tables* for Swansea. Say whether you would expect a flood stream or an ebb stream in the vicinity of Swansea at:

i) 1500 January 1st. ii) 1300 January 2nd. iii) 2315 January 2nd.

i) Ebb stream. ii) Flood stream. iii) Flood stream.

The diagram indicates the general direction of the main flood stream around the British Isles. The actual direction in a particular locality may be considerably different and it is always necessary to refer to the chart or tidal atlas of the area for detailed information. (Information can also be found in *Admiralty Sailing Directions* — also known as *"Pilots".)*

There are tidal atlases for all the waters around the British Isles; for other areas such atlases are available where the tidal stream can be related to a Standard Port and where sufficient observations have been made. The changing patterns of the tidal streams are shown hour-by-hour on each page. (See next page.)

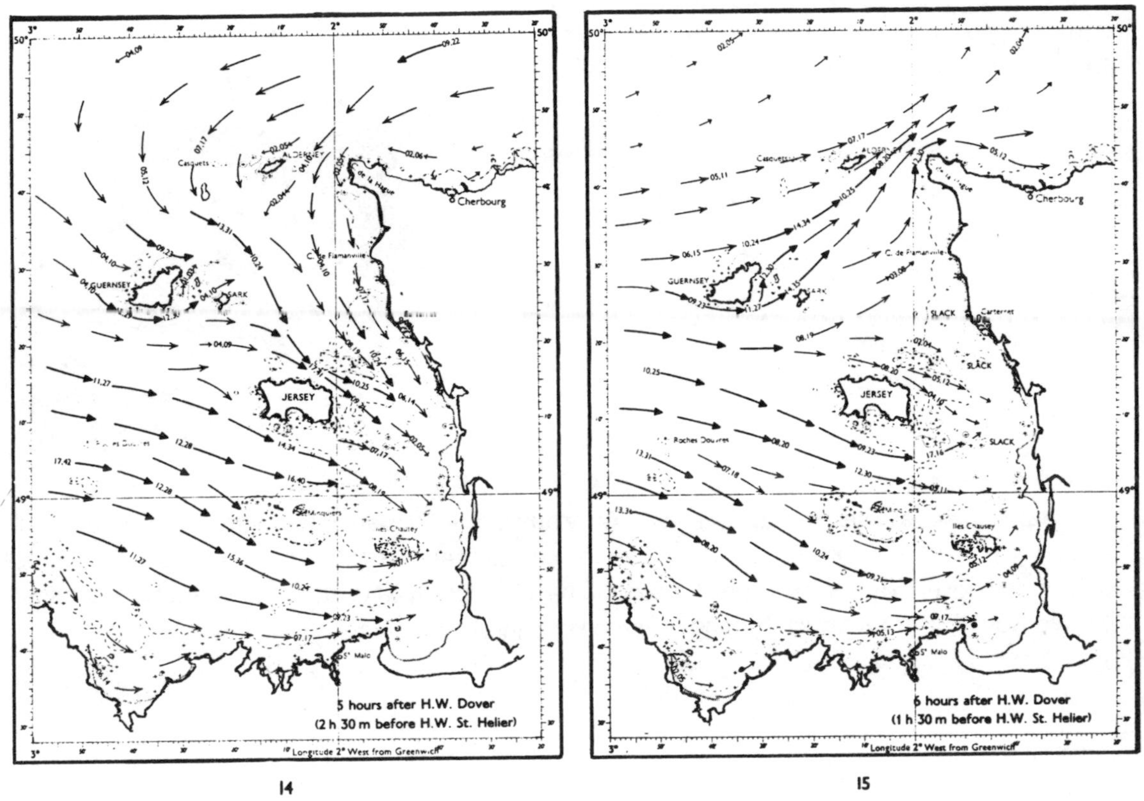

14 15

Excerpt from *The Tidal Stream Atlas: The Channel Islands and Adjacent Coasts of France,* showing the direction of the tidal stream for two consecutive hours.

A labelled diamond on a chart indicates that detailed tidal-stream information for that point is given in a table in a corner of the chart. This particular table gives a good illustration of the fact that the rate (i.e. speed) and direction of the tidal stream vary continuously throughout the period between high and low water. You can also see that tidal streams are stronger at springs than at neaps.

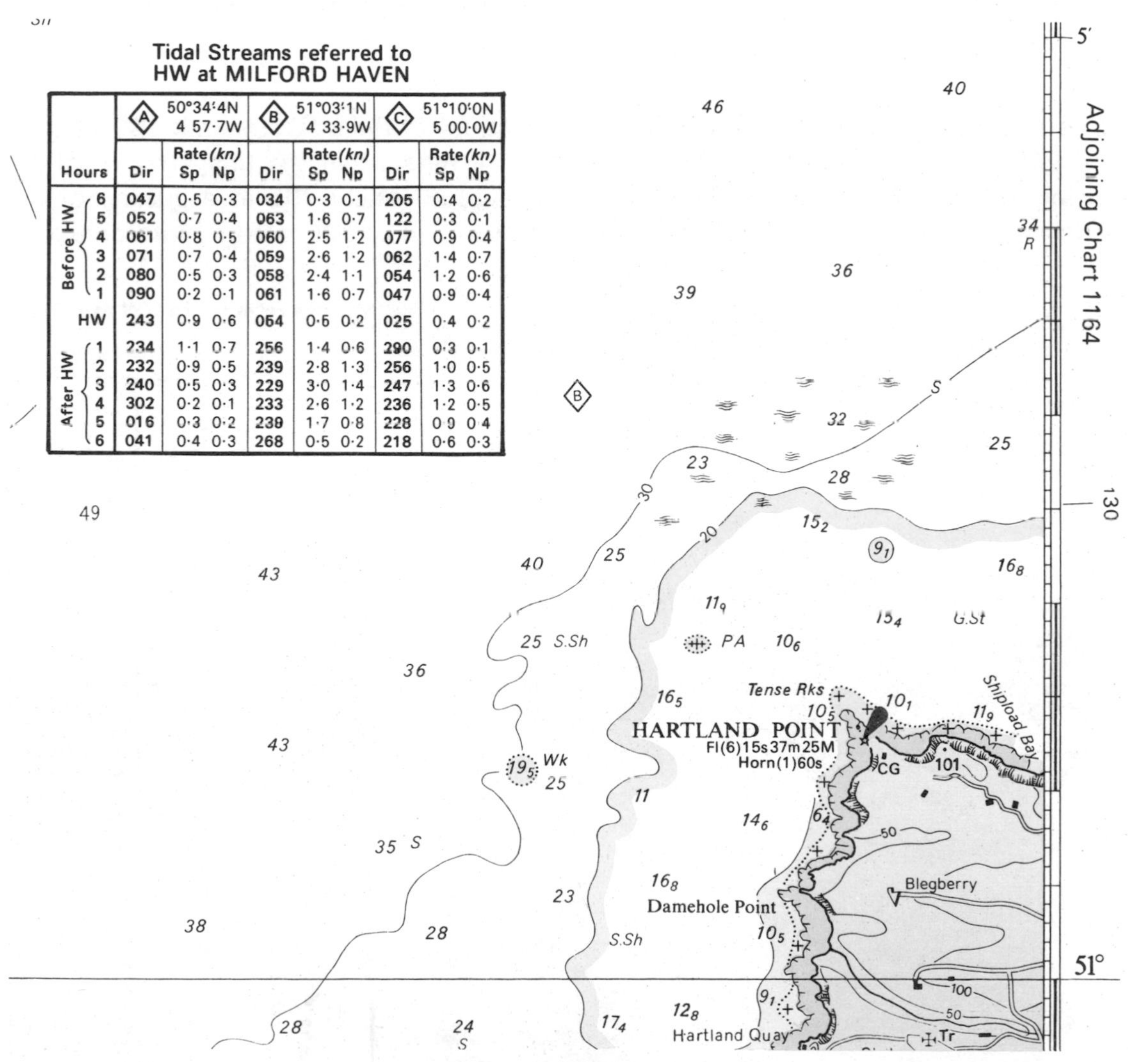

Tidal Streams referred to HW at MILFORD HAVEN

Hours	A 50°34'·4N 4 57·7W			B 51°03'·1N 4 33·9W			C 51°10'·0N 5 00·0W		
	Dir	Rate (kn) Sp	Np	Dir	Rate (kn) Sp	Np	Dir	Rate (kn) Sp	Np
Before HW 6	047	0·5	0·3	034	0·3	0·1	205	0·4	0·2
5	052	0·7	0·4	063	1·6	0·7	122	0·3	0·1
4	061	0·8	0·5	060	2·5	1·2	077	0·9	0·4
3	071	0·7	0·4	059	2·6	1·2	062	1·4	0·7
2	080	0·5	0·3	058	2·4	1·1	054	1·2	0·6
1	090	0·2	0·1	061	1·6	0·7	047	0·9	0·4
HW	243	0·9	0·6	054	0·5	0·2	025	0·4	0·2
After HW 1	234	1·1	0·7	256	1·4	0·6	290	0·3	0·1
2	232	0·9	0·5	239	2·8	1·3	256	1·0	0·5
3	240	0·5	0·3	229	3·0	1·4	247	1·3	0·6
4	302	0·2	0·1	233	2·6	1·2	236	1·2	0·5
5	016	0·3	0·2	238	1·7	0·8	228	0·9	0·4
6	041	0·4	0·3	268	0·5	0·2	218	0·6	0·3

What would be the direction and the rate of the tidal stream in the vicinity of ⟨B⟩ 4 hours after H.W. at Milford Haven? (Assume a neap tide.)

233° 1·2 Knots

As the tidal stream will affect the course steered by the ship, the navigating officer will need to know the direction and rate of the tidal stream at <u>any</u> particular point in coastal waters. Reference to the chart may produce no suitably placed tidal-stream diamonds or helpful arrows. In this situation he must <u>interpolate between</u> tidal diamonds.

If he finds out from the table that the set (direction) of the tidal stream is 190° at ◇J and 215° at ◇G then (by interpolation) he can estimate that the tidal stream will be setting 202° at a point half-way between, and approximately 196° at a quarter of the distance from ◇J. The rate of the tidal stream can also be estimated by interpolation.

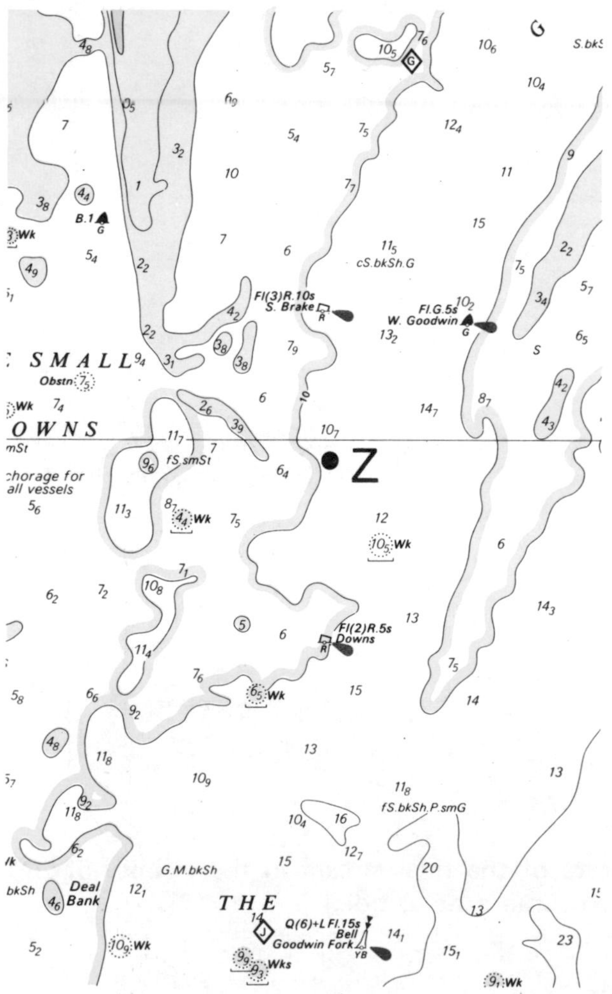

Tidal Streams referred to HW at DOVER

Hours		◇J 51°13'·3N 1 26·6E Dir	Rate (kn) Sp	Np
Before HW	6	181	1·6	0·9
	5	183	2·1	1·1
	4	186	2·1	1·2
	3	188	1·9	1·0
	2	190	0·8	0·5
	1	007	0·9	0·5
HW		001	2·1	1·2
After HW	1	001	2·3	1·3
	2	003	2·3	1·3
	3	002	1·4	0·8
	4	017	0·6	0·3
	5	161	0·3	0·2
	6	180	1·3	0·7

Hours		◇G 51°16'·3N 1 27·4E Dir	Rate (kn) Sp	Np
Before HW	6	195	2·0	1·1
	5	197	2·6	1·5
	4	197	2·8	1·5
	3	202	2·4	1·3
	2	215	1·0	0·6
	1	012	1·3	0·7
HW		017	2·7	1·5
After HW	1	027	3·2	1·7
	2	018	2·6	1·4
	3	022	1·7	0·9
	4	037	0·6	0·3
	5	205	0·4	0·2
	6	197	1·6	0·9

Estimate the rate and direction of the tidal stream at point Z. The time is 3 hours after H.W. and it is a spring tide.

012°, 1·6 Knots.

In this section a simplified account of tidal theory has been given. For further information see Chapter XII *Admiralty Manual of Navigation Volume I* and Introduction to *Admiralty Tide Tables Volume 1.*

Section 4 : Self-test

1. What is the difference between 'tide' and 'tidal stream'?
2. What is the 'range' of the tide?
3. What do the following terms mean?
   i) 'spring tides'.
   ii) 'neap tides'.
4. How long does it take for a succession of two high and two low tides to occur?
5. What tides would you expect at i) full Moon ii) last quarter?

6. i) What is the height of high water at Narvik on Saturday 4th May 1985.
   ii) This is the height above – what?
   iii) What is the height of the tide on the same day at 1500?
   (Refer to page 93 to help you answer these questions.)

7. On the chart below, what are the direction and rate of the tidal stream at X? (The time is 1 hour before H.W. at Immingham and it is a spring tide.)

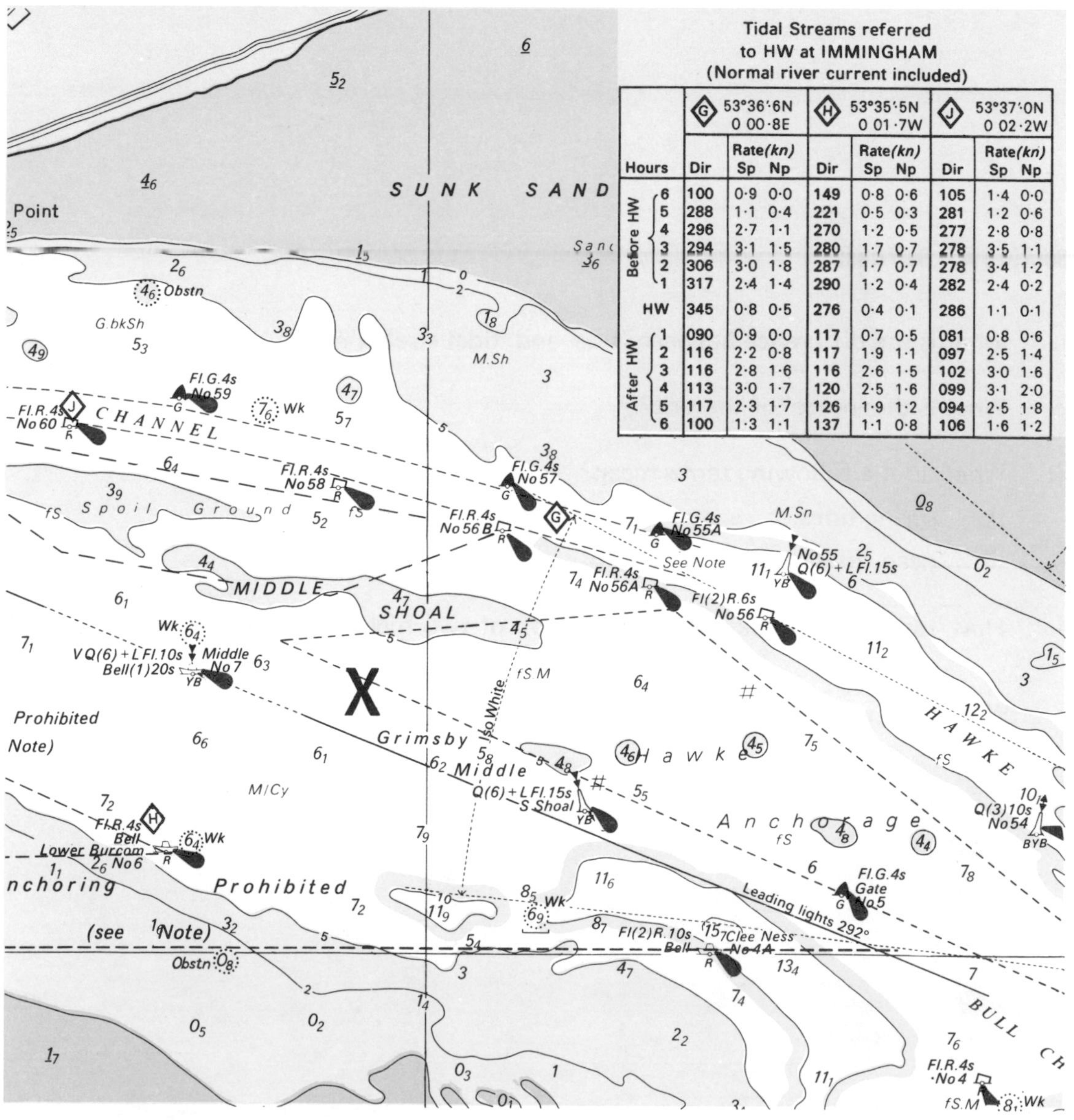

Tidal Streams referred to HW at IMMINGHAM (Normal river current included)

Hours	G 53°36'·6N 0 00·8E			H 53°35'·5N 0 01·7W			J 53°37'·0N 0 02·2W		
	Dir	Rate (kn) Sp	Np	Dir	Rate (kn) Sp	Np	Dir	Rate (kn) Sp	Np
Before HW 6	100	0·9	0·0	149	0·8	0·6	105	1·4	0·0
5	288	1·1	0·4	221	0·5	0·3	281	1·2	0·6
4	296	2·7	1·1	270	1·2	0·5	277	2·8	0·8
3	294	3·1	1·5	280	1·7	0·7	278	3·5	1·1
2	306	3·0	1·8	287	1·7	0·7	278	3·4	1·2
1	317	2·4	1·4	290	1·2	0·4	282	2·4	0·2
HW	345	0·8	0·5	276	0·4	0·1	286	1·1	0·1
After HW 1	090	0·9	0·0	117	0·7	0·5	081	0·8	0·6
2	116	2·2	0·8	117	1·9	1·1	097	2·5	1·4
3	116	2·8	1·6	116	2·6	1·5	102	3·0	1·6
4	113	3·0	1·7	120	2·5	1·6	099	3·1	2·0
5	117	2·3	1·7	126	1·9	1·2	094	2·5	1·8
6	100	1·3	1·1	137	1·1	0·8	106	1·6	1·2

Now turn to page 94 for answers.

NORWAY - NARVIK

LAT 68°26'N   LONG 17°25'E

TIME ZONE **-0100**   TIMES AND HEIGHTS OF HIGH AND LOW WATERS   YEAR **1985**

MAY

	TIME	M		TIME	M
1	0318	1.0	**16**	0429	1.0
	0933	2.6		1024	2.6
W	1553	0.6	TH	1653	0.7
	2215	2.7		2254	2.6
2	0417	0.8	**17**	0509	0.9
	1025	2.9		1057	2.6
TH	1641	0.4	F	1719	0.7
	2300	3.0		2327	2.7
3	0505	0.6	**18**	0543	0.9
	1109	3.0		1131	2.7
F	1729	0.2	SA	1754	0.6
	2341	3.1			
4	0553	0.5	**19**	0002	2.8
	1151	3.2		0618	0.8
SA	1807	0.1	**SU**	1206	2.7
○			●	1818	0.6
5	0023	3.3	**20**	0033	2.9
	0631	0.4		0645	0.8
SU	1236	3.2	M	1241	2.7
	1851	0.1		1849	0.6
6	0103	3.3	**21**	0105	2.9
	0715	0.3		0717	0.8
M	1317	3.2	TU	1312	2.7
	1932	0.2		1917	0.6
7	0144	3.3	**22**	0136	2.9
	0756	0.4		0748	0.8
TU	1357	3.1	W	1349	2.7
	2013	0.3		1944	0.6
8	0221	3.2	**23**	0213	2.9
	0844	0.5		0825	0.8
W	1439	2.9	TH	1426	2.6
	2059	0.5		2021	0.7
9	0307	3.0	**24**	0250	2.8
	0936	0.7		0906	0.8
TH	1531	2.6	F	1511	2.5
	2150	0.8		2106	0.8
10	0359	2.7	**25**	0335	2.7
	1038	0.8		[illegible]	0.9
F	1626	[illegible]			

JUNE

	TIME	M		TIME	M
1	0431	0.8	**16**	0501	1.1
	1039	2.9		1052	2.5
SA	1655	0.4	**SU**	1701	0.8
	2314	3.0		2329	2.7
2	0522	0.7	**17**	0545	1.0
	1127	3.0		1133	2.5
SU	1743	0.4	M	1741	0.8
3	0002	3.1	**18**	0004	2.8
	0618	0.6		0623	0.9
M	1216	3.0	TU	1215	2.6
○	1832	0.4	●	1820	0.7
4	0044	3.2	**19**	0045	2.9
	0707	0.5		0704	0.9
TU	1302	3.0	W	1256	2.7
	1918	0.4		1904	0.7
5	0130	3.1	**20**	0123	3.0
	0758	0.5		0743	0.8
W	1346	2.9	TH	1338	2.7
	2006	0.5		1946	0.7
6	0214	3.1	**21**	0202	3.0
	0850	0.6		0827	0.7
TH	1438	2.8	F	1422	2.7
	2054	0.7		2024	0.7
7	0258	3.0	**22**	0243	3.0
	0938	0.6		0908	0.7
F	1526	2.6	SA	1509	2.7
	2145	0.8		2110	0.8
8	0346	2.8	**23**	0326	3.0
	1036	0.7		0958	0.7
SA	1624	2.4	**SU**	1601	2.7
	2239	1.0		2202	0.8
9	0434	2.7	**24**	0414	2.9
	1134	0.8		1050	0.7
SU	1722	2.3	M	1655	2.6
	2345	1.1		2303	0.9
10	0533	2.5	**25**	0504	2.8
	1233	[illegible]		1144	0.7
M	1831	[illegible]		[illegible]	2.6

JULY

	TIME	M		TIME	M
1	0512	0.9	**16**	0511	1.2
	1113	2.7		1110	2.4
M	1729	0.7	TU	1711	0.9
	2348	3.0		2344	2.8
2	0617	0.8	**17**	0610	1.0
	1205	2.8		1158	2.6
TU	1828	0.6	W	1807	0.8
○			●		
3	0036	3.0	**18**	0026	2.9
	0712	0.7		0651	0.8
W	1300	2.8	TH	1243	2.7
	1919	0.6		1851	0.7
4	0124	3.1	**19**	0107	3.1
	0804	0.6		0732	0.7
TH	1344	2.8	F	1327	2.9
	2007	0.7		1936	0.6
5	0202	3.1	**20**	0148	3.2
	0849	0.6		0813	0.5
F	1430	2.8	SA	1412	2.9
	2049	0.7		2020	0.6
6	0248	3.1	**21**	0228	3.2
	0935	0.6		0857	0.4
SA	1516	2.7	**SU**	1456	3.0
	2139	0.8		2101	0.6
7	0327	3.0	**22**	0309	3.2
	1016	0.7		0934	0.4
SU	1600	2.6	M	1539	2.9
	2216	0.9		2148	0.7
8	0407	2.8	**23**	0352	3.1
	1100	0.8		1025	0.4
M	1645	2.5	TU	1626	2.9
	2304	1.1		2234	0.8
9	0455	2.7	**24**	0439	3.0
	1142	0.8		1112	0.5
TU	1737	2.4	W	1720	2.8
	2350	1.2		2328	0.9
10	0541	2.5	**25**	0530	2.9
	1221	[illegible]		[illegible]	0.6

AUGUST

	TIME	M		TIME	M
1	0028	3.0	**16**	0004	3.0
	0707	0.6		0630	0.7
TH	1252	2.8	F	1228	2.9
	1917	0.7	●	1837	0.6
2	0112	3.1	**17**	0045	3.2
	0755	0.5		0708	0.5
F	1336	2.9	SA	1309	3.1
	1955	0.7		1918	0.5
3	0150	3.1	**18**	0126	3.3
	0834	0.5		0745	0.3
SA	1414	2.9	**SU**	1350	3.2
	2034	0.7		1958	0.4
4	0229	3.1	**19**	0203	3.4
	0905	0.5		0822	0.2
SU	1453	2.8	M	1431	3.2
	2112	0.8		2036	0.5
5	0300	3.0	**20**	0240	3.4
	0940	0.6		0902	0.2
M	1528	2.7	TU	1514	3.1
	2143	0.9		2115	0.5
6	0335	2.9	**21**	0320	3.2
	1011	0.7		0949	0.3
TU	1603	2.6	W	1557	3.0
	2215	1.0		2202	0.7
7	0406	2.7	**22**	0407	3.0
	1039	0.9		1036	0.5
W	1636	2.5	TH	1644	2.8
	2248	1.2		2252	0.9
8	0444	2.5	**23**	0457	2.8
	1116	1.0		1126	0.7
TH	1721	2.4	F	1742	2.6
	2329	1.3		2354	1.0
9	0521	2.4	**24**	0559	2.6
	1153	1.1		1231	0.9
F	1812	2.3	SA	1856	2.5
10	0008	1.4	**25**	[illegible]	
	0612	2.2			
SA	1235				

NARVIK

MEAN SPRING AND NEAP CURVES

Springs occurs 2 days after New and Full Moon

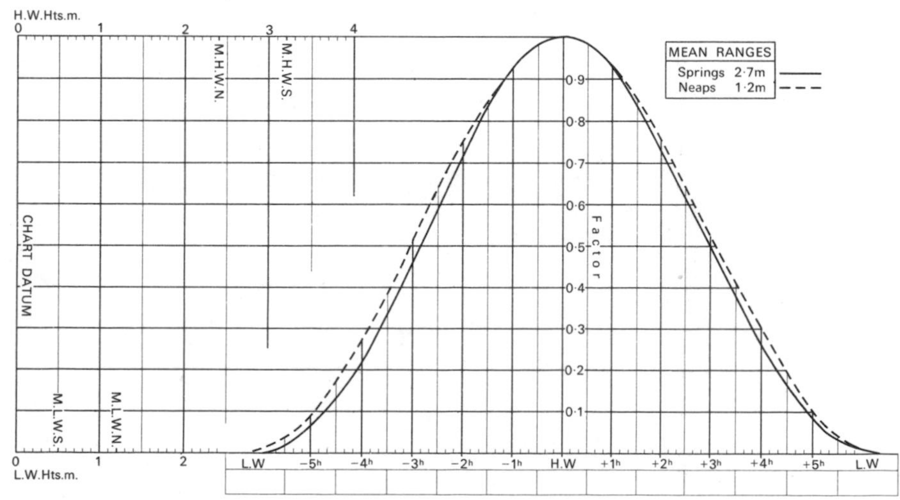

Section 4: Answers to Self-test

1. 'Tide' is the vertical movement of water. 'Tidal stream' is the horizontal movement of water.

2. The range of the tide is the vertical distance between successive high and low water.

3. i) Spring tides are those where the range is greatest.

   ii) Neap tides are those where the range is least.

4. Just over 24 hours.

5. i) Spring tides.

   ii) Neap tides.

6. i) 3·2m

   ii) Chart Datum.

   iii) 1·6m.

7. 303° (or 304°) 1·8 Knots.

Section 5: Levels

There is now in progress a programme for metricating Admiralty charts, and the old charts with depths expressed in fathoms are gradually being replaced by charts of improved design using metric units. However, as there are few fathoms charts left, all charts in this book are metric charts.

The most obvious distinguishing feature of a fathoms chart is the colouring. Grey instead of yellow is the colour for the land, and the foreshore is represented by shading.

ENGLAND — EAST COAST

ENTRANCE TO THE

RIVER HUMBER

DEPTHS IN METRES

SCALE 1:50 000

You can see that 'DEPTHS IN METRES' is written under the title of this metric chart; a fathoms chart will have______ __ _______under the title.

DEPTHS IN FATHOMS

It is not only the depths which are in metres on a metric chart. All heights and land contours are in metres as well.

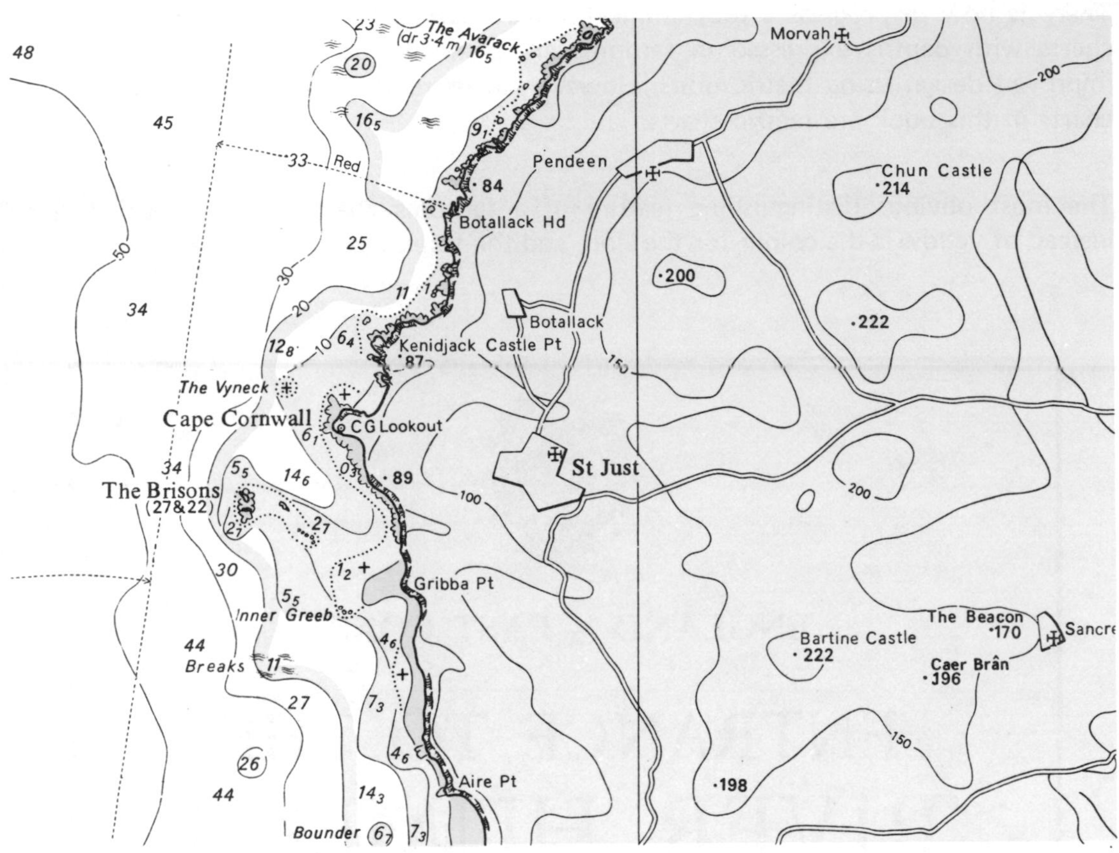

What is the height of Chun Castle?

214 metres.

You will have noticed that on almost all the examples of charts illustrated in this book, the sea areas are covered with a host of figures. These represent the depths of water at different points.

The chart below, as well as showing depths at particular points, also gives the submarine contours. The convention on metric charts is to show depths below 5 metres in blue, and to line the 10 metre depth contour with a ribbon of blue tint.

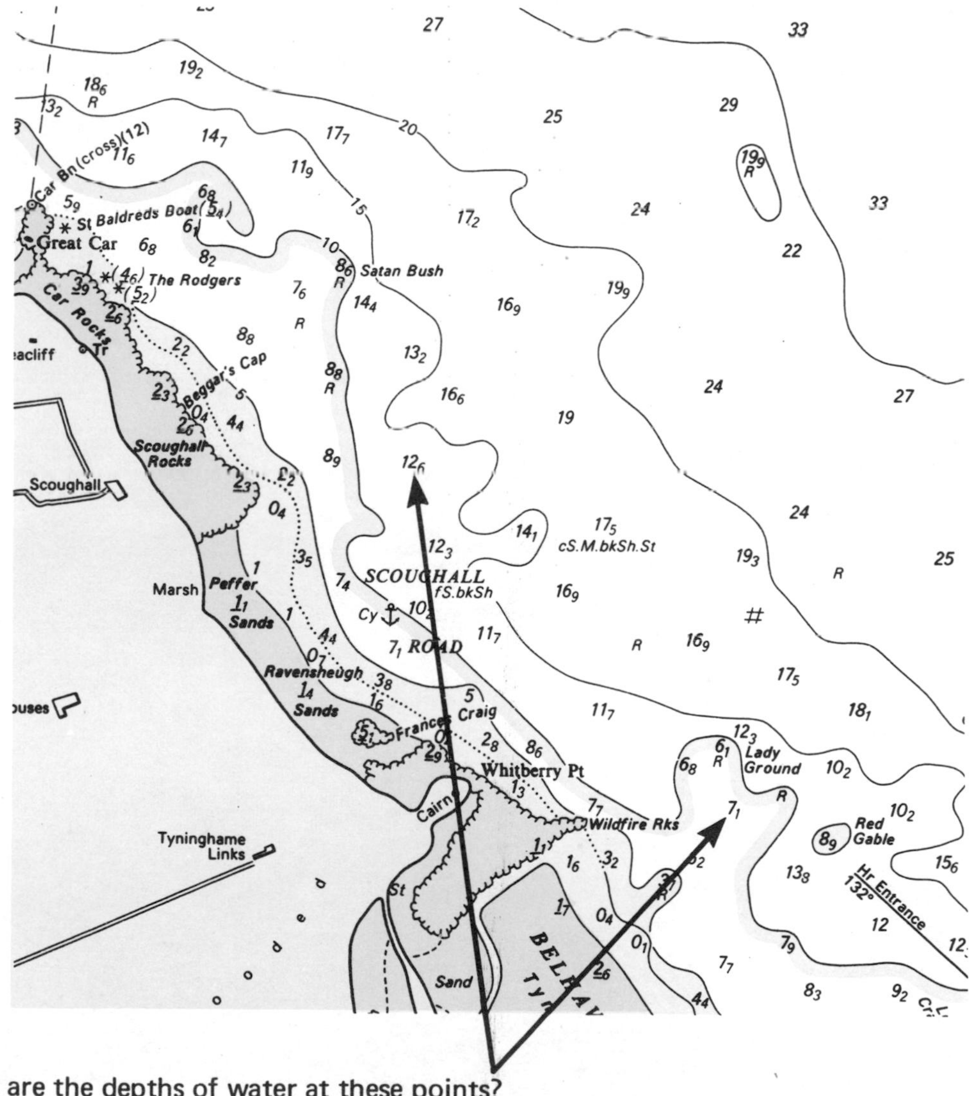

What are the depths of water at these points?

7·1 metres.   12·6 metres.

As the actual depth of water at any point is constantly changing because of the tide, a datum line is used to which all depths are referred. Depths shown on a chart are expressed as depths below Chart Datum and heights of tide are measured above Chart Datum.

What is Chart Datum?

Chart Datum is an arbitrarily fixed level (different for every port) below which the tide seldom, if ever, falls.

As the tide rises and falls, certain parts of the shore are alternately covered and uncovered by the water-level. These parts are called the *foreshore* and are coloured green on metric charts. (On the chart below note how sand is represented when it is part of the shore.)

Other features besides the foreshore may lie exposed between high and low water e.g. rocks, wrecks etc. All such features have what is called a *drying height*, that is their height is above Chart Datum. Drying heights are given as underlined figures.

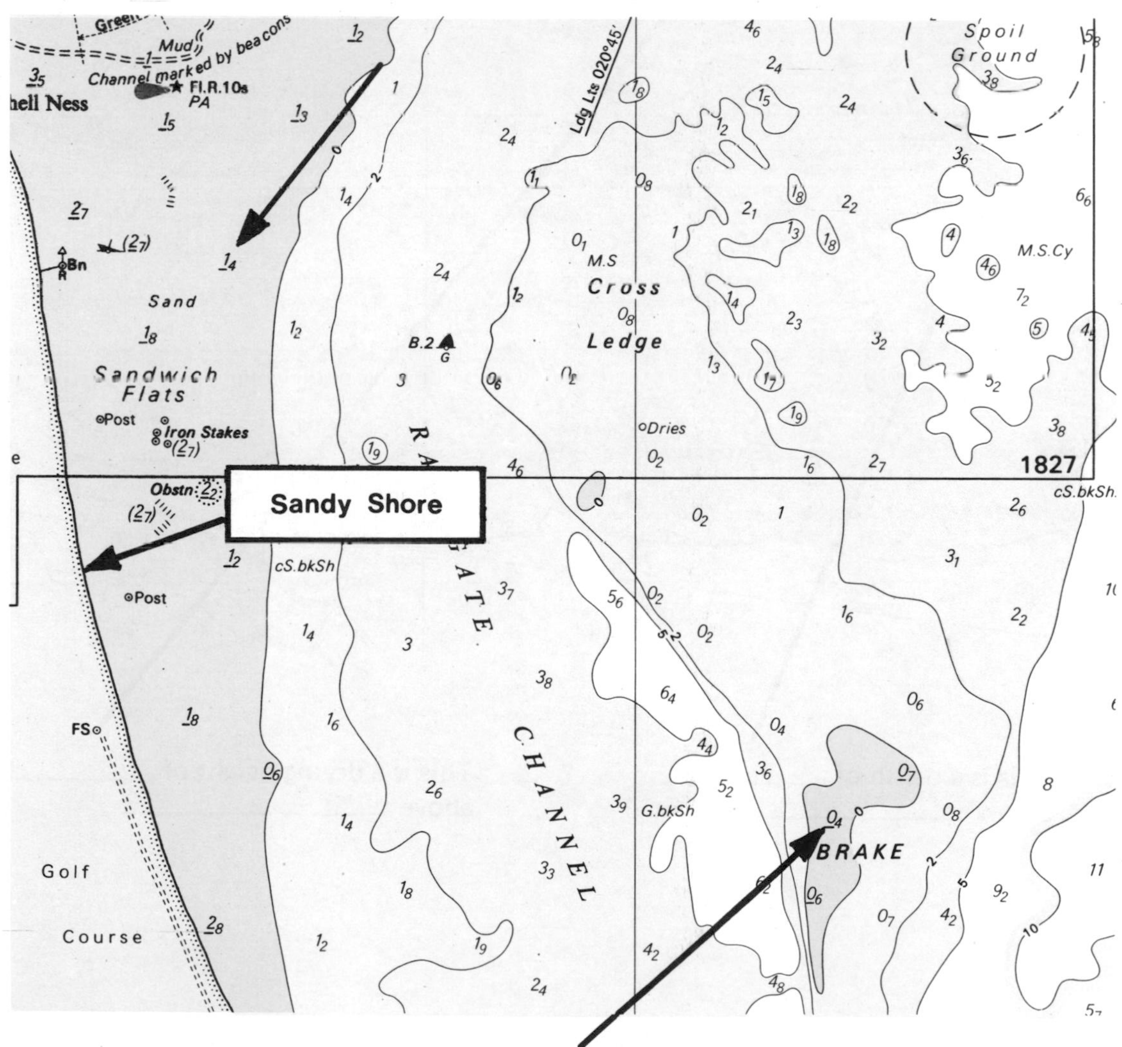

What will be the depth of water at this point with a height of tide of 2m?

1·6 metres.

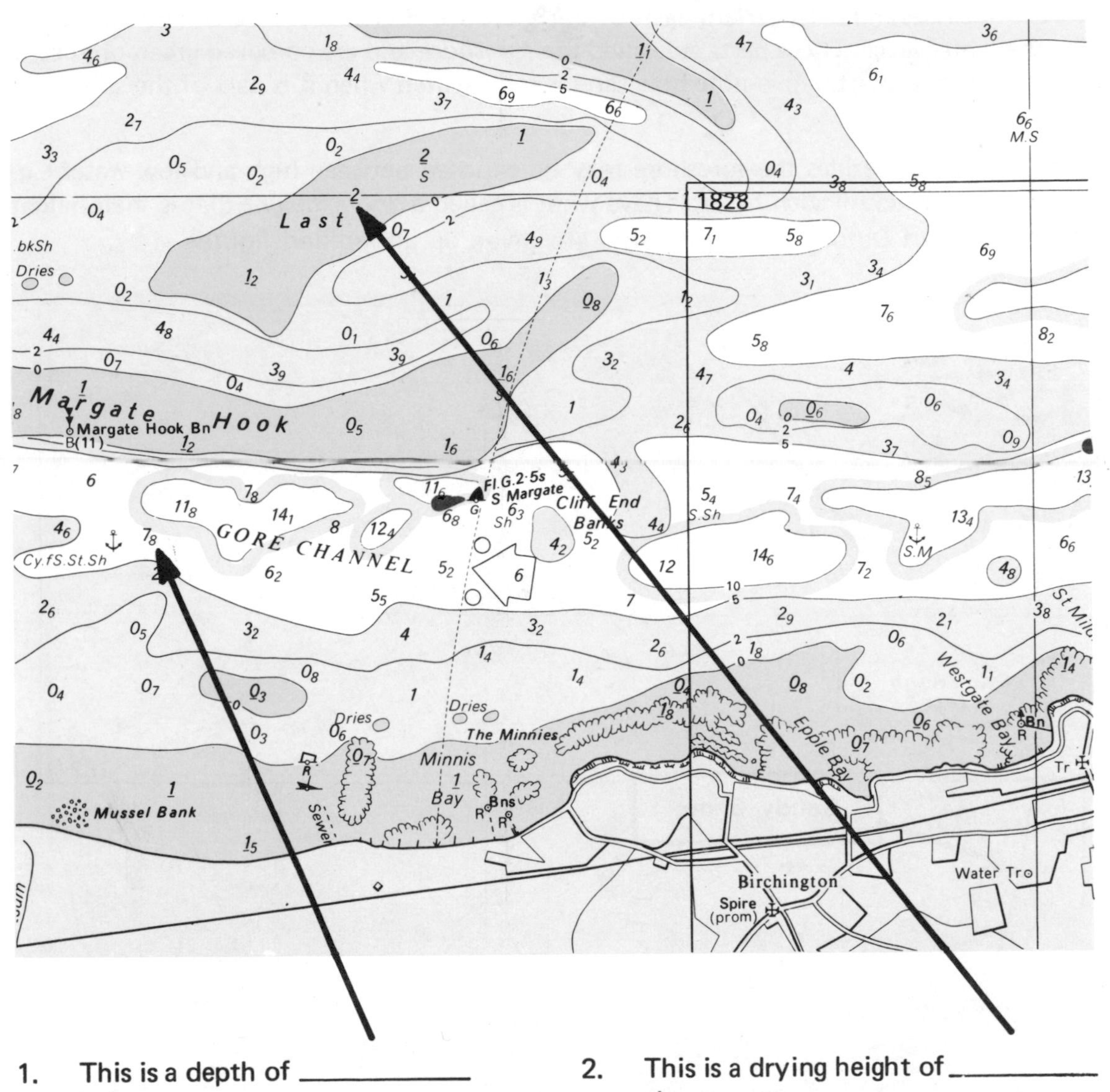

1. This is a depth of ____________ below ______ __________ .

2. This is a drying height of ____________ above ______ __________ .

1. 7·8 metres.
   Chart Datum.

2. 2 metres.
   Chart Datum.

To summarise so far: Chart Datum is an arbitrarily fixed level used in the measurement of depths, drying heights and heights of tide.

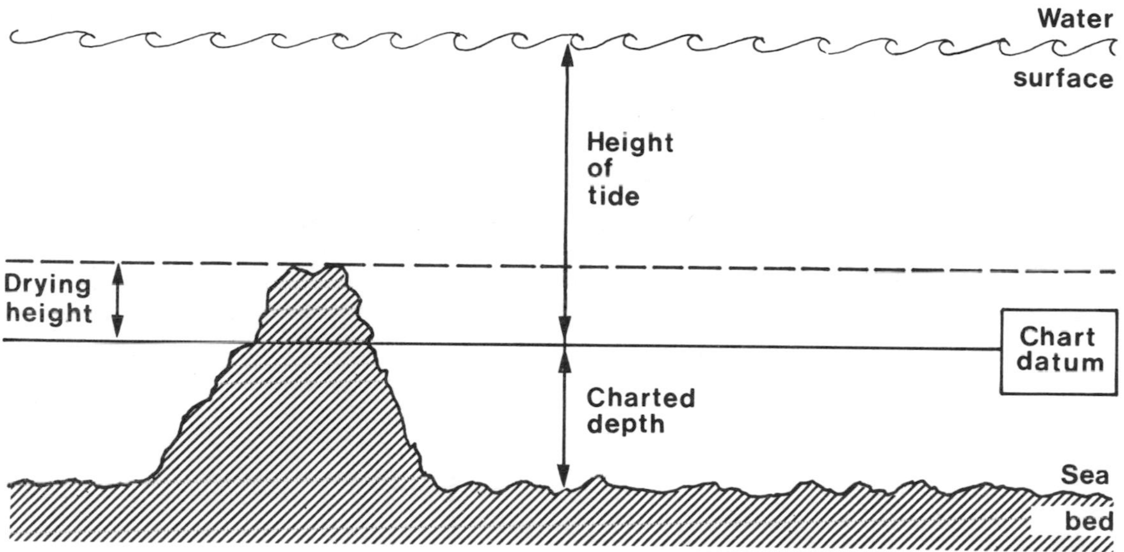

The diagram shows the relationship between Chart Datum and height of tide. Think back to the definition of Chart Datum that you have already learnt and then answer this question. Would you expect to find a low tide prediction of e.g., minus 0·1 metres, in the *Admiralty Tide Tables?*

Never.

Very rarely.

Often.

Choose the correct answer and then turn to page 102

Very rarely. (It is possible because, except for very low tides, Chart Datum is below low-tide level. If you study the pages of the *Admiralty Tide Tables,* you will be able to find a few predicted low tides that are below Chart Datum.)

In planning your passage there will be times when you want to know if there will be sufficient water under the keel. The chart will tell you the depth below Chart Datum. To translate this figure into the actual depth of water at any particular time, you will need to consult the *Admiralty Tide Tables* to find the height of tide.

Calculate the amount of clearance below the ship's keel when:

depth according to chart = 25·0m,
height of tide according to the *Admiralty Tide Tables* = 3·0m,
draught of vessel = 10·0m.

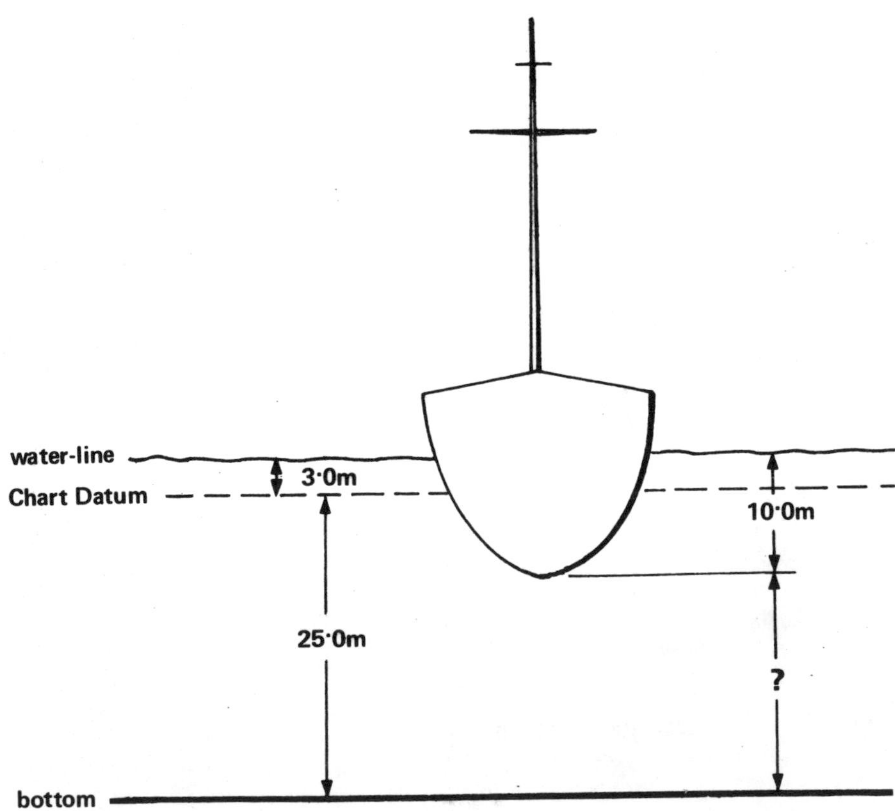

Depth under keel = 18m (25 + 3 – 10).

This sort of calculation is one that you will make in planning your passage. To find out the actual depths of water beneath your ship, you will need to take soundings, and these are obtained by an Echo Sounder. This works on the principle that if a sound impulse is transmitted underwater, the time taken for it to be reflected off the sea-bed and received again by the ship will give a measure of the depth of water. Readings are taken from a sheet of paper on which the depths are recorded automatically by a stylus.

(See the *Admiralty Manual of Navigation Volume I* for further information.)

It is important that there should be sufficient clearance not only for the ship's keel but also for the ship's mast-head. Shipping has to pass under bridges, overhead cables, etc. and if you discover from the chart or *Sailing Directions* that these or other overhead obstructions will be encountered on your planned passage, you will need to calculate the amount of clearance.

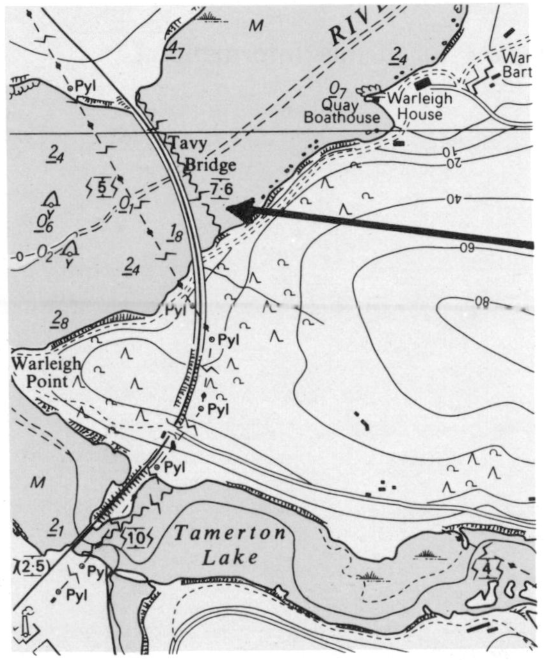

The overhead clearance of this bridge, as the chart shows, is 7·6 metres. The actual distance between the bridge and the water will be larger than this on most occasions. That is, 7·6 metres is the minimum height of the bridge above the water. Bearing this in mind, which of these levels would be the datum used for the clearance of this bridge?

BRIDGE

average high-water level at springs

average low-water level at neaps

Chart Datum

The average high-water level at springs.

This is the datum used for all heights on charts (except drying heights). It is commonly referred to as *Mean High Water Springs (M.H.W.S.).* The actual water-level will rarely be higher than this, and so the actual clearance under a bridge at any one time is likely to be greater than the figure given on a chart.

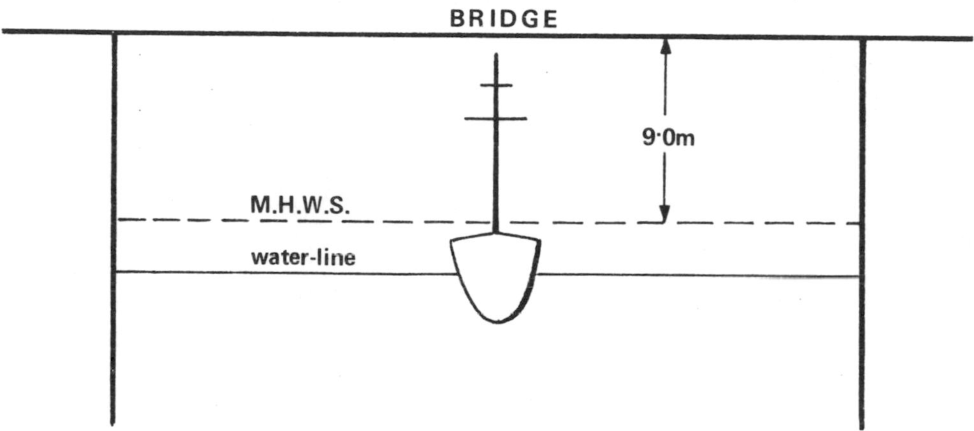

What is the datum used for the heights and depths on this chart?

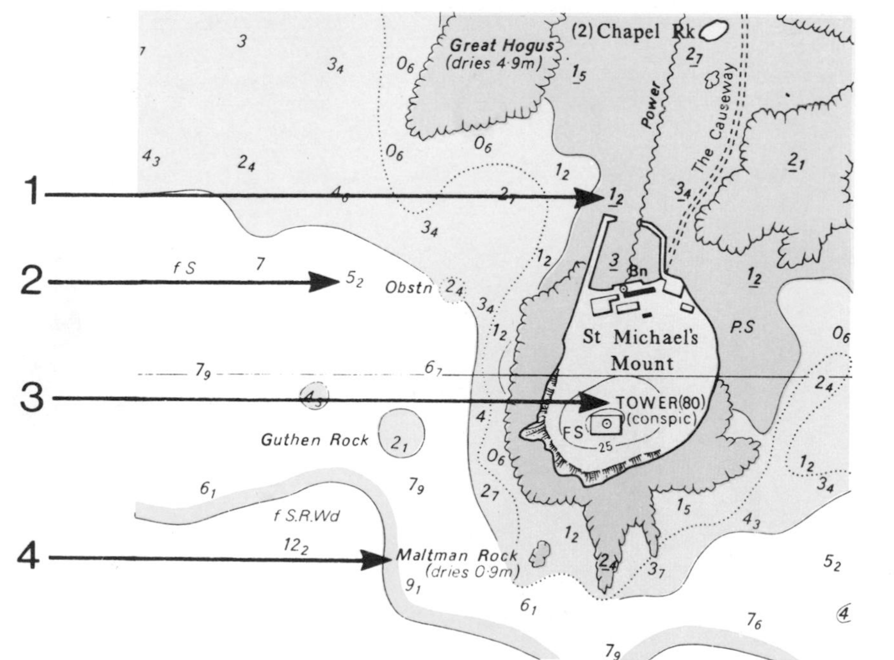

1. Chart Datum.
2. Chart Datum.
3. M.H.W.S.
4. Chart Datum.

The height of a structure above M.H.W.S. is called its *charted elevation* (to distinguish it from the height above Ordnance Datum used on land maps).

What is the difference between this and a drying height?

The drying height is the height of the foreshore and other features exposed between tides. It is measured above Chart Datum. The charted elevation is the height of all other features shown on a chart. It is measured above M.H.W.S.

You have the following information, and you want to calculate the amount of clearance between a bridge and the ship's mast-head.

Charted elevation of bridge = 23·8m.

Height of tide = 1·0m.

Distance from water-line
to mast-head = 32·0m.

What other information do you need before you can carry out this calculation? (Draw a diagram of the levels to help you answer this question.)

The height of M.H.W.S. above Chart Datum.

This information is given in Table V on page xli of the *Admiralty Tide Tables* and you will need to refer to this in order to make your calculation. (You will notice that other tidal levels are also given in Table V, e.g. Mean Low Water Springs (M.L.W.S.).

The other facts you were given were:

Charted elevation of bridge = 23·8m.

Height of tide according to the *Admiralty Tide Tables* = 1·0m.

Distance from water-line to mast-head = 32·0m.

The bridge is just outside Devonport. How far will the mast-head be below or above the bridge? Always draw a diagram before attempting these problems.

The mast-head will be 3·7m above the bridge.

This is how the calculation is done:

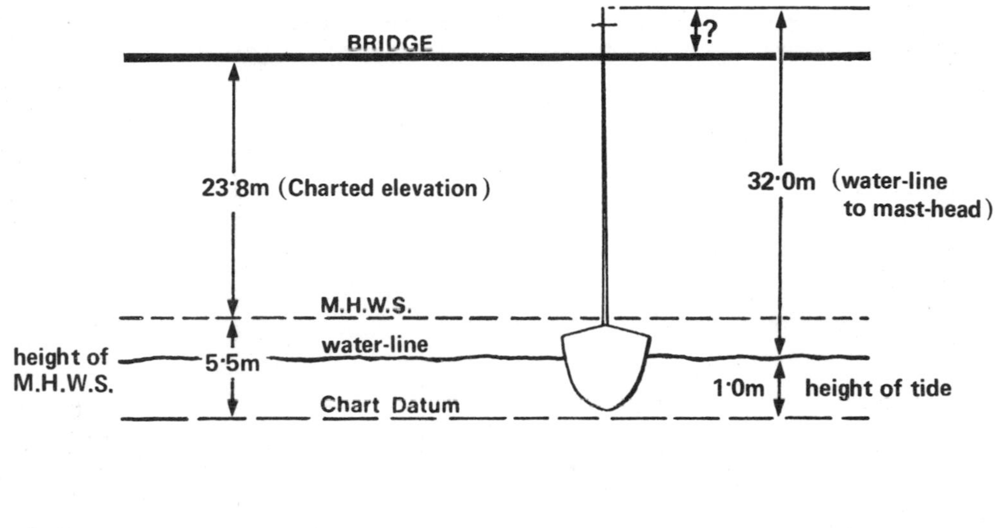

According to Table V the height of M.H.W.S. above Chart Datum at Devonport is 5·5m.

The height of the bridge above the water-line = (23·8 + 5·5 – 1·0)m = 28·3m.

Distance from the water-line to the mast-head = 32·0m.

Thus the mast-head will be 3·7m above the bridge.

Here are two more practice questions. Calculate the clearances. (Remember to draw a diagram first.)

1. Charted height of bridge 21·0m.
   Height of tide = 1·9m.
   Distance from water-line to mast-head = 17·5m.
   Height of M.H.W.S. above Chart Datum = 4·9m.

2. Charted elevation of overhead cable at Milford Haven = 27·4m.
   Distance from water-line to mast-head = 32·0m.
   Height of tide = 0·5m.

(You will need to refer to Table V in the Admiralty Tide Tables to complete this problem.)

1. Clearance = 6·5m.
2. Clearance = 1·9m.

State what datum is used in measuring each of the following levels:

i) Charted depth.
ii) High water.
iii) Drying height.
iv) M.H.W.S.
v) Low water.
vi) Charted elevation.

i)
ii)
iii) } Chart Datum
iv)
v)
vi) M.H.W.S.

Section 5 : Self-test

1. The labelled lines on the diagram below represent the following: a particular neap low water, a particular neap high water, M.H.W.S., M.L.W.S., and Chart Datum. Which lines represent which levels?

A

B

C

D

E

2. The charted elevation of a bridge is 30·5 m. The distance of a ship's mast-head to the water-line is 32·0 m. Using the *Admiralty Tide Tables* work out the clearance, if the bridge is just outside Devonport and is passed under at low water on June 24th 1985 (1·5 m).

3. On a metric chart what do these figures mean: i) $\underline{3}$? ii) 7_5 ?

4. If the draught of a ship is 8m, how much clearance below the keel will there be if the depth of water according to the chart is 12·5m? (Height of tide = 3·5m.)

Now turn to page 112 for the answers.

Section 5 : Answers to Self-test

1.

A	M.H.W.S.
B	neap high water
C	neap low water
D	M.L.W.S.
E	Chart Datum

2. 2·5m.

3. i) A drying height of 3 metres.
   ii) A depth of 7·5 metres.

4. 8m.

Here is a diagram of the principle levels for reference.

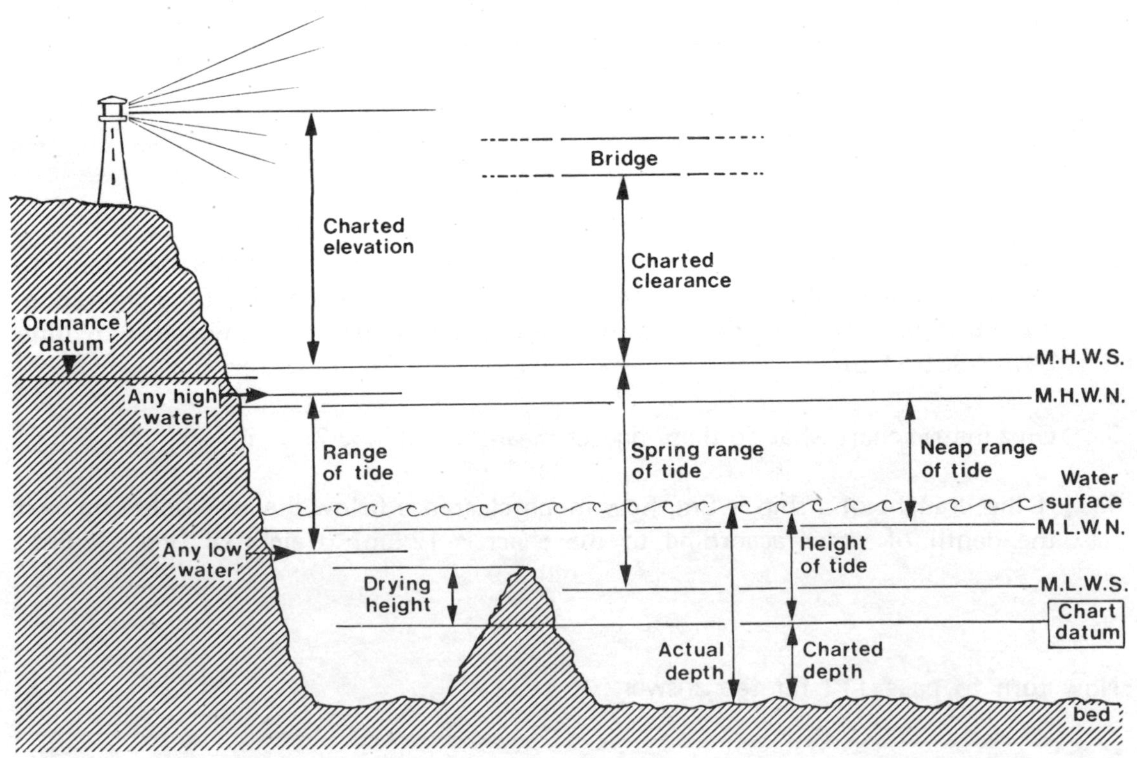

Section 6: Buoys – IALA Maritime Buoyage – Region 'A'

Buoys are used to mark channels, dangers and special areas.

A revised system of Buoyage, System 'A' was adopted for use in the waters of NW Europe from 1977, after years of study by the International Association of Lighthouse Authorities (IALA). System 'A' combines the previously separate Cardinal and Lateral Systems with some additions.

The system is made up of:

1. Lateral marks
2. Cardinal marks
3. Isolated danger marks
4. Safe water marks
5. Special marks

More information on buoyage can be found in *IALA Maritime Buoyage System 'A' (NP 735),* in the *Mariner's Handbook* (NP 100) and in the appropriate volume of the *Admiralty Sailing Directions (Pilots).*

However, as the system involves replacement of many buoys, and extensive chart amendments, it will not be complete in United Kingdom waters until 1980.

Where else do you suppose information on buoys could be found other than in books of reference?

If you said 'on a chart' you were right. (The chart is the authority for the buoyage of any particular area).

The mariner needs to know not only where a shoal, bank or other danger is but how far it extends. Thus buoys marking dangers are placed at the extremities of the dangers, and in the case of a lateral system buoy this means that you must pass it on one side and not on the other.

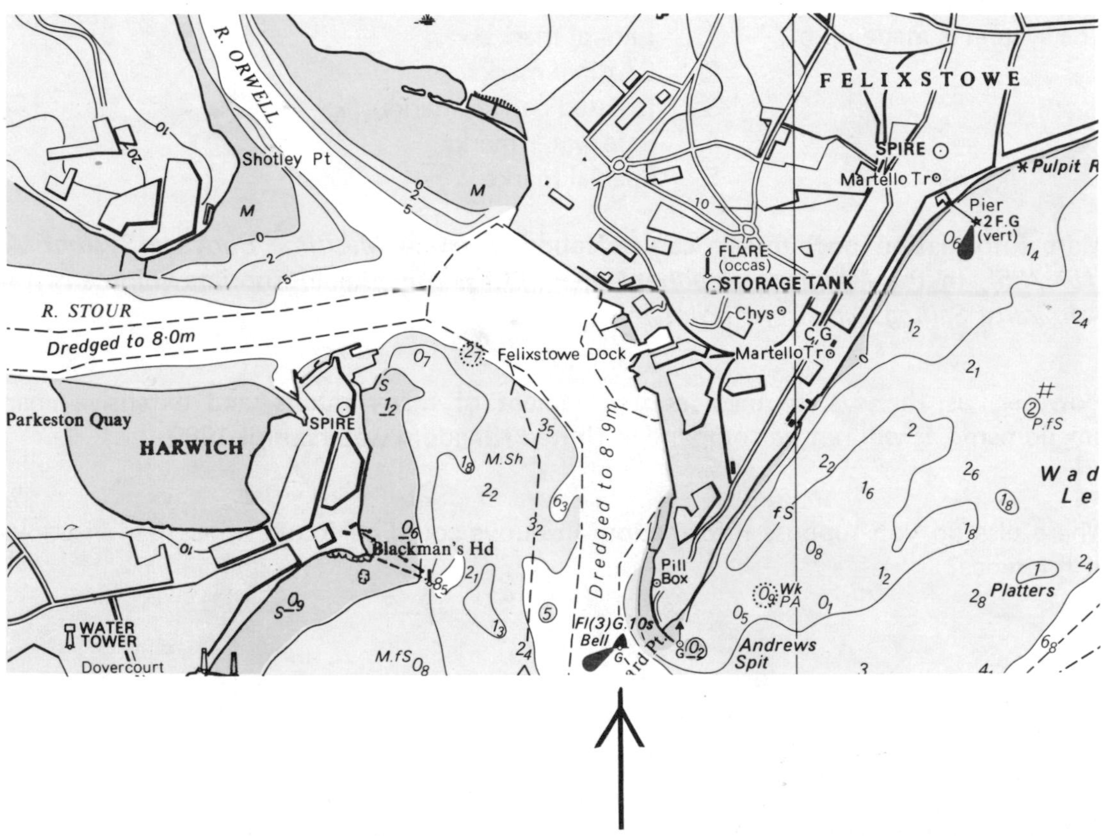

If you were approaching Felixstowe Dock from the south, as shown, on which side of your ship would you leave the buoy marked ▲ ?

The starboard side

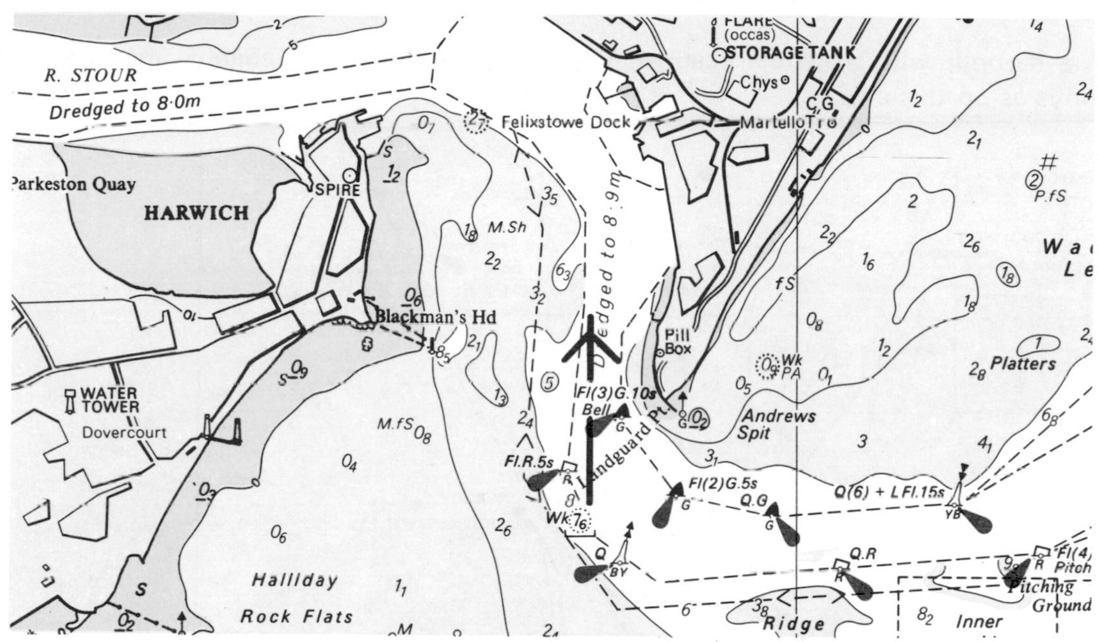

You would steer so that the buoy is on your starboard side as you pass it, i.e. you would leave it to starboard. Hence this type of buoy is called a starboard hand buoy.

As you can see the chart symbol 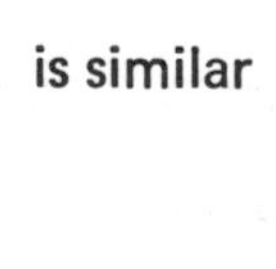 is similar in shape to the actual buoy, that is, conical. It may carry a cone-shaped topmark

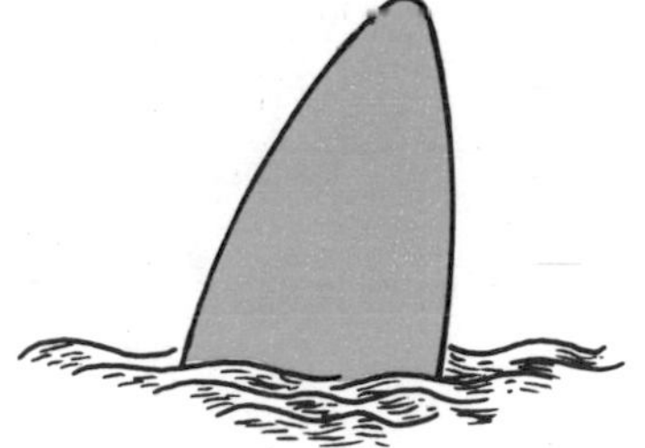

A starboard hand buoy may be a pillar or spar with a cone-shaped top mark.

Buoys are represented on charts by the appropriate symbol (which depends on the shape) and can be accompanied by additional information, e.g. G for green. Starboard hand buoys are always green in British waters: elsewhere they may sometimes be black.

Where else on the chart above can you find another starboard hand buoy?

To the north of the Pitching Ground or south of Landguard point.

In a harbour with a narrow channel, you will usually find the channel marked with buoys as on this chart.

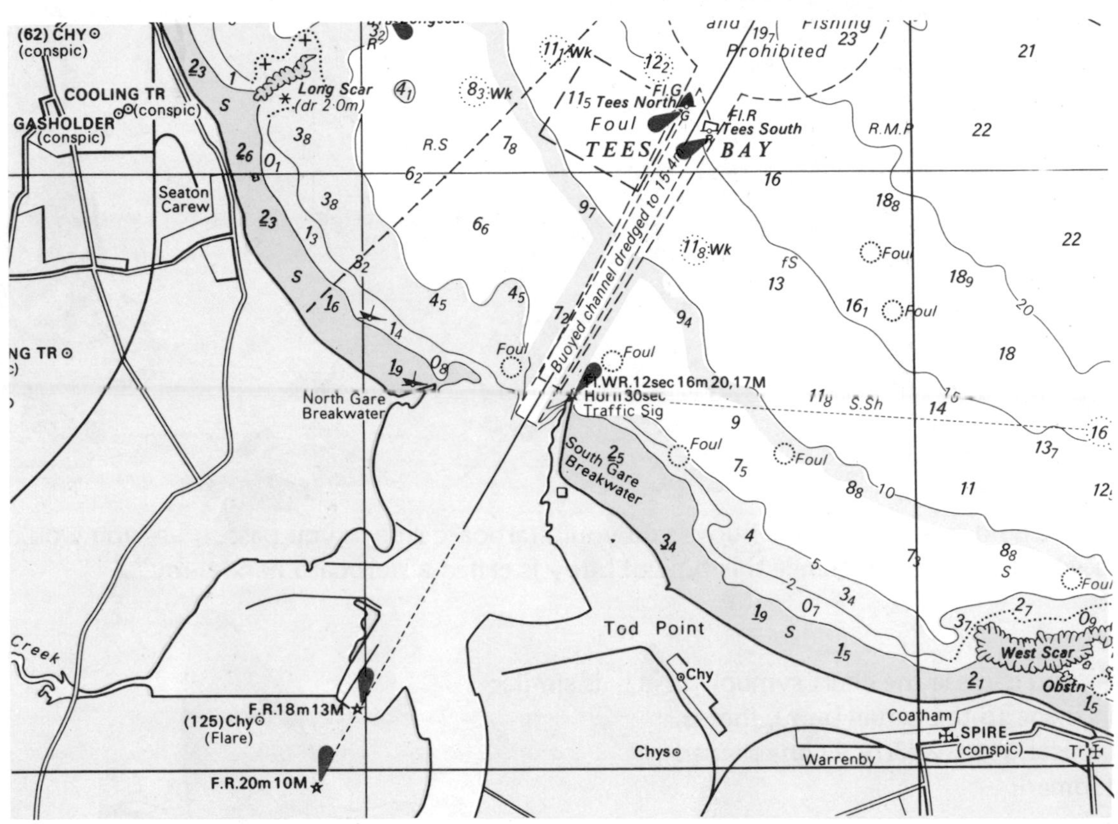

You will notice that not all the buoys here are the same shape and that a ship following the dredged channel passes between them.

Buoys represented on a chart like this ______ you should leave to ________.

Buoys represented on a chart like this ______ you should leave to ________.

starboard
port

This is a port hand buoy. It is red and can shaped.

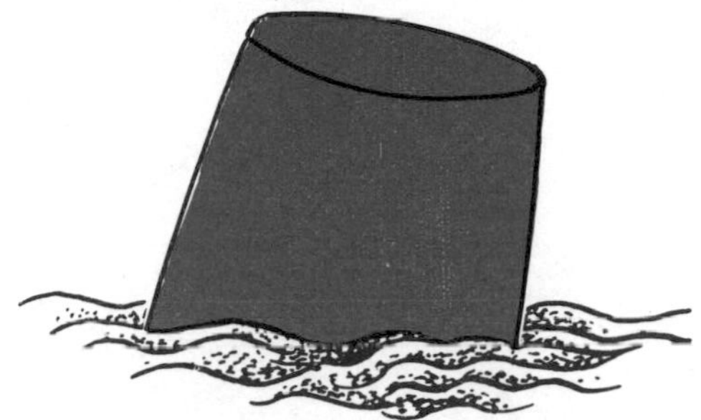

The top mark, if one is carried, will also be can shaped. A port hand buoy that is pillar or spar shaped will always have a can shaped top mark.

The actual position of the buoy is shown on the chart by the small circle at the base of the symbol.

You should leave starboard hand buoys to starboard and port hand buoys to port, but as you will have realised, this rule only applies when the ship is approaching the buoy from one direction. What direction?

When entering harbour.

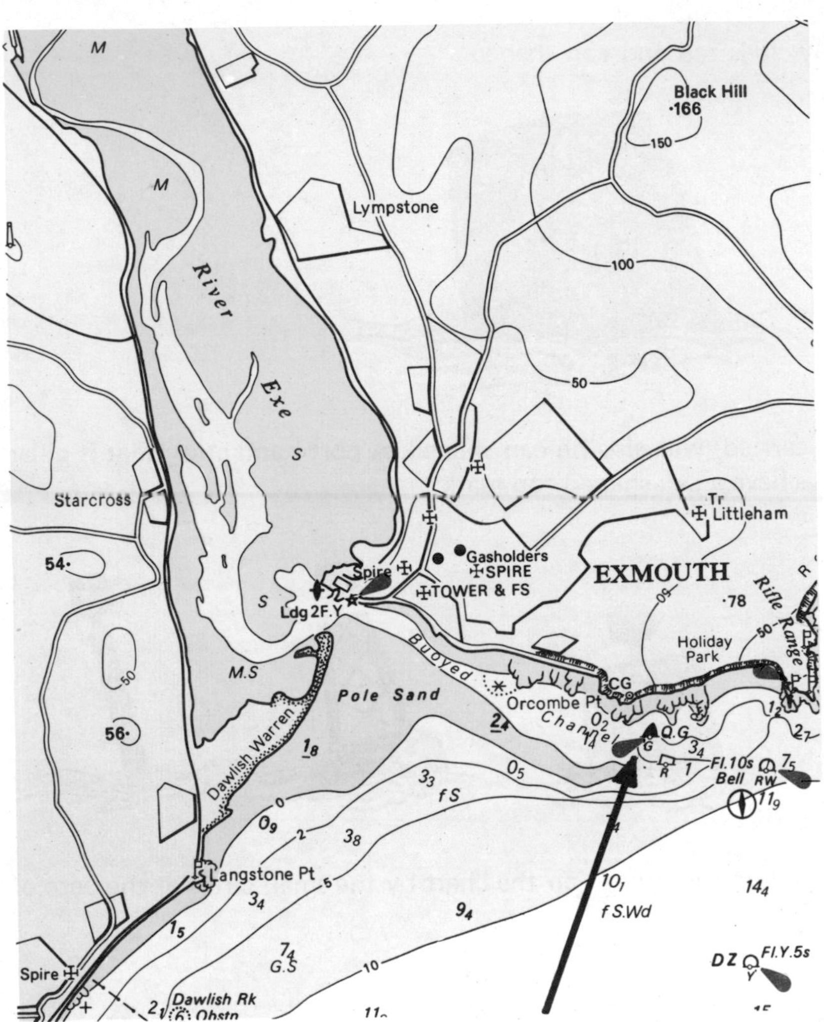

On which side would you leave the buoy when leaving harbour?

To starboard ——→ Turn to page 119.

To port ——→ Turn to page 122.

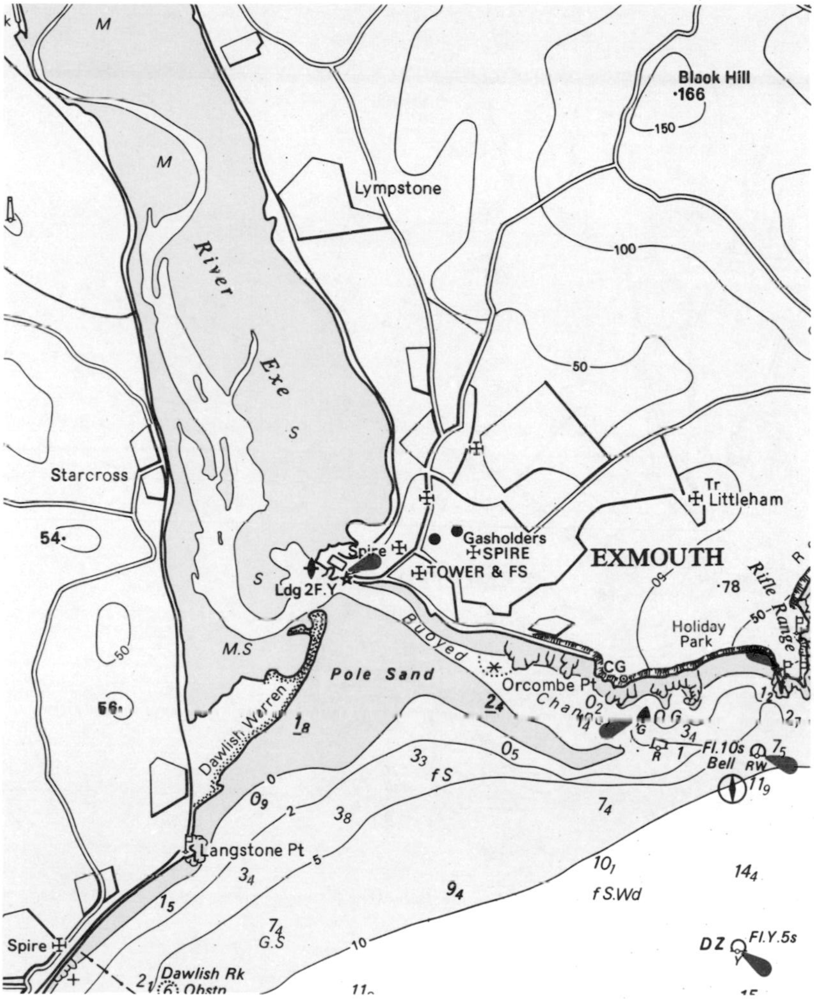

No, you should not leave the buoy to starboard. There are two possible reasons why you went wrong, depending on whether you identified the buoy as a port hand buoy or a starboard hand buoy.

If you thought that this was a port hand buoy turn to 120.

If you thought that this was a starboard hand buoy turn to 121.

Your mistake lay in identifying the buoy on the chart as a port hand buoy, when in fact it was a starboard hand buoy.

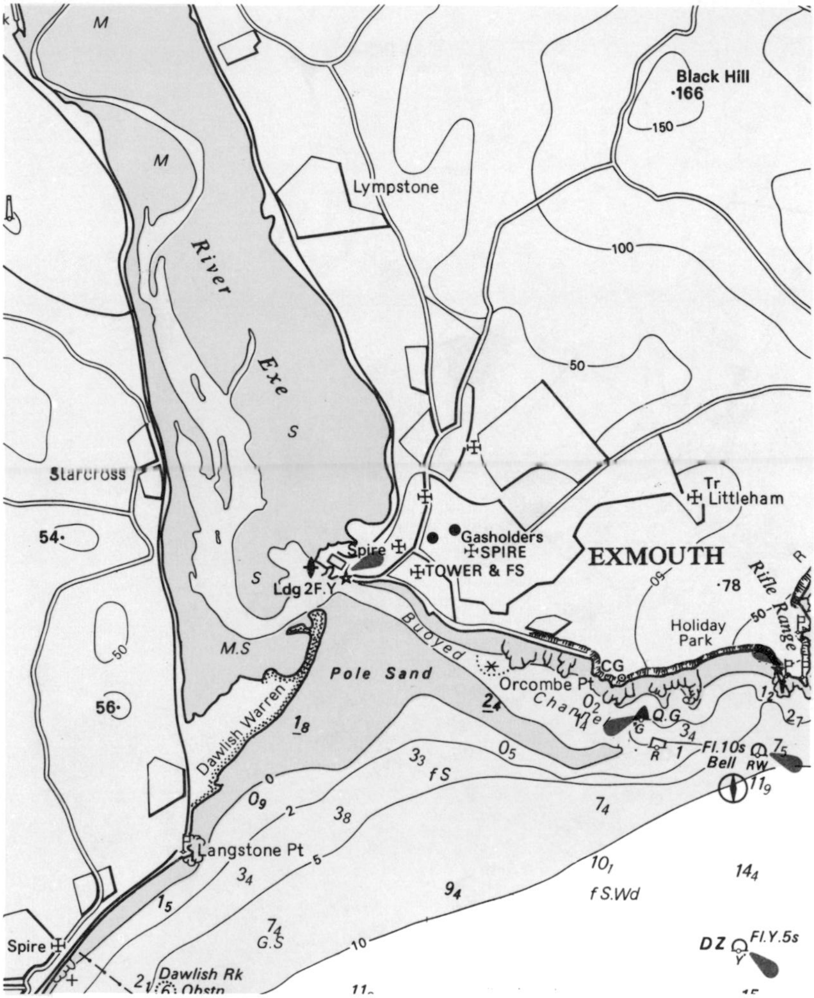

You should leave a starboard hand buoy to starboard when entering harbour, but – as you seem to have grasped–this rule is reversed when leaving harbour.

Before continuing, make sure you remember that:

this stands for a port hand buoy, ...and this stands for a starboard hand buoy.

Turn to 123.

Good, you correctly identified the buoy on the chart as a starboard hand buoy. Your mistake in the original question lay in passing it on the wrong side.

When entering harbour the ship left this starboard hand buoy to starboard. But if it takes the same track when departing, it will leave it to port.

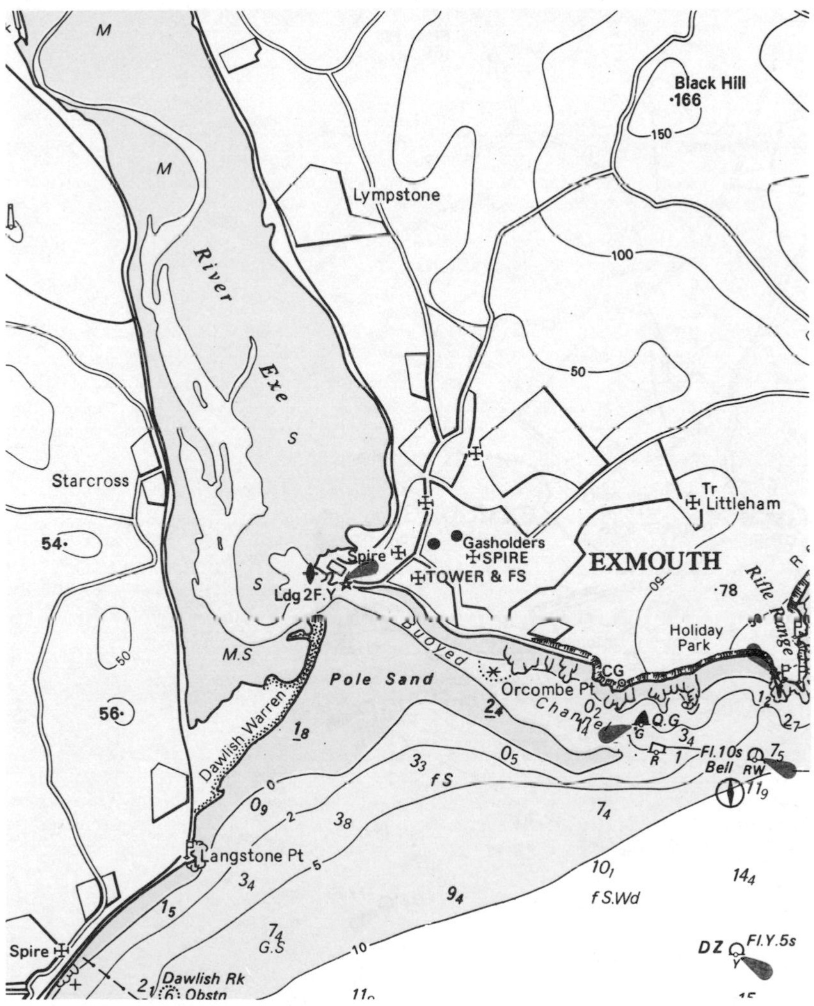

Turn to 123.

Very good, the correct procedure would be to leave the buoy to port. On entering harbour, you would leave a starboard hand buoy like this to starboard, but the rule is reversed when departing from harbour.

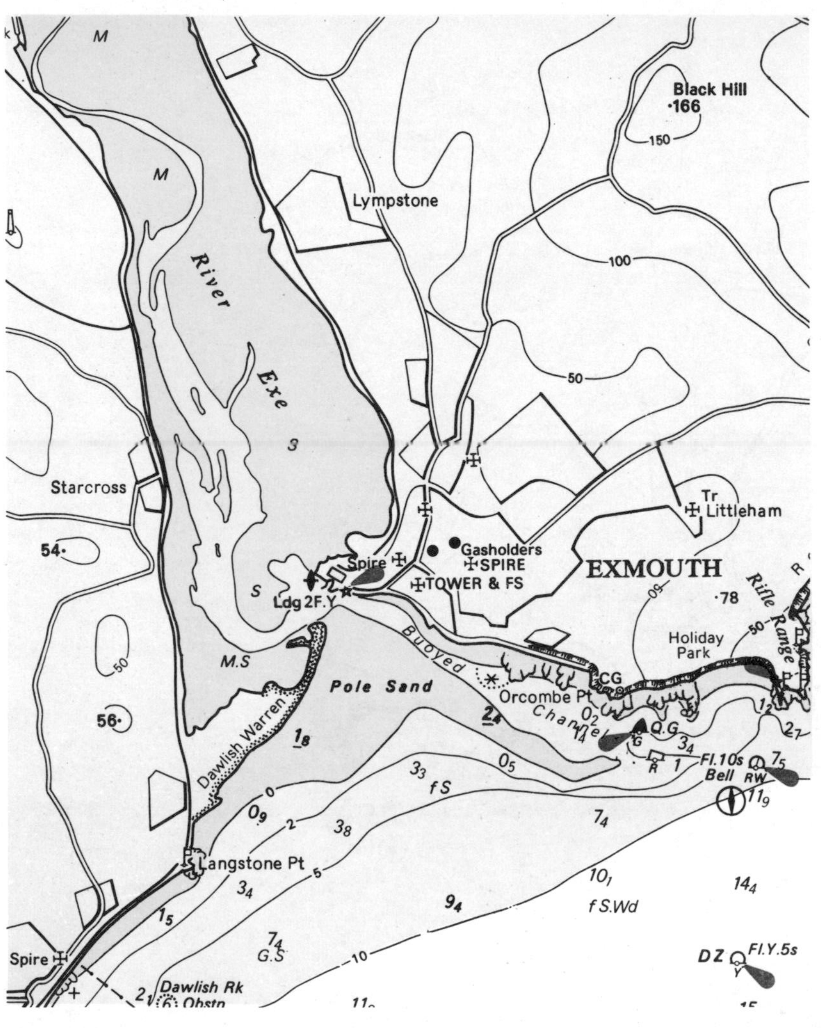

The ship leaves a starboard hand buoy to starboard when it is approaching a harbour or other waterway from seaward. This is called the local direction of buoyage.

In open water the direction of buoyage is called the General direction and is laid down by the buoyage authorites. Around the British Isles the General direction of buoyage runs as shown below.

The General direction of buoyage runs Northward along the East and West coasts and ___________ through the English Channel.

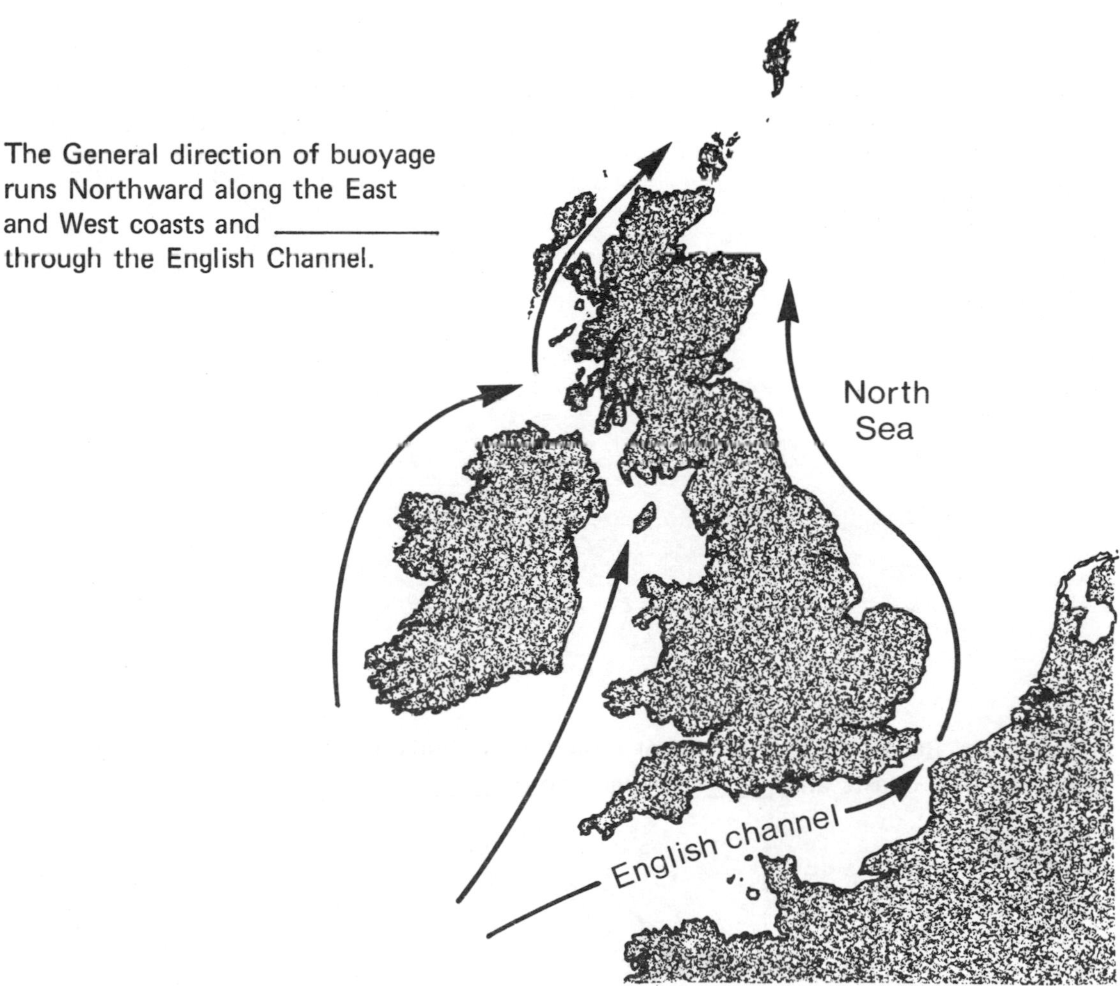

eastward

When the ship is neither entering nor leaving harbour, the rule to follow is that you leave a port hand buoy to port and a starboard hand buoy to starboard when going with the general direction of buoyage.

When there is any doubt about the direction it will be marked on charts with this symbol.

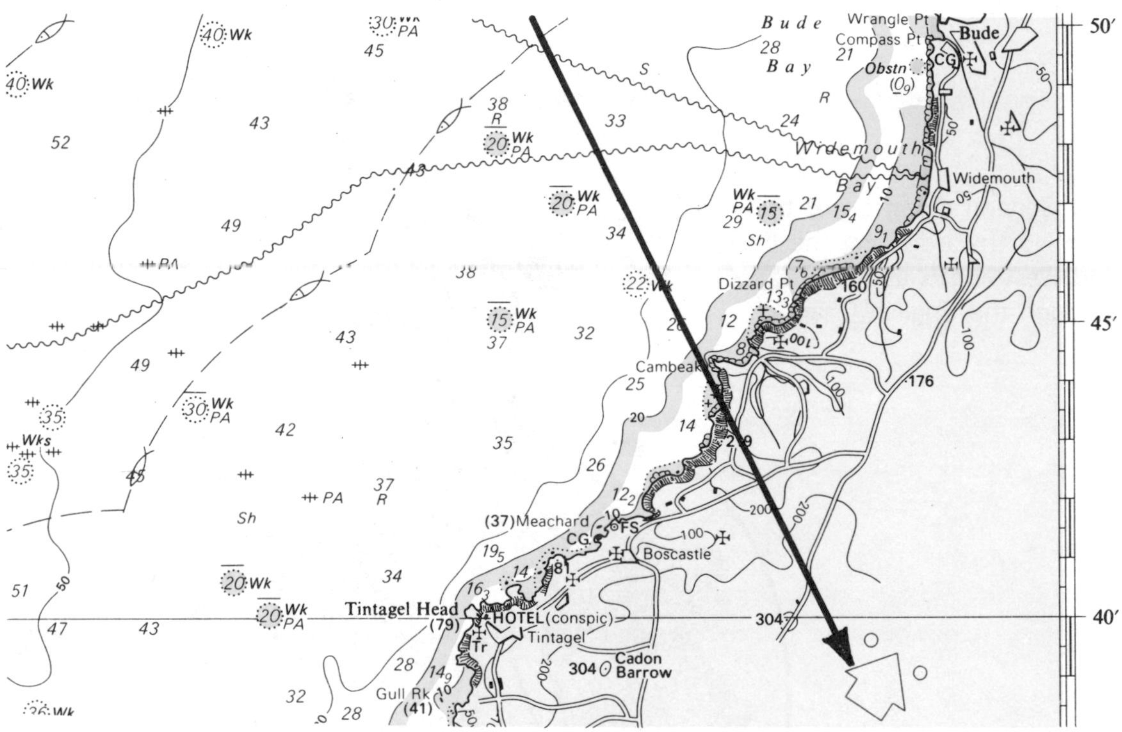

Around the British Isles the general direction of buoyage runs __________along the west and east coasts and ______through the ________ ________ .

northward

eastward

English Channel

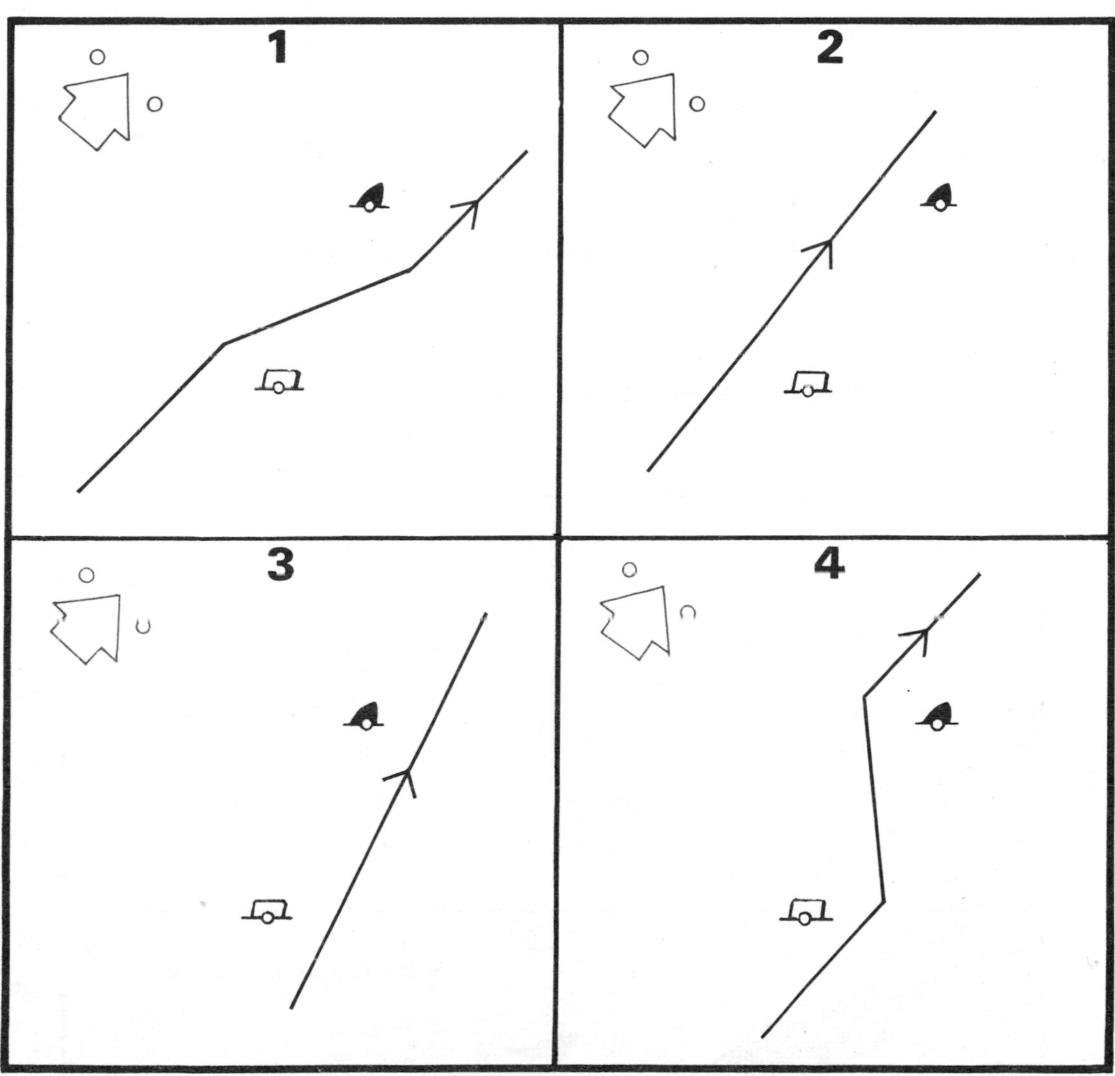

Approaching from the direction indicated, which is the correct track for the ship to follow? (Note the general direction of buoyage.)

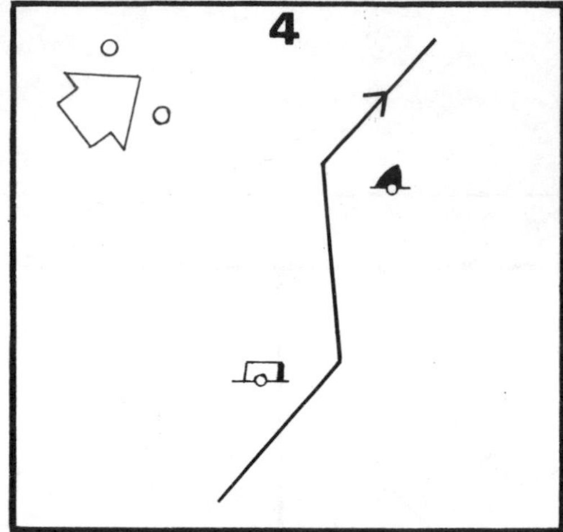

Approaching from the direction indicated, in each case say whether you would leave the buoy to port or starboard.

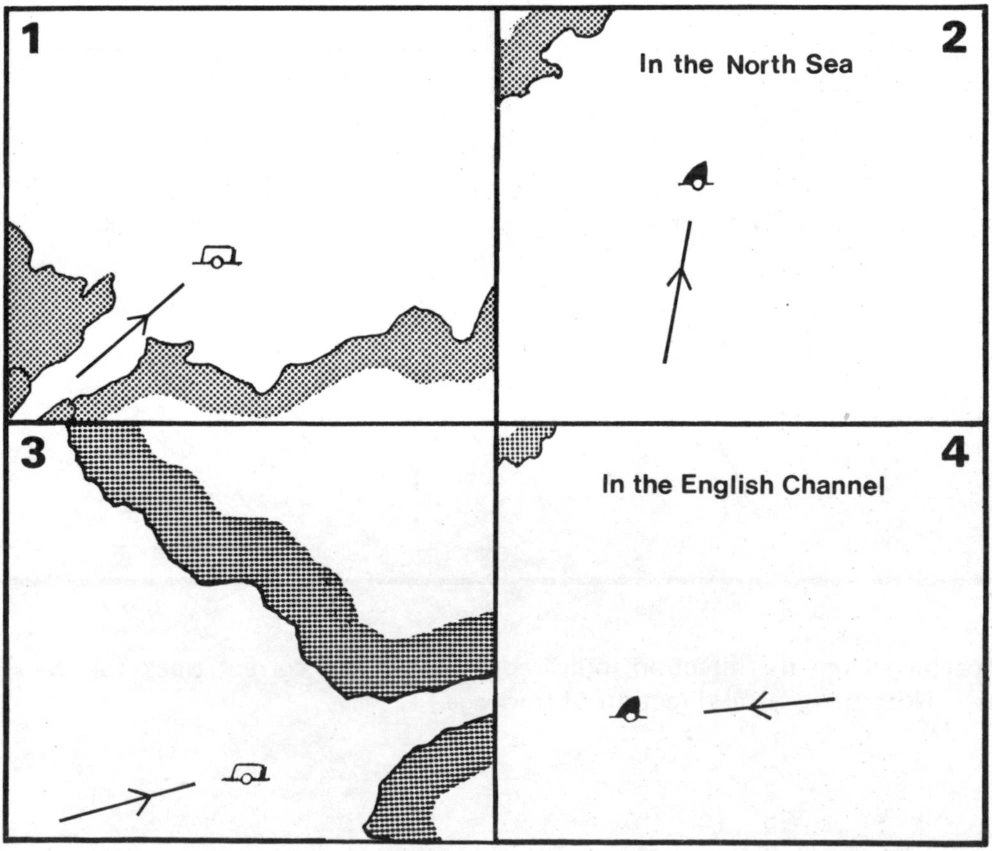

1

2 In the North Sea

3

4 In the English Channel

1. Leave buoy to starboard.
2. Leave buoy to starboard.
3. Leave buoy to port.
4. Leave buoy to port.

It is important to note that where there are one way shipping lanes the general direction of buoyage does not change to conform with the direction of shipping and so may run counter to it. For example the general direction of buoyage in the English Channel is eastward and this is so even in the westbound shipping lane.

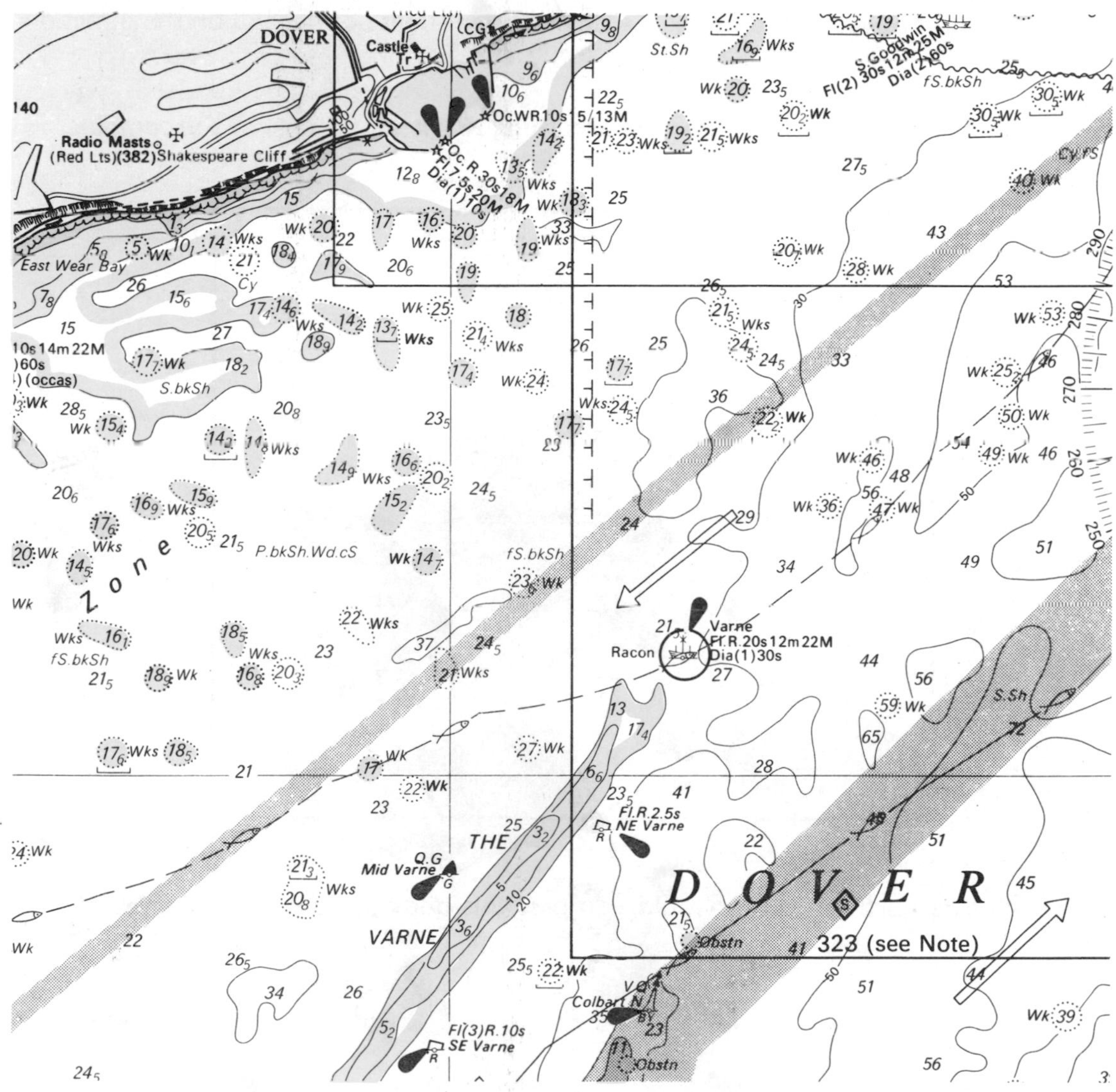

The NE Varne buoy is in a westbound shipping lane in the English Channel. You would always leave it to ________.

starboard (Remember the general direction of buoyage in the English Channel is to the east.)

There will obviously be a change over from the area in which the General Direction of buoyage operates to the area in which the local direction operates. This may not be marked on the chart, so in case of doubt you should see on which side of the danger the buoy is placed and pass it on the appropriate side.

However, there should seldom be any doubt, because the Cardinal System is used to reduce the possibility of error in open waters. Unlike the Lateral System of port and starboard hand buoys the use of the Cardinal System does not depend on the direction of buoyage.

Cardinal buoys always indicate direction according to the four points of the compass.

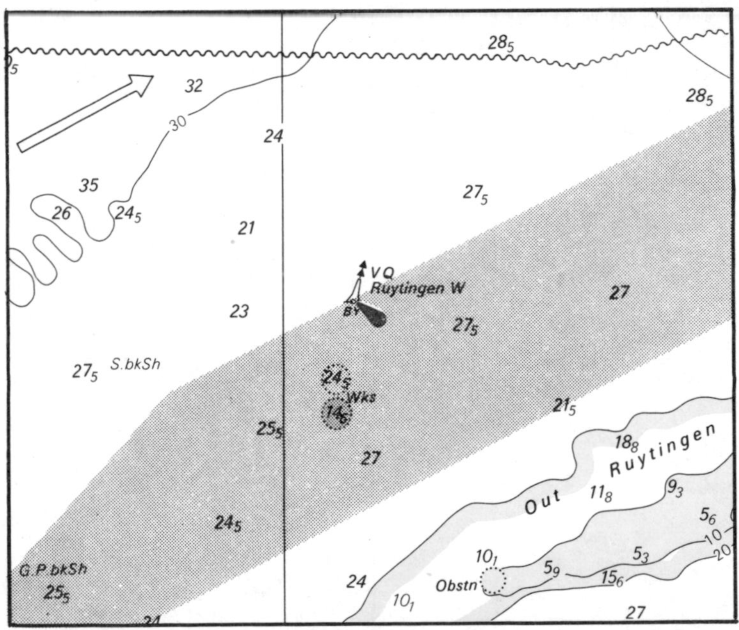

On which side, north or south, would you pass this buoy in a deep draught vessel?

To the north.

Cardinal marks can be used to mark hazards and dangers and they indicate the navigable water to the named side of the mark. All cardinal marks are either pillar or spar buoys - cone and can buoys are not used.

A North mark is coloured black above yellow (BY) and has a double cone top mark, with points upmost.

It indicates navigable water to the ______ of the buoy.

north

You can remember the symbol for a north mark because it points north on the chart, i.e. towards navigable water.

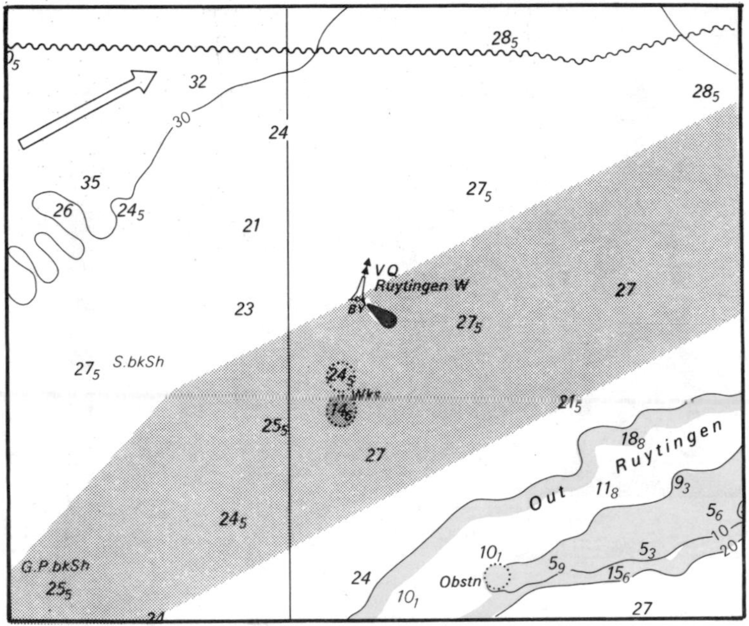

The symbol on the chart below indicates navigable water to the_______of the buoy.

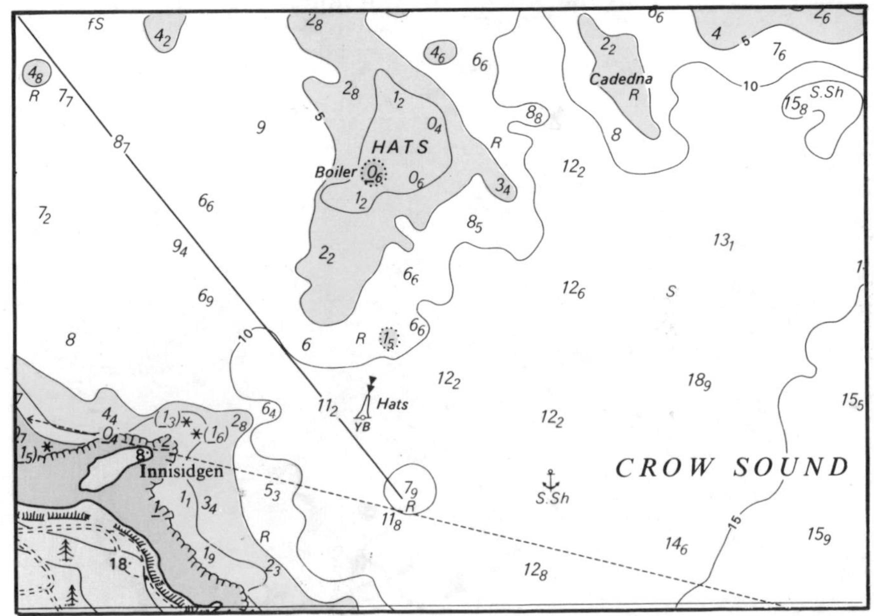

south

This is a summary of the top marks of cardinal buoys showing the quadrants in which they are placed.

The black cone top marks of the cardinal buoys are their most noticeable distinguishing features by day.

North and South can easily be remembered but West and East 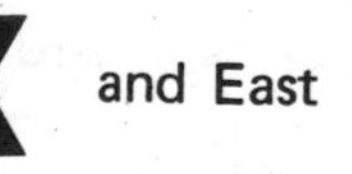 are less obvious.

It may help to remember the West mark looks like a Wineglass or a W on its side.

Is the side on which you should pass a cardinal buoy affected by;

1. the local direction of buoyage ?
2. the general direction of buoyage ?

1. No
2. No

(The direction of buoyage only affects lateral marks.)

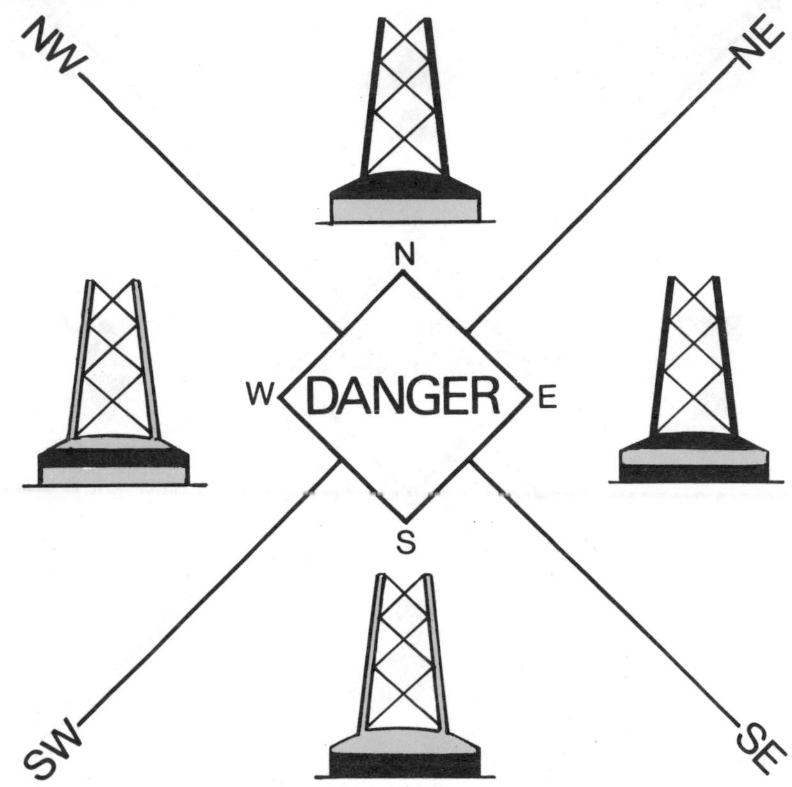

Cardinal marks may be either pillar or spar buoys and are always coloured yellow and black in horizontal bands. The position of the black band, or bands, is related to the <u>points</u> of the black top marks.

North – Points up	Black band above yellow band. (BY)
South – Points down	Black band below yellow band. (YB)
West – Points inward	Black band with yellow bands above and below. (YBY)

Which of these spar buoys is an east mark?

It is B. (The east top mark is  )

Which diagram shows the correct track for the ship to follow?

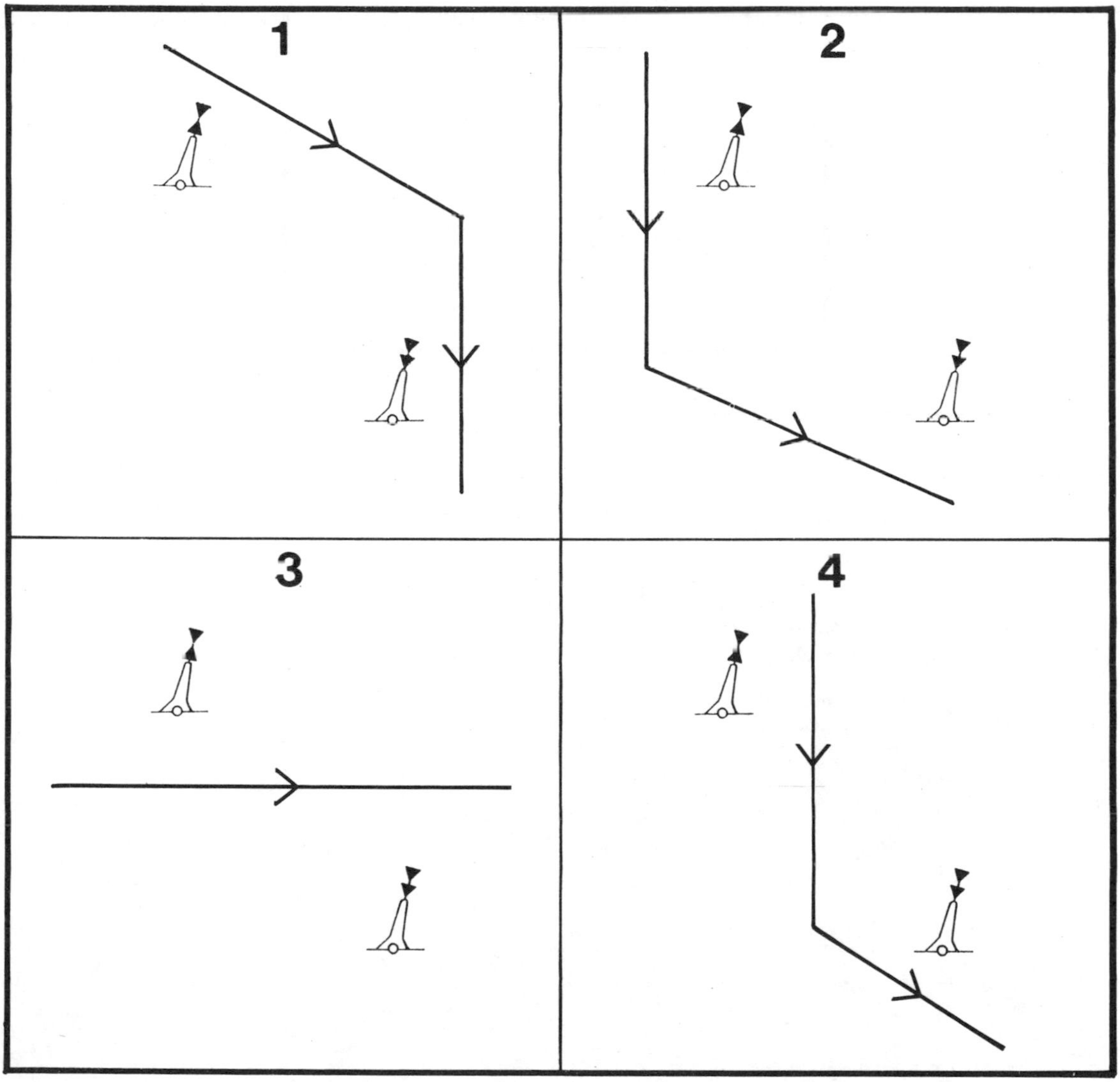

1

2

3

4

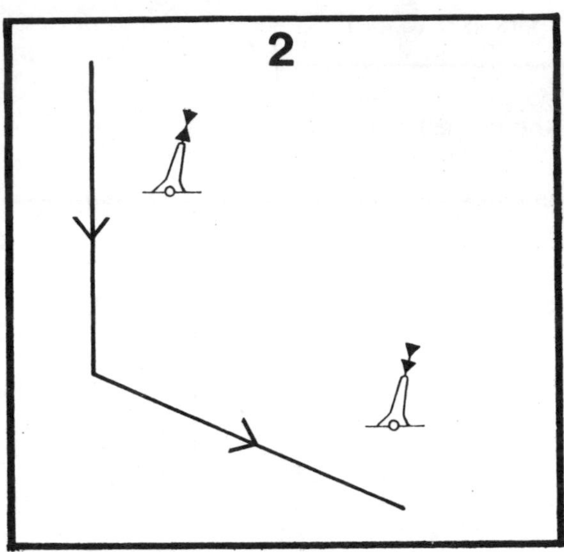

Cardinal marks can be used in conjunction with lateral marks in a channel to mark a point of special interest such as the point of a shore or the bend of a channel.

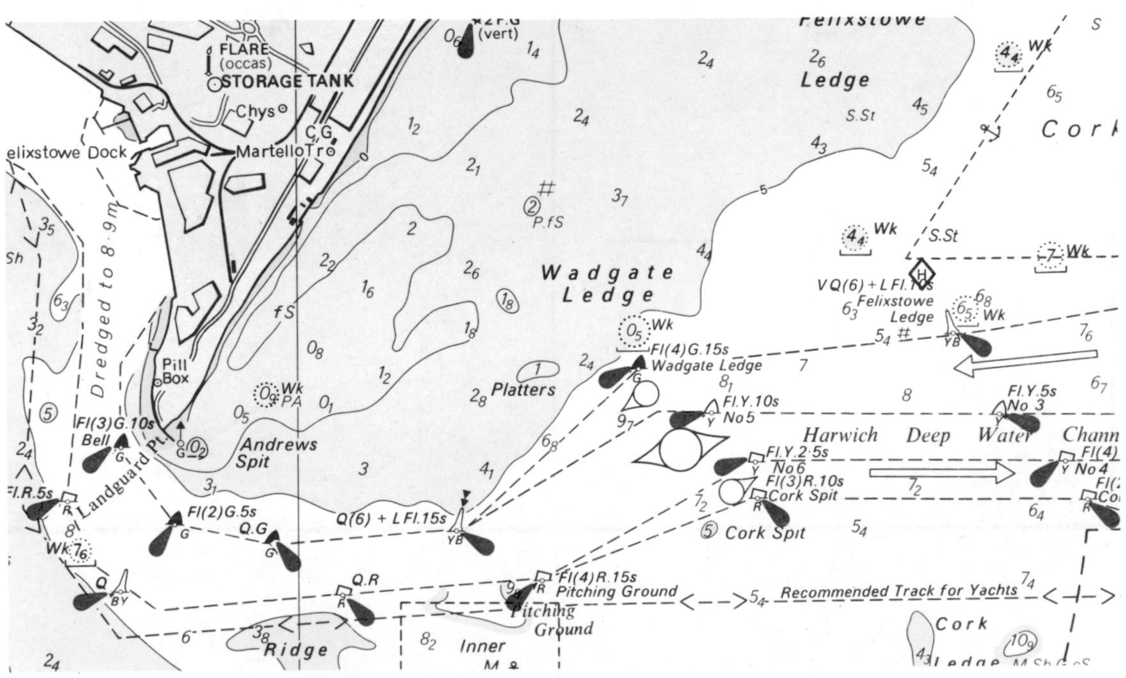

In this portion of a chart we have blacked out the top marks of two of the cardinal buoys one south of Andrews Spit and the other marking Felixstowe Ledge. What should these top marks be?

South of Andrews Spit ▲▲

Felixstowe Ledge ▼▼

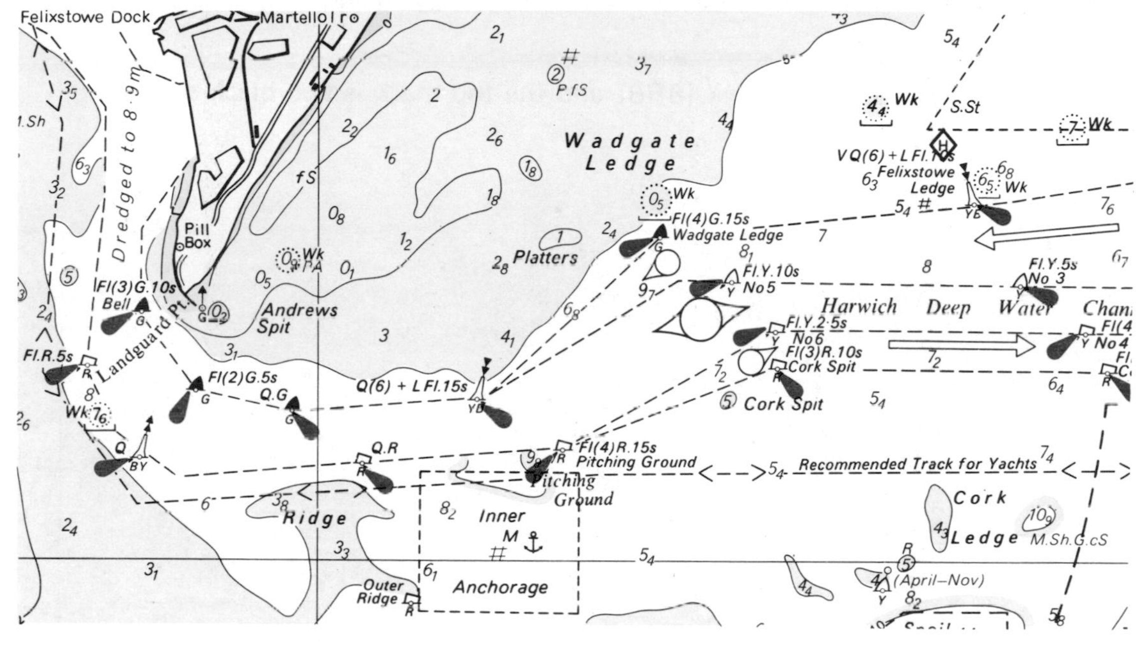

On which side of the South Edinburgh buoy is there navigable water?

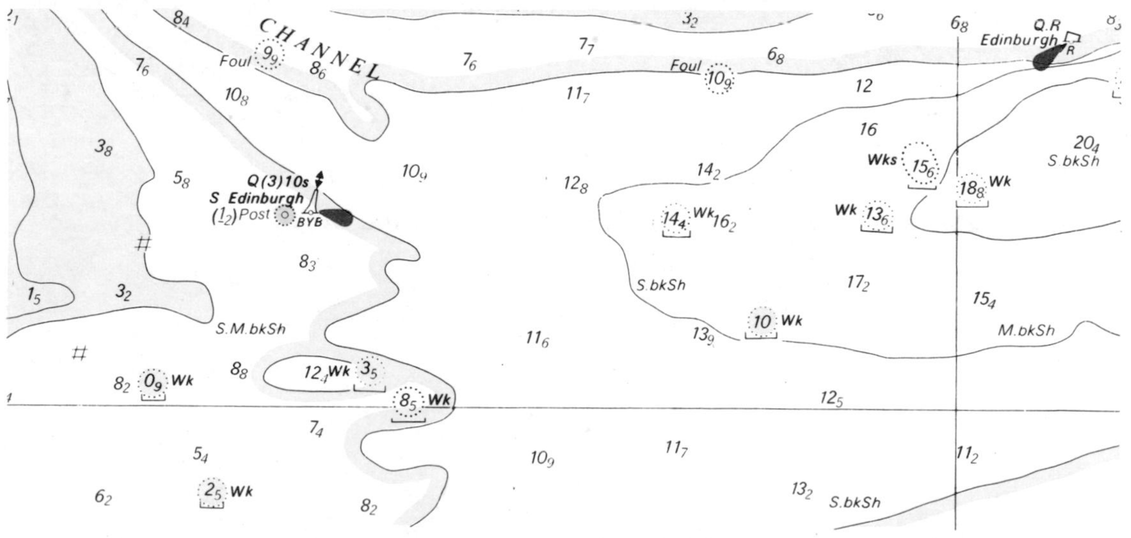

On the east side.

The next type of buoy to consider is the isolated danger mark.

The colours are black, red, black (BRB) and the top mark is two black spheres.

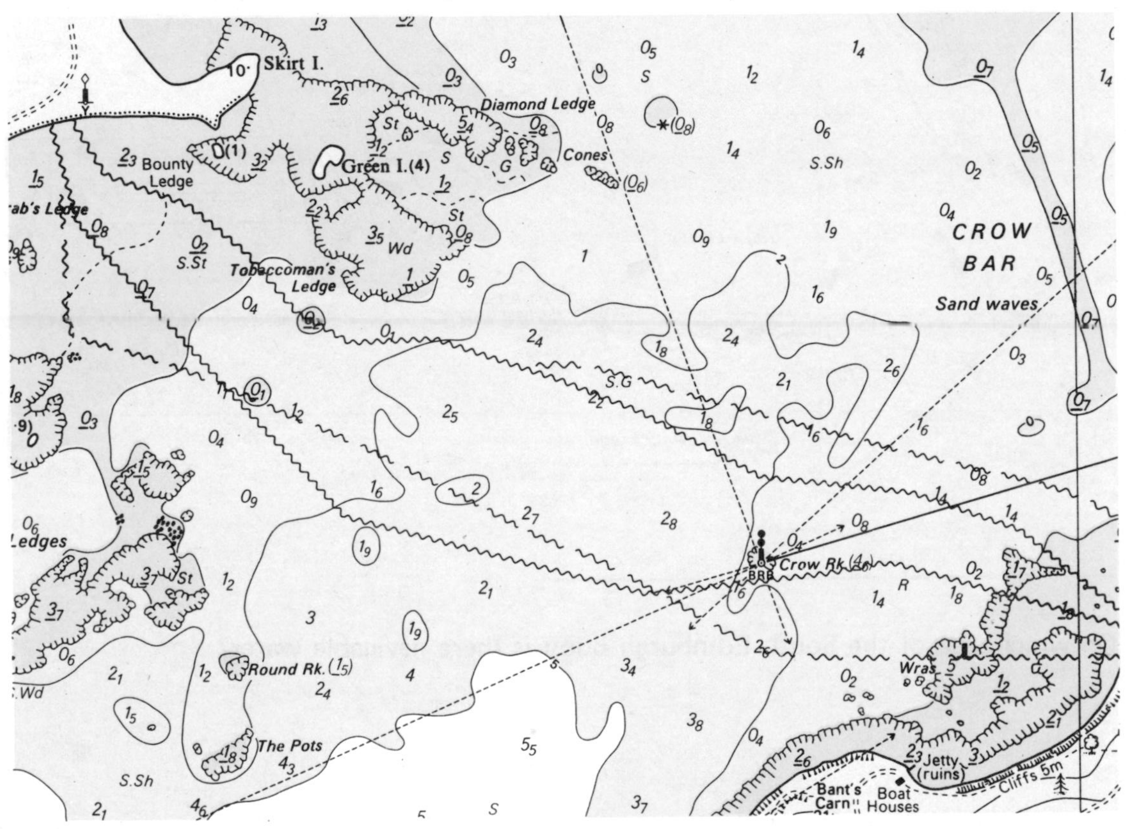

Is there safer water on one side of Crow Rock than the other?

No. (Provided there was enough water for your ship
you could pass any side.)

Isolated Danger Mark

It always marks an isolated danger of limited extent (e.g. a shoal or rock) with navigable water on all sides.

All the buoys described so far mark navigational hazards and indicate where it is safe for the mariner to pass.

This next group comprises the marks which can be passed on all sides. They are used as landfall and mid-channel markers and shown on charts as follows:

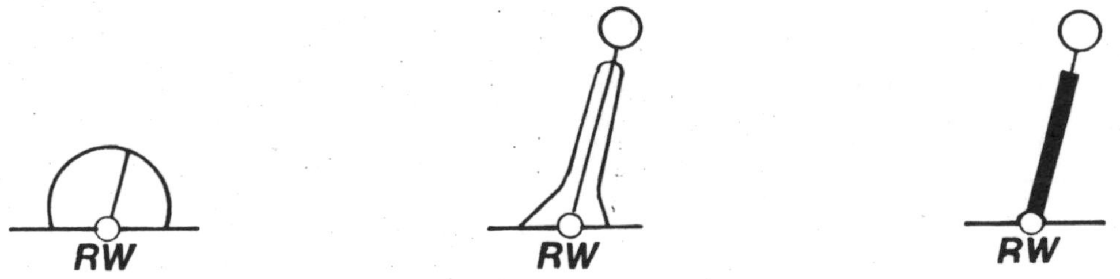

They can be distinguished by their red and white ________stripes.

Pillar or spar shaped safe water buoys have a single_____sphere for a top mark.

vertical

red

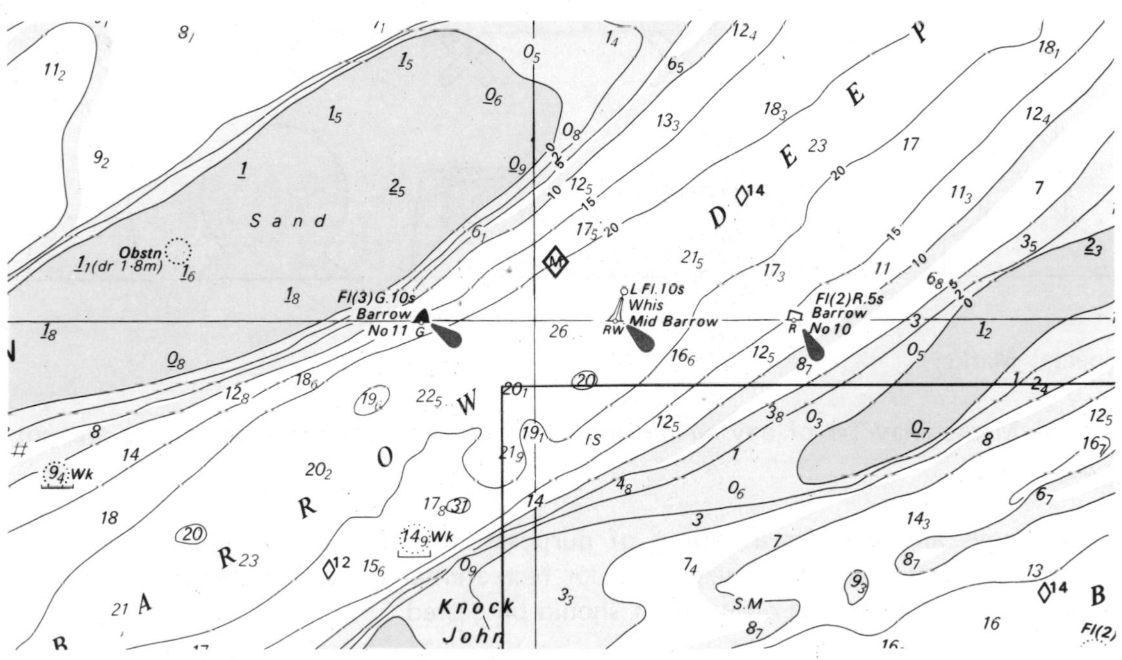

Which is the safe water buoy?

The Mid Barrow Buoy.

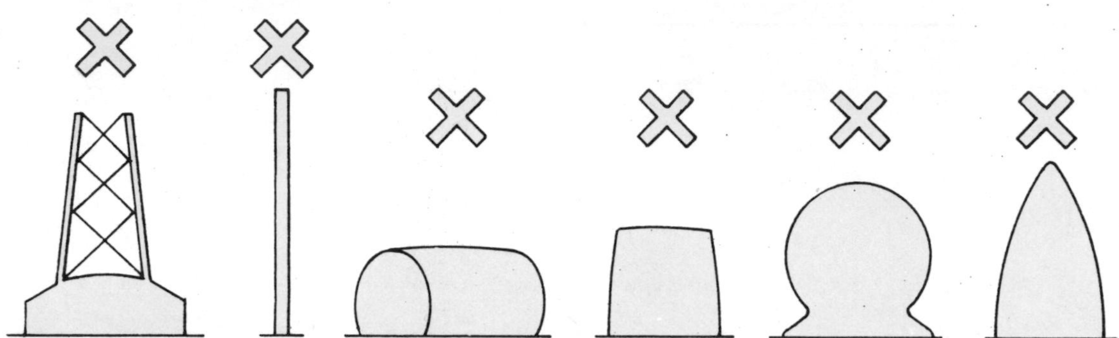

Special Marks

Special Marks may be of any shape but their colour is yellow. (Top marks are not always used.)

These buoys are used for a variety of purposes, for instance, to separate different shipping lanes or mark military exercise or recreational zones. The shape of a special buoy can indicate the side on which it should be passed.

A deep-draught channel within a wider navigable area could be marked by special buoys. If you were following such a channel into port which of the buoys below would you take to mark:

1. The port hand side of the channel ?
2. The starboard side ?
3. The centre line ?

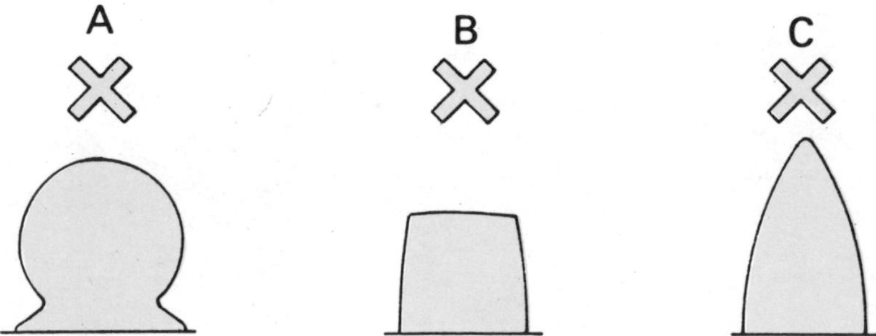

1. B. 2. C. 3. A.

A spherical special buoy may be used as a centre line mark, because the only other spherical buoy is a safe water buoy, which is also used for that purpose.

Section 6 : Self-test

1. Say in each case whether you would pass the buoy to port or starboard.

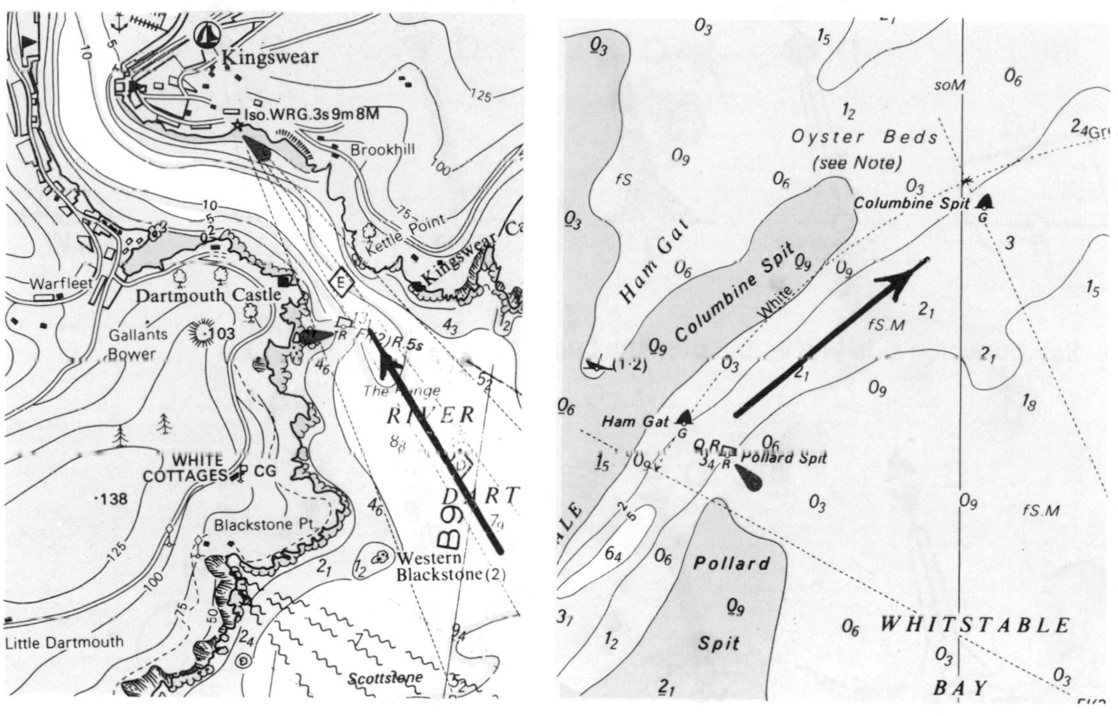

2. Which of these chart symbols shows:

i a starboard hand buoy

ii a north mark

iii an isolated danger buoy

iv a safe water mark

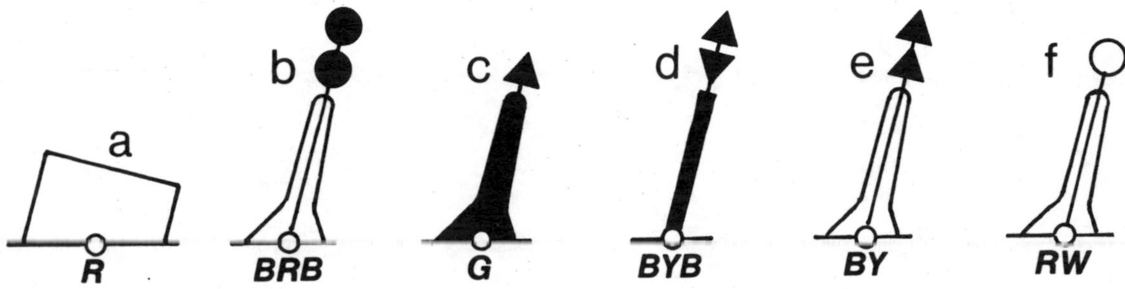

3. Say on which side you would pass the buoy.

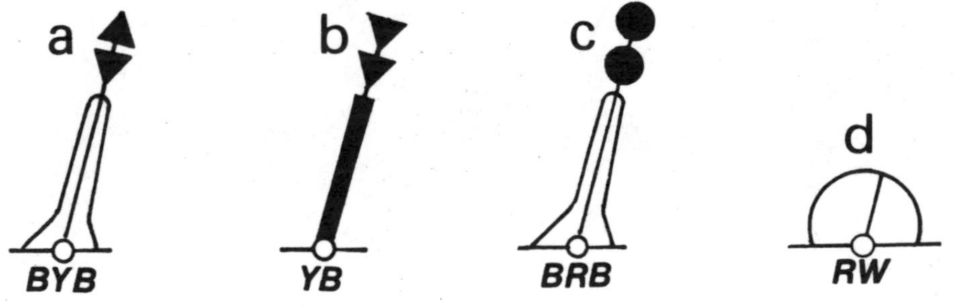

4. What are the colours appropriate for:

i a starboard hand buoy in British waters

ii a safe water buoy

iii a special buoy

iv a west buoy

Section 6 : Answers to Self-test

1. a Port

   b Port

2. i c (if you were wrong about this turn back to page 115)

   ii e

   iii b

   iv f

3. a To the East of the buoy.

   b To the South of the buoy.

   c Either side of the buoy.

   d Either side of the buoy.

4. i Green

   ii Red and white vertical stripes.

   III Yellow.

   iv A black band between yellow bands.

Section 7: Lights

Lights play an important part in night-time navigation. In order to be able to find his position the navigating officer must be able to identify land features and be able to take bearings of them. An easily identifiable light will serve his purpose and he will refer to the chart for the exact position of the light — this is immediately obvious by the flare which will be coloured *magenta* on the chart attached to the symbol for a light ☆ or ★ or the symbol for a buoy or a light vessel:

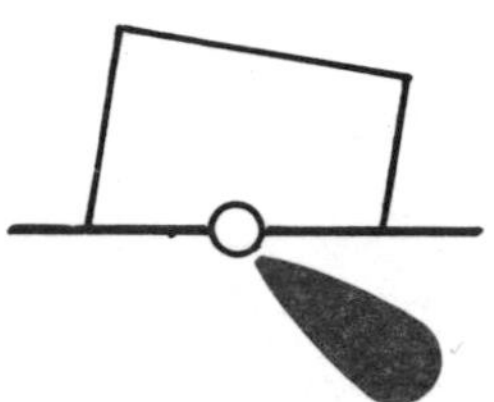

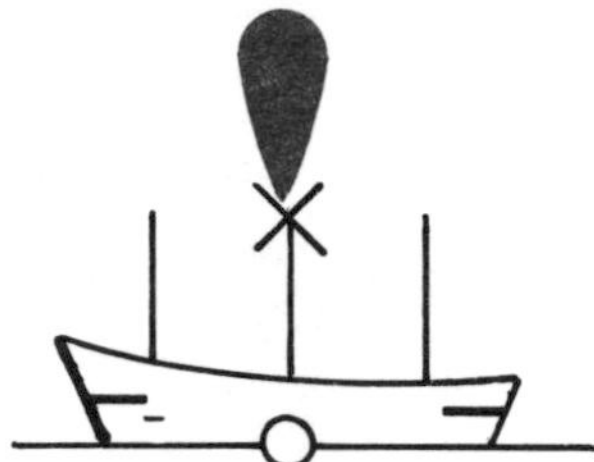

Quite a variety of lights are displayed around the coast: they can be white or coloured, they can be fixed or flashing, they can flash at intervals and in different patterns — and some even flash in Morse code. There is good reason for this variety of light *characteristics* (as they are called). For instance, approaching Grimsby Harbour the untrained eye will see just a confused array of lights — but reference to the chart will enable the navigator to identify each one by its distinguishing characteristic.

How many lights are shown on this portion of chart?

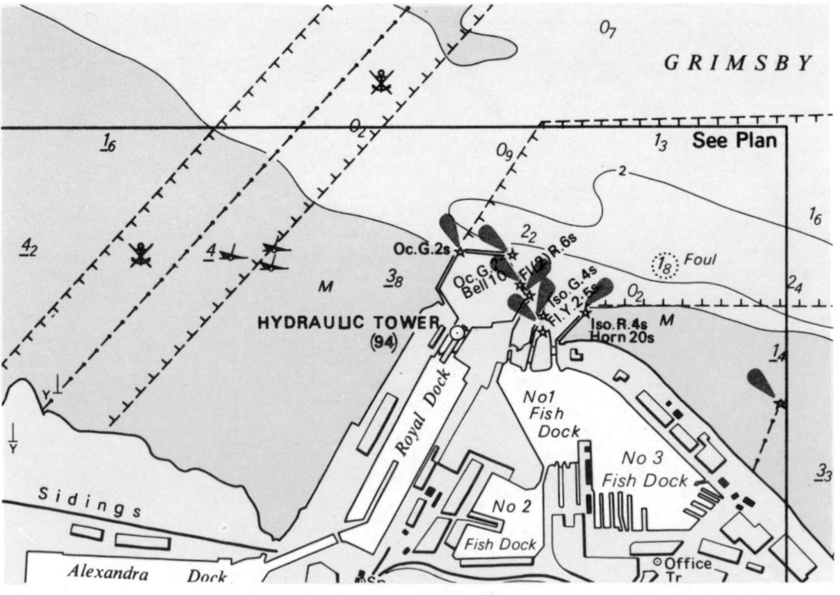

Eight.

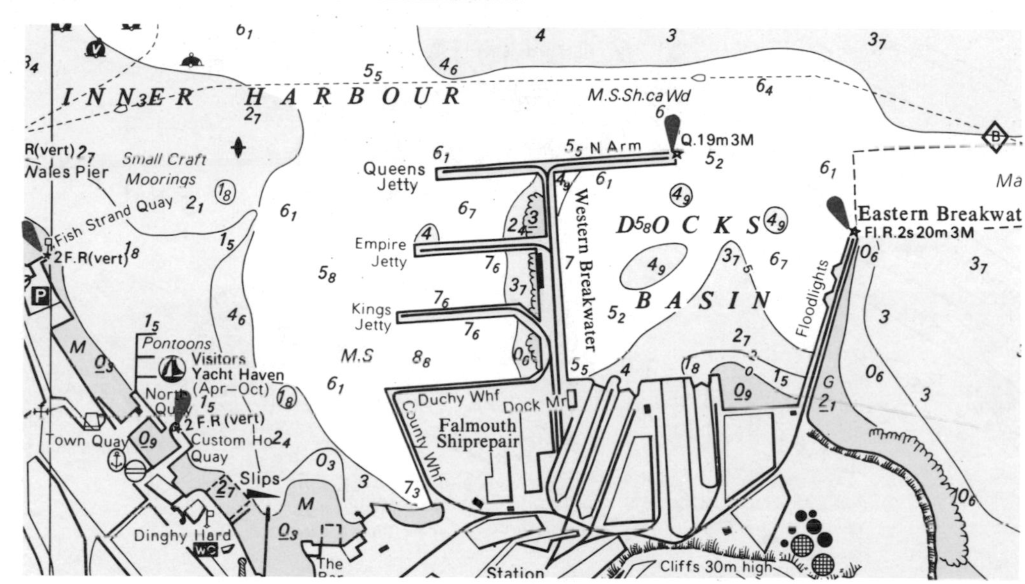

The abbreviations next to a light symbol tell you the characteristic of the light. For instance, two of the lights on the chart above exhibit flashes (denoted by **Fl** for flashing or **Q** for quick flashing); another two have the letter **F**, denoting a fixed light.

A fixed light has the simplest characteristic; a stationary observer will see a continuous light. With an occulting light, however, the light is switched off at regular intervals (called occultations). A flashing light is quite the opposite to this: most of the time it is dark but there are flashes of light.

Which of the lights on the chart below does not show a continuous steady light?

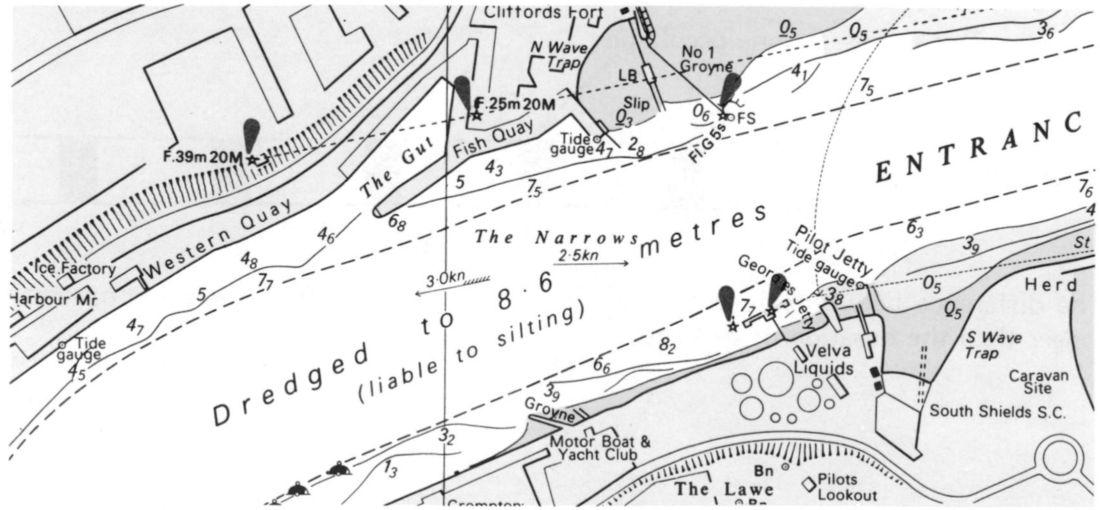

The light ringed is a flashing light. The others all show continuous steady light.

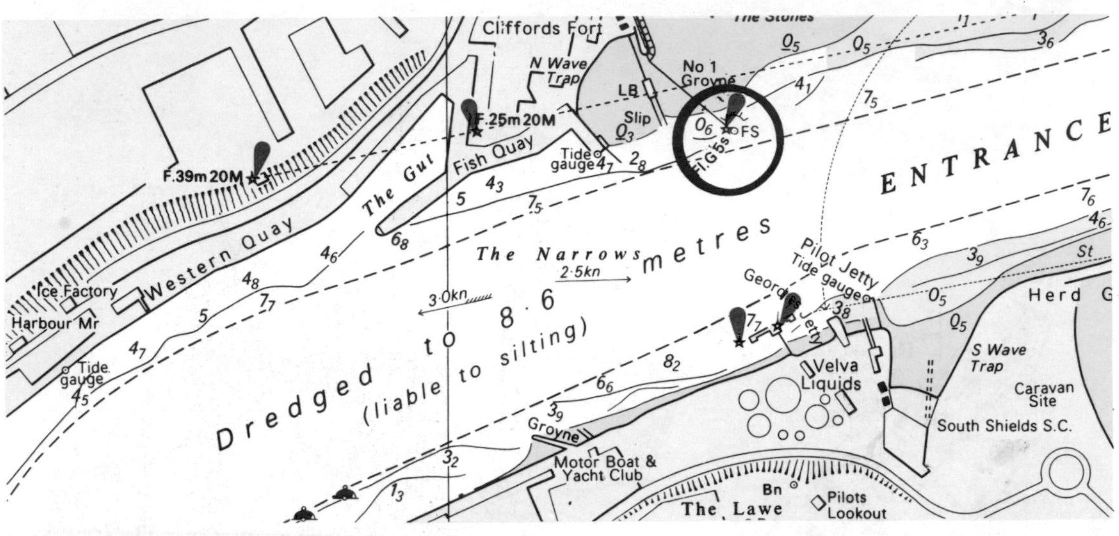

The difference between a flashing light and an occulting light can be seen from these diagrams which represent what the observer sees:

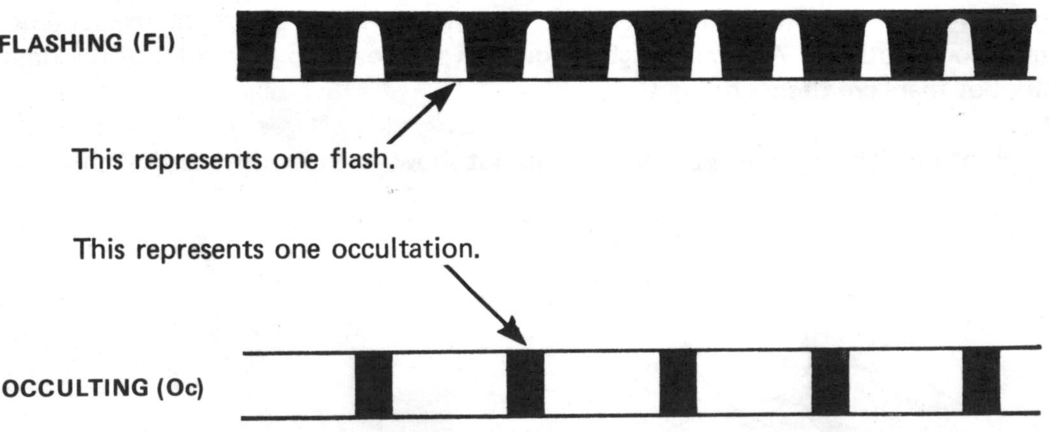

The difference between the two is that with __________ lights the duration of light is longer than the duration of darkness.

occulting

Quite often you will encounter lights where the flashes and occultations occur in groups. For instance, you may find the abbreviation **Fl (3)** beside a light on a chart.

The characteristic this denotes is a group of three flashes followed by an interval of darkness (eclipse).

What does **Oc (2)** signify?

A group of two occultations followed by an interval of light.

This is one complete sequence and it will be repeated continuously - the light occults twice in quick succession, maintains a steady light, occults twice in quick succession, maintains a steady light .... and so on.

The time taken for a rhythmic light to exhibit one complete sequence is called the period of the light. The following illustrations represent the light mentioned above. On which diagram is the period correctly indicated?

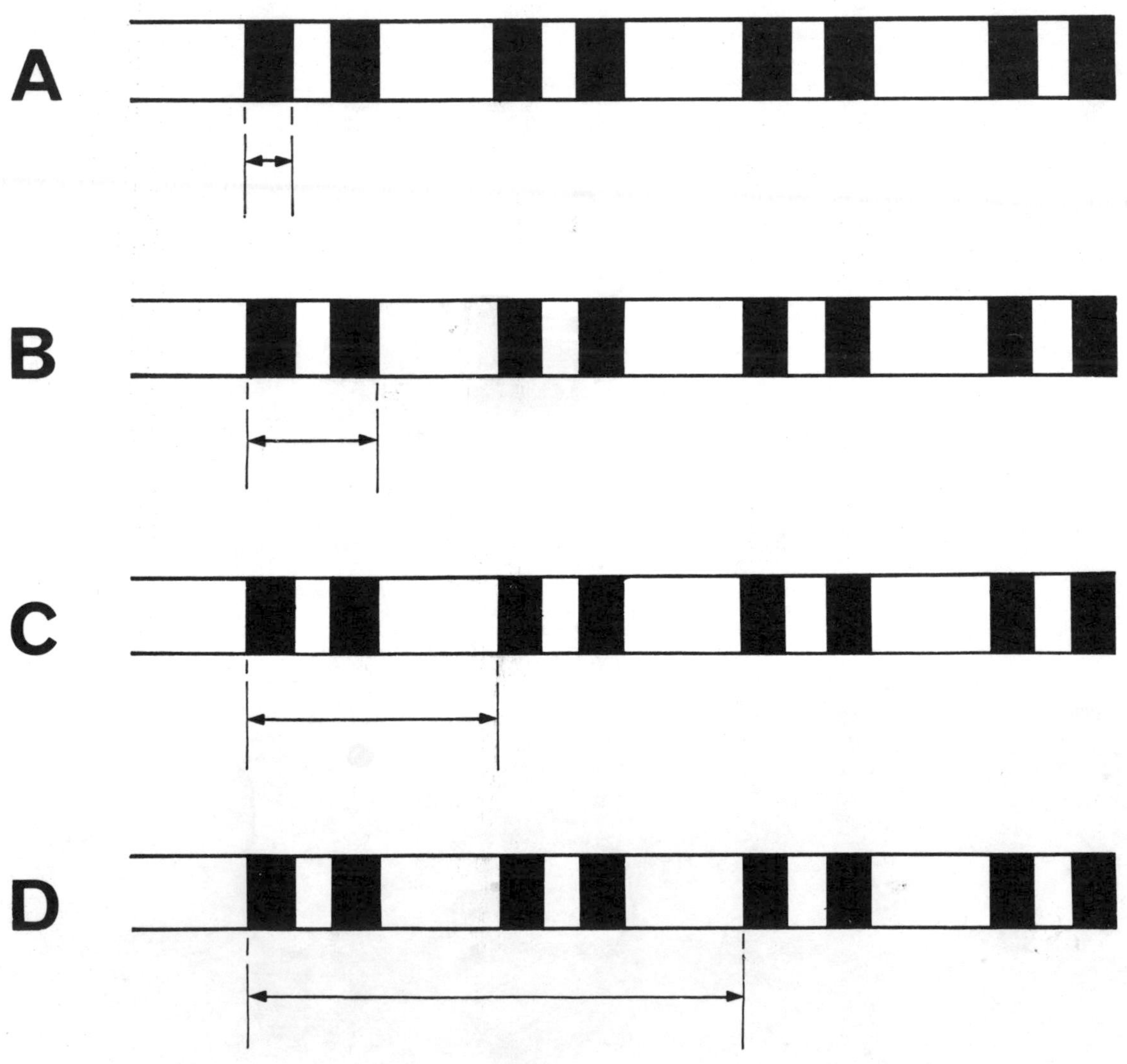

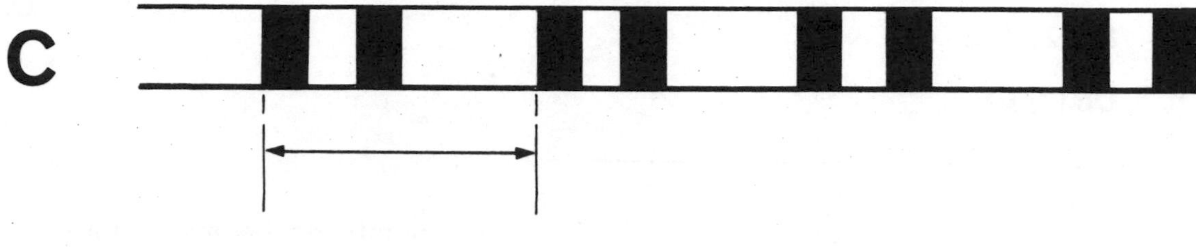

To give you an idea of the duration of flashes etc., the illustrations below break down a period into its elements.

A

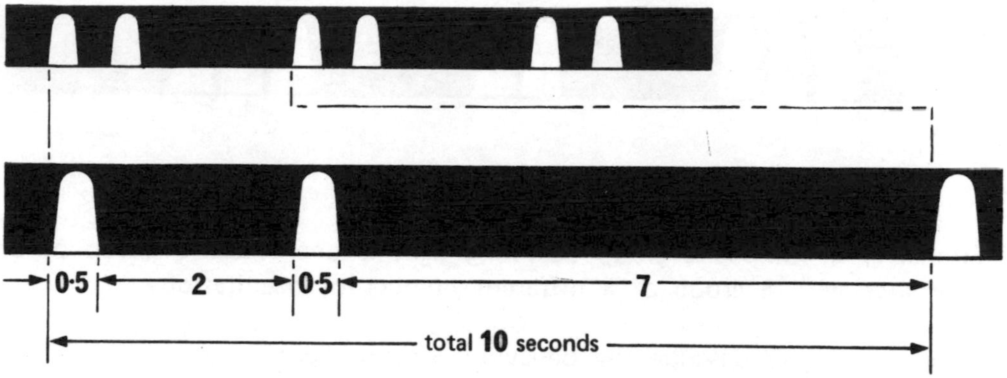

0·5 2 0·5 7

total **10** seconds

B

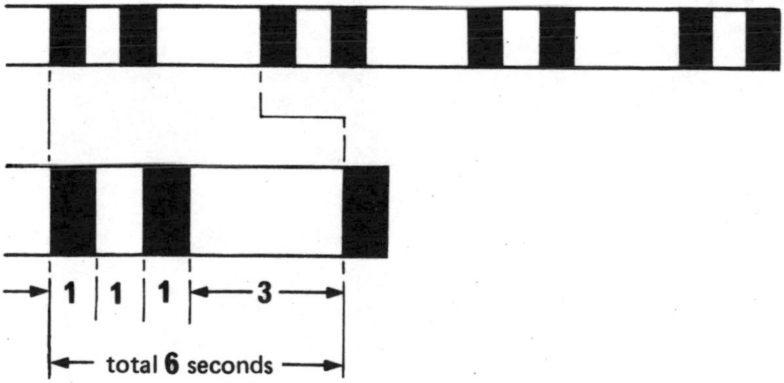

1 1 1 3

total **6** seconds

Where a light is shown on a chart the characteristic of the light is stated followed by the length of the period. Both are given in abbreviated form. The abbreviation ' s ' stands for seconds.

Which of the abbreviations below match the lights shown in diagrams A and B?

Fl (2) 7s   **Oc (2) 6s**   **Fl (2) 10s**   **Oc (2) 3s**

a. **Fl (2) 10s**

b. **Oc (2) 6s**

The arrangement of flashes and occultations can sometimes be even more complicated. A light such as this one **Fl (3+2)** is called a composite group flashing light and would look like this:

Similarly, a composite group occulting light is one where a group of occultations alternates with a group of a different number of occultations.

How would you describe the behaviour of this light?

Oc (1 + 2) 12s

One occultation followed by a group of two occultations occuring within a period of 12 seconds.

An isophase light **(Iso)** is one which has an equal duration of light and darkness and looks like this:

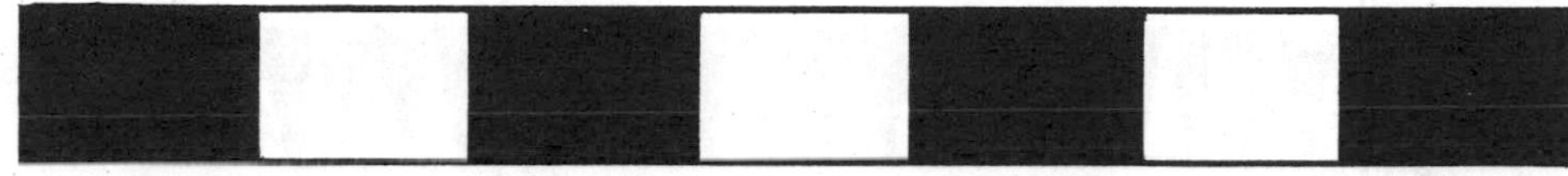

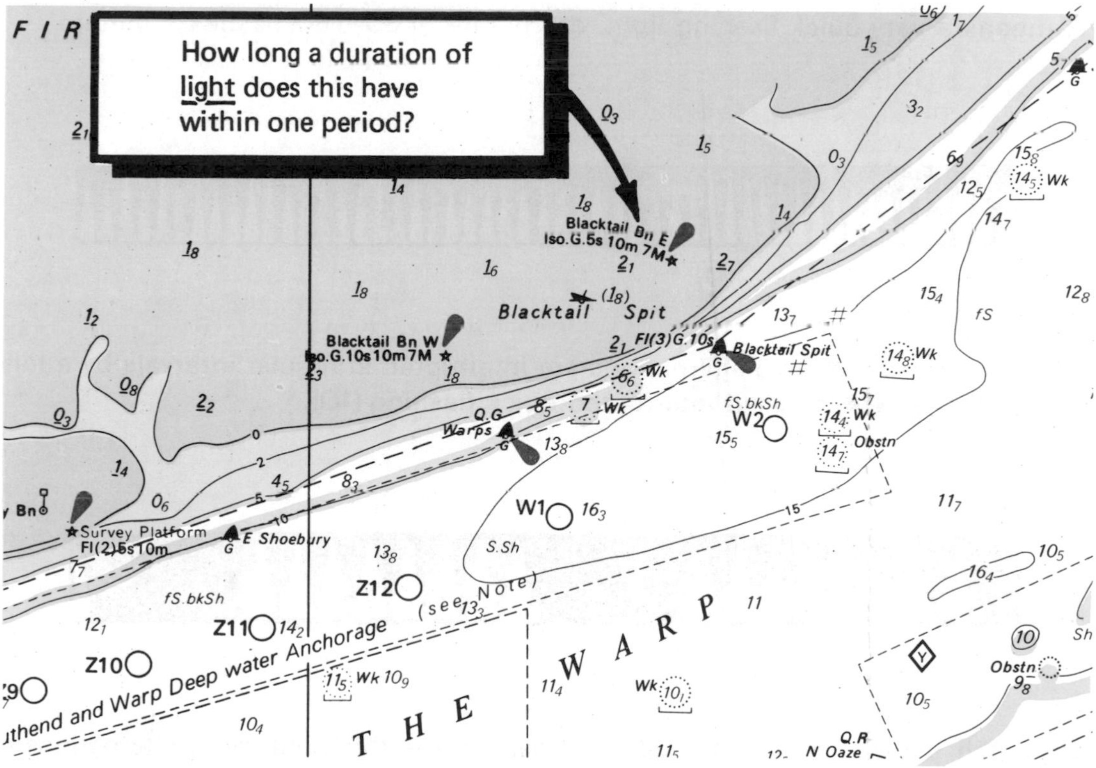

How long a duration of <u>light</u> does this have within one period?

2½ seconds (The period is 5 seconds long.)

The abbreviation **Q** denotes a quick flashing light; its characteristics are regular alternations of light and darkness, flashing at a rate of between 50 and 80 flashes per minute.

VQ means a very quick flashing light, at the rate of 80–160 flashes a minute.

A light in which the rapid alternations are interrupted at regular intervals by a long period of darkness is called interrupted quick flashing **(IQ)**.

You watch a light for five seconds. In that time nothing but rapid alternations of light and darkness occur at about 1 second intervals. What light could it be?

There are two possibilities:

1. It could be a quick flashing light.
2. It could be an interrupted quick flashing light. The period of darkness (eclipse) may not yet have occurred.

A quick flashing light with a group rhythm is written **Q(3) 10s** and would look like this:

In the same way, a very quick flashing light may be written **VQ (9) 10s** which would look like this:

There is also a long flash which is written **L Fl** and lasts at least two seconds. A composite group flashing light may include a long flash.

How would you describe this light?

VQ (6) + L Fl 10s

Six very quick flashes (about 120 to the minute) followed by one long flash within a period of 10 seconds.

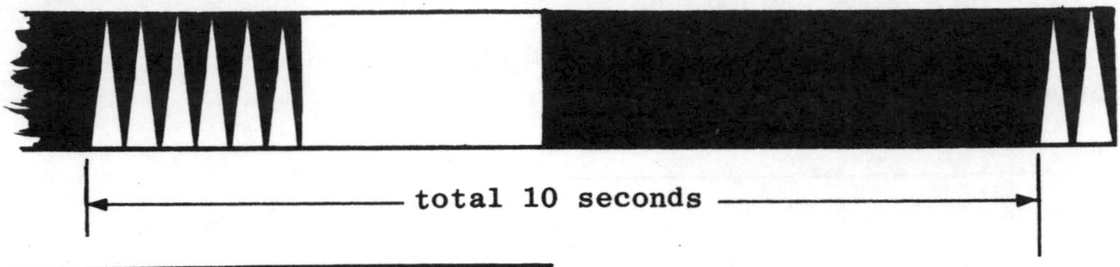

After the abbreviation for the characteristic of a light there will be the abbreviation for the colour of the light. The absence of such an abbreviation means a white light.

Abbreviations of light colours on charts

W	White
R	Red
G	Green
Bu	Blue
Y	Yellow, Amber or Orange
Vi	Violet

1. State the characteristics and colours of the following lights.

a. **Fl (6) 30s**

b. **Oc Y 12·5s**

c. **F.G**

d. **Oc (1 + 3) R 12s**

e. **Iso R**

f. **QR**

g. **L Fl Y 15s**

h. **VQ (3) 10s**

2. What is the general name given to the abbreviations 30s, 12·5s, 12s and 10s in the descriptions above ?

1. a. A group of six white flashes every 30 seconds.
   b. A yellow, amber or orange light with one occultation every 12½ seconds.
   c. A fixed green light.
   d. A red light with one occultation followed by a group of three occultations every 12 seconds.
   e. A red light with an equal duration of light and darkness. (Isophase)
   f. Rapid alternations of red light and darkness. (Quick flashing)
   g. One long flash of yellow amber or orange light every 15 seconds.
   h. Three very quick flashes of white light every 10 seconds.

2. A number followed by s gives the period of the light.

Some buoys are lit for night-time recognition.

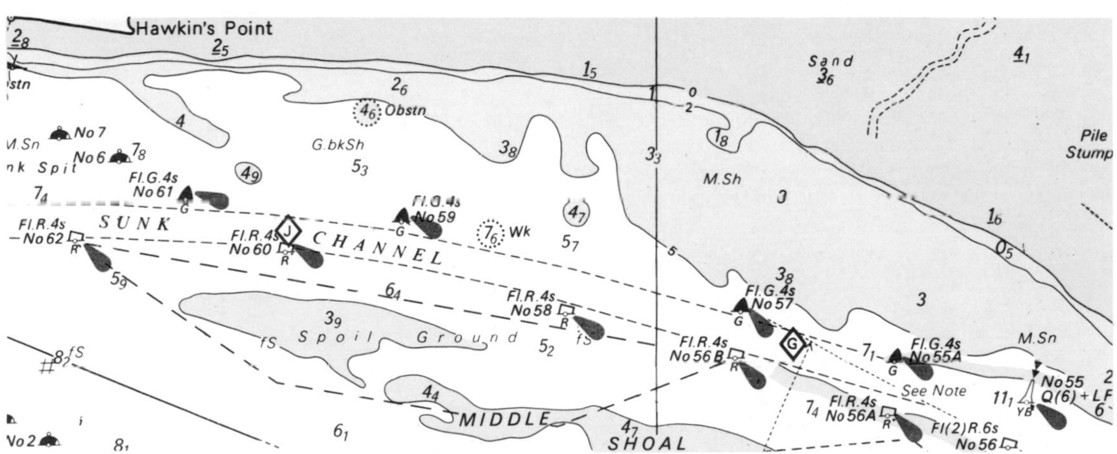

What colour lights do port and starboard hand lateral buoys show in IALA Region A?

Port hand buoys show red lights.

Starboard hand buoys show green lights.

It is by colour that a lateral buoy can be recognised. A lit port hand buoy always has a red light, whatever its rhythm, and a lit starboard hand buoy a green light.

If fixed lights are used they are frequently shown in pairs so that they are not mistaken for ships' lights.

Which buoys show these lights ?

a. **Iso R**

b. **Oc (2) G 6s**

a. A port hand buoy.

b. A starboard hand buoy.

On the other hand, cardinal buoys always have white lights either quick flashing or very quick flashing and are identified by rhythm. Each of the four cardinal buoys has a specific rhythm, which can be remembered by association with a clock face.

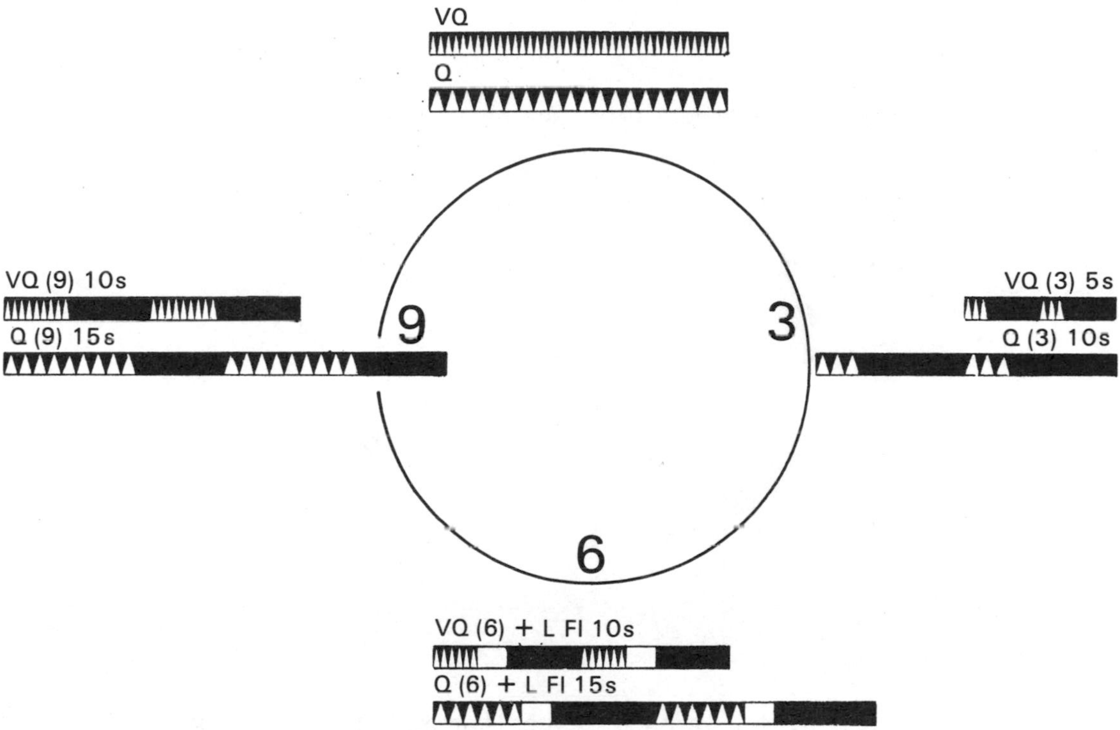

Note that the periods of these lights are standard and may be omitted on some charts.

Match the topmarks with the correct lights.

1. ⧗ 2. ▼▼ 3. ▲▼ 4. ▲▲

a. **VQ (6) + L Fl 10s**

b. **Q (3) 10s**

c. **Q (9) 15s**

d. **VQ**

1. c.
2. a.
3. b.
4. d.

Remember that, while lights of cardinal buoys are always white and are identified by their rhythm, lights of lateral buoys are identified by colour only.

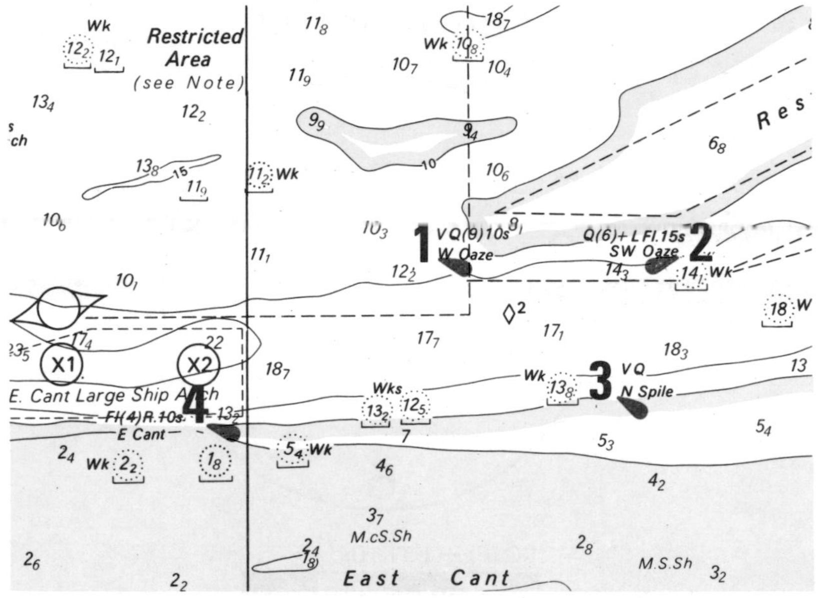

This chart shows part of the entrance to the Thames. All the lights shown here are exibited by buoys whose other identifying characteristics we have erased.

On which side would you pass each buoy ?

W. Oaze to the west
S.W. Oaze to the south
N. Spile to the north
E. Cant to port

This table shows the light characteristics of the remaining Region 'A' buoys.

Type of Buoy	Colour of Light	Rhythm	Identifying Feature
Isolated Danger	White	Group flashing 2	Rhythm
Safe Water	White	Isophase, Occulting, or 1 long flash in period of 10 seconds	Rhythm
Special	Yellow	Any rhythm not used by a white light	Colour and Rhythm

1. Use the table to identify these lights. (The colour of the light is not specified.)

2. Which buoys from the table have these light characteristics ?

a. **Fl Y 6s**
b. **Oc (2) 15s**
c. **L Fl 10s**

1. a. Safe Water buoy.
   b. Isolated Danger buoy.
   c. Special buoy.
2. a. Special buoy.
   b. Safe Water buoy.
   c. Safe Water buoy.

First, cover the page opposite, then complete this diagram with the correct abbreviations for appropriate lights.

Remember, the periods for cardinal lights may be **5s**, **10s** or **15s** only.

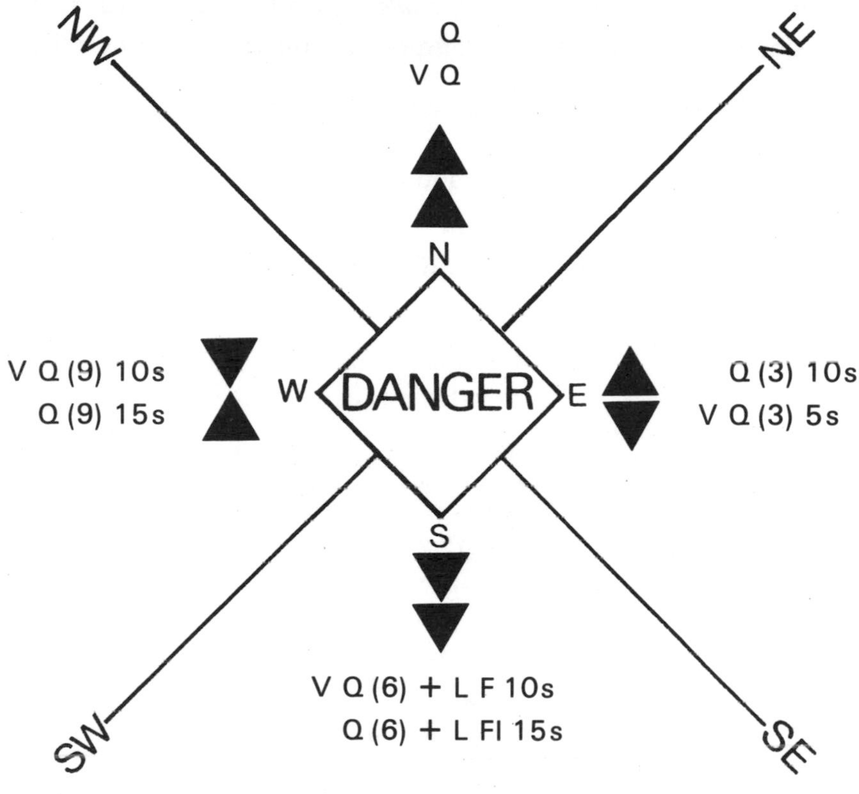

Please turn to page 162

If you wanted to find more details about a particular light (e.g. its elevation, description of its appearance) than is given on a chart, you would refer to the appropriate volume of the *Admiralty List of Lights and Fog Signals* (usually referred to as the *List of Lights).* Every light is listed there except light-buoys (unless the light on the light-buoy has an elevation of 8 metres or more).

Refer to your copy of the ***List of Lights*** and find out.

i. What sort of structure is Saint Anthony Head Light (shown below)?

ii. What is its elevation?

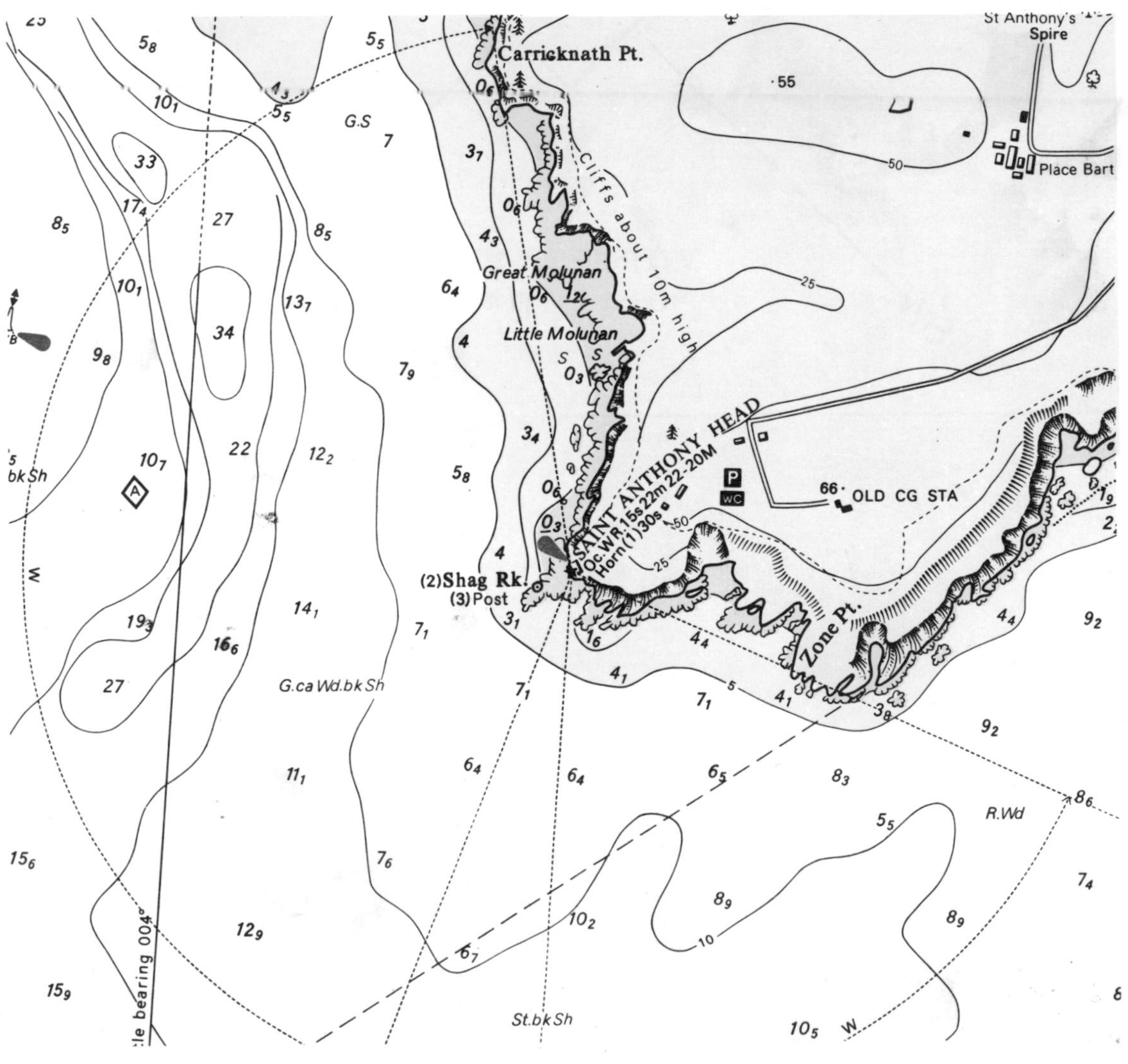

i. A white 8-sided tower.

ii. 22 metres.

You will notice that the elevation is also printed on the chart (22 m) immediately after the period of the light.

The Saint Anthony Head Light is a white and red occulting light and this abbreviation, **Oc W R**, tells you that it <u>changes colour in sectors.</u> This means that if two observers were simultaneously watching from different directions they would see different colours.

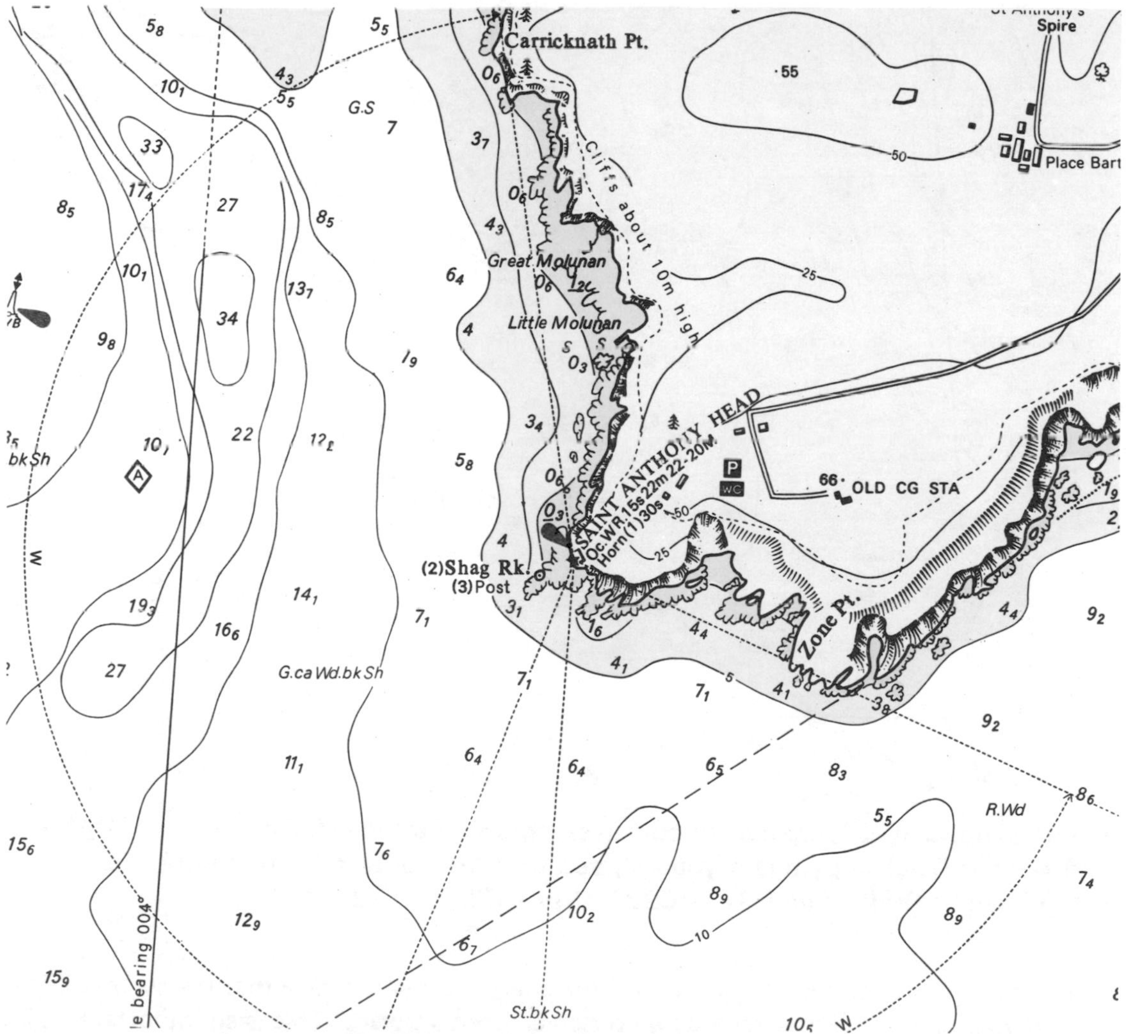

Which of the following lights changes colour in sectors ?

1. **Fl (2) R 10s**
2. **FWG**
3. **Iso Bu 2s**

2. FWG (A fixed light coloured white in one sector and green in another.)

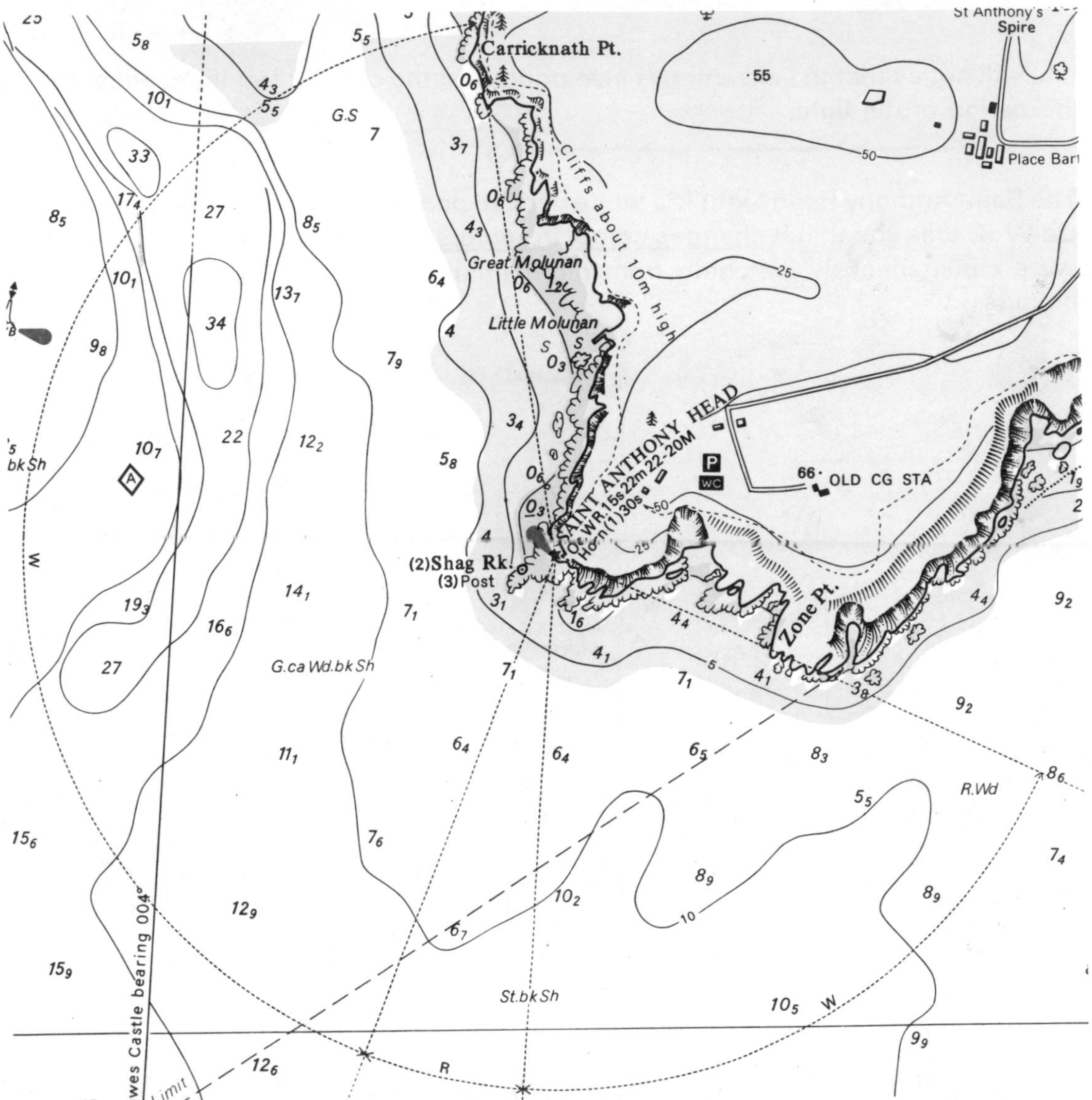

Limits of lights which change colours in sectors are stated in full in the *List of Lights.* If you refer to your copy again you will see that the sectors for this light are: White 295° - 004°, Red 004° - 022°, White 022° - 172°.

Compare this with the sectors shown on the chart: you will notice that the sectors in the *List of Lights* are given as seen by an observer from seaward. This is an important point to remember.

If the *List of Lights* tells you that the white sector of a light is 295° - 028°, would you see it as white - when you are directly north of it, or when you are directly south of it ?

Directly south of it.

Not only do you find lights that change colour in sectors but also ones that change colour on the same bearing. Such lights are called *alternating* lights e.g.,

Al Fl WR 20s

Al W R 6s

The first example (**Al Fl WR 20s**) is like an ordinary flashing light, except that it appears as a white flash and then as a red flash and then as a white flash again . . . . and so on.

Describe the appearance of each of these lights:

1. **Al Fl (3) WGR**
2. **Fl (2) WR**

1. A group of three flashes alternately coloured, white green and red.
2. A group of two flashes, coloured white in one sector and red in another. (Not a white flash followed by a red flash.)

Other lights that you might encounter are those which flash a Morse code signal (e.g. the signal for the letter A) or exhibit a flash or flashes while maintaining a continuous light. Further information on these is given on *page 19* of the *List of Lights.*

Aero – indicates an aero light. It is usually brighter than navigational lights and is not designed for marine navigation.

Occas – denotes an occasional light: a light exhibited only when specially needed e.g. a privately maintained light or a fishing light.

Fog signals are often associated with lights, and can be identified on a chart by an abbreviation denoting the type. A full description of the sounds associated with these types is provided in the front of the *List of Lights.*

Abbreviations of fog signals found on charts are:

Dia
Siren
Reed
Explos
Bell
Gong
Whis
Horn

The *Diaphone* generally emits a powerful low-pitched sound – often terminating with a grunt . Like the *Siren* and *Reed,* it uses compressed air to produce a sound. The *Explosive* emitter produces short reports by the firing of explosive charges.

In addition some of these sounds may be produced in Morse code, e.g. Horn Mo (A) 30s indicates a horn fog signal in the form of the letter A produced every 30 seconds.

From the chart extracts below find:

1. Which of the lights are associated with fog signals?
2. Which of the lights are not designed for general navigation purposes?

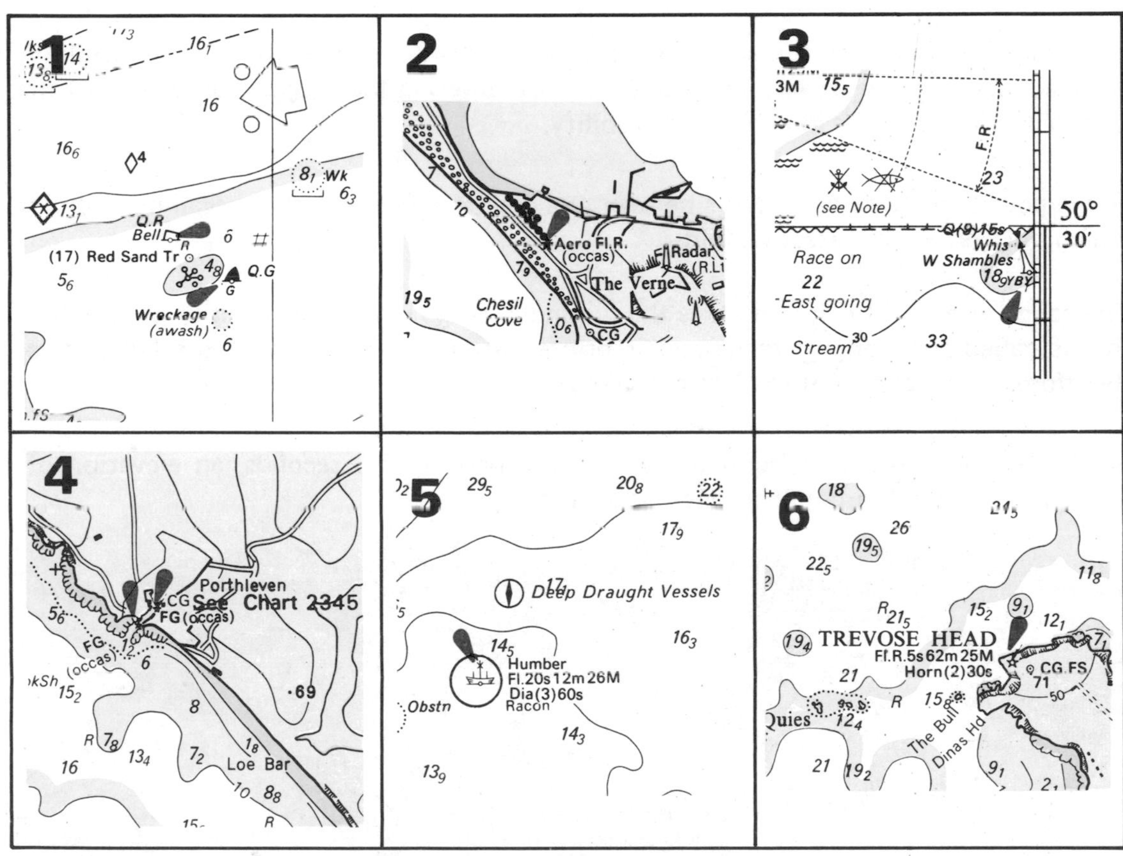

1. Those in drawings 3, 5 and 6.
2. Those in drawings 2 (Aero light) and 4 (Occasional lights).

You will often want to know how far away you can see a light. Two factors to consider are the brightness, or intensity of the light, and the prevailing visibility.

In navigational terms 'visibility' means perfect visibility without haze.

The range at which you can see a light of given intensity in different states of visibility, is called the luminous range. You can find it by entering the diagram on page 4 of the *List of Lights* with the intensity and visibility.

Remember that lights can always be seen at a greater range than the prevailing visibility, which only refers to perfect visibility.

The range given on British charts is the luminous range when the visibility is 10 miles - this is called the nominal range and is printed after the elevation of the light. It is, therefore, a special case of the luminous range.

Iso 5s 12m 4M means as isophase light with a period of 5 seconds, an elevation of 12 metres and with a nominal range of 4 miles.

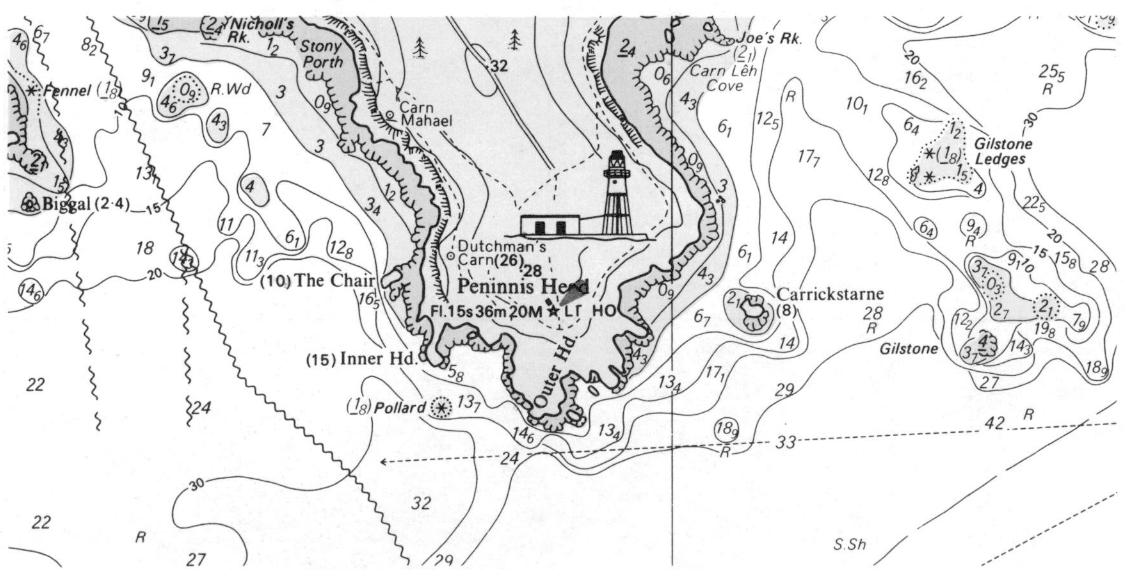

1. What is the nominal range of Peninnis Head Light?
2. In what visibility could the light be seen at this distance?

1. 20 miles.
2. In atmospheric conditions such that daylight visibility would be 10 miles.

However, the range at which the observer actually sights the light may be neither the nominal nor the luminous range, because of a third factor - the curvature of the earth.

As you approach St.Mary's, there will be a point where the light is just appearing over the horizon (provided the luminous range is sufficient). Conversely, when you are steering away from the lighthouse there will be a point where the light is on the verge of disappearing over the horizon. The distance from this point to the lighthouse is called the geographical range of the light.

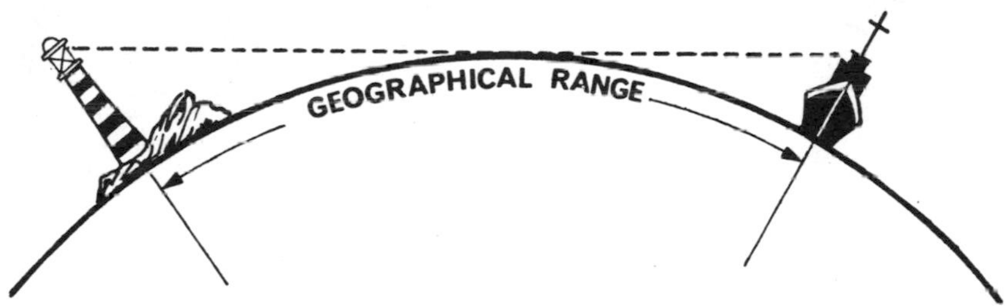

Now this distance, the geographical range, will depend on the height of the observer's eye. What other height will it depend upon?

The height (elevation) of the light.

The higher an observer is the greater is his horizon. The higher an object, the further away it can be seen. Consequently the height of both the observer and a light will affect the geographical range — which is the distance at which an observer sees the light appear or disappear over the horizon.

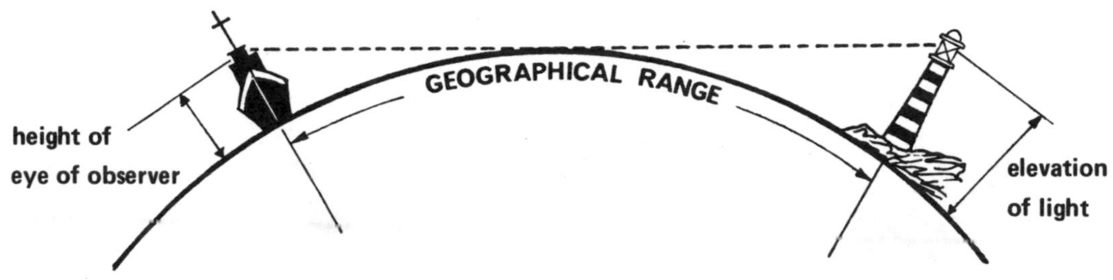

You can thus work out the geographical range of a light provided you know:

- your height of eye above sea level.
- the elevation of the light.

This is done by using a geographical range table (see pages 2 and 3 of the *List of Lights*).

What is the geographical range of a light with an elevation of 30m:

i. when the height of eye of observer is 2m?

ii. when the height of eye of observer is 20m?

(Note that you will use the part of the geographical range table dealing in <u>metres.</u>)

i. 14·0 miles

ii. 20·2 miles

From the geographical range tables you can see that in order to see St. Mary's Island light from 24 miles away (the nominal range) the observer's eye would have to be at a height of approximately 35 metres.

Where necessary, use the Geographical Range Table at the front of the Admiralty *List of Lights* to answer the following questions. Assume atmospheric conditions equivalent to 10 miles visibility in daytime.

1. The elevation of a light is 9 metres and its nominal range is 18 miles. The height of eye of an observer is 16 metres and he is 12 miles from the light. Will he be able to see it ?

2. The elevation of a light is 25 metres and its nominal range is 20 miles. The height of eye of an observer is 4 metres and he is 16 miles from the light. Will he be able to see it ?

1. Yes 2. No

More information about ranges and visibility is given in the *List of Lights* (pages 13-16).

Section 7: Self-test

1. What does this symbol stand for? 

2. What information do these abbreviations convey ?
(Describe the light - do not just say what the abbreviations stand for.)

    (i) **Fl (4) 20s 15m 12M**

    (ii) **Oc (1 + 2) 12s 35m 20M**

    (iii) **F W R 4m 5M**

3. Describe these lights and say what sort of buoy each belongs to:

    (i) **Iso G 4s**

    (ii) **Q**

    (iii) **Fl (2) 10s**

4. Explain what is meant by nominal range.

5. What is the geographical range of a light with an elevation of 40m when the eye of the observer is 14m ?

6. What do these symbols and abbreviations denote ?

    (i) 

    (ii) (occas)

    (iii) Dia

    (iv) Explos

7. Where would you look for further information about lights ?

Section 7 : Answers to Self-test

1. A light.

2. (i) There is a group of 4 flashes in each period of twenty seconds. Elevation is 15 metres. Luminous range is 12 miles.

   (ii) There is one occultation followed by a group of two occultations in each period. The period lasts for 12 seconds. Elevation is 35 metres. Luminous range is 20 miles.

   (iii) There is a fixed light, white in one sector, red in another. The elevation is 4 metres and the luminous range 5 miles.

3. (i) There is an equal duration of light and darkness in a period of 4 seconds. The light is green. This light is on a starboard buoy.

   (ii) There are continuous quick flashes of light. This denotes a North buoy.

   (iii) There are two flashes of light in a period of ten seconds. The light is on an isolated danger buoy.

4. Nominal Range is luminous range of a light in sea miles when the atmospheric conditions are such that daylight visibility would be 10 miles.

5. 20·4 miles

6. (i) A light vessel.

   (ii) An occasional light.

   (iii) Diaphone fog signal.

   (iv) Explosive fog signal.

7. In *The Admiralty List of Lights and Fog Signals.*

Section 8: Charts

You have already met some of the chart symbols, the comprehensive list is given in *Symbols and Abbreviations used on Admiralty Charts (Chart 5011).*

There are a number of symbols and abbreviations relating to anchorages in ports and harbours – three important ones which should be learnt are illustrated on this portion of chart 871 (Rivers Tamar, Lynher and Tavy).

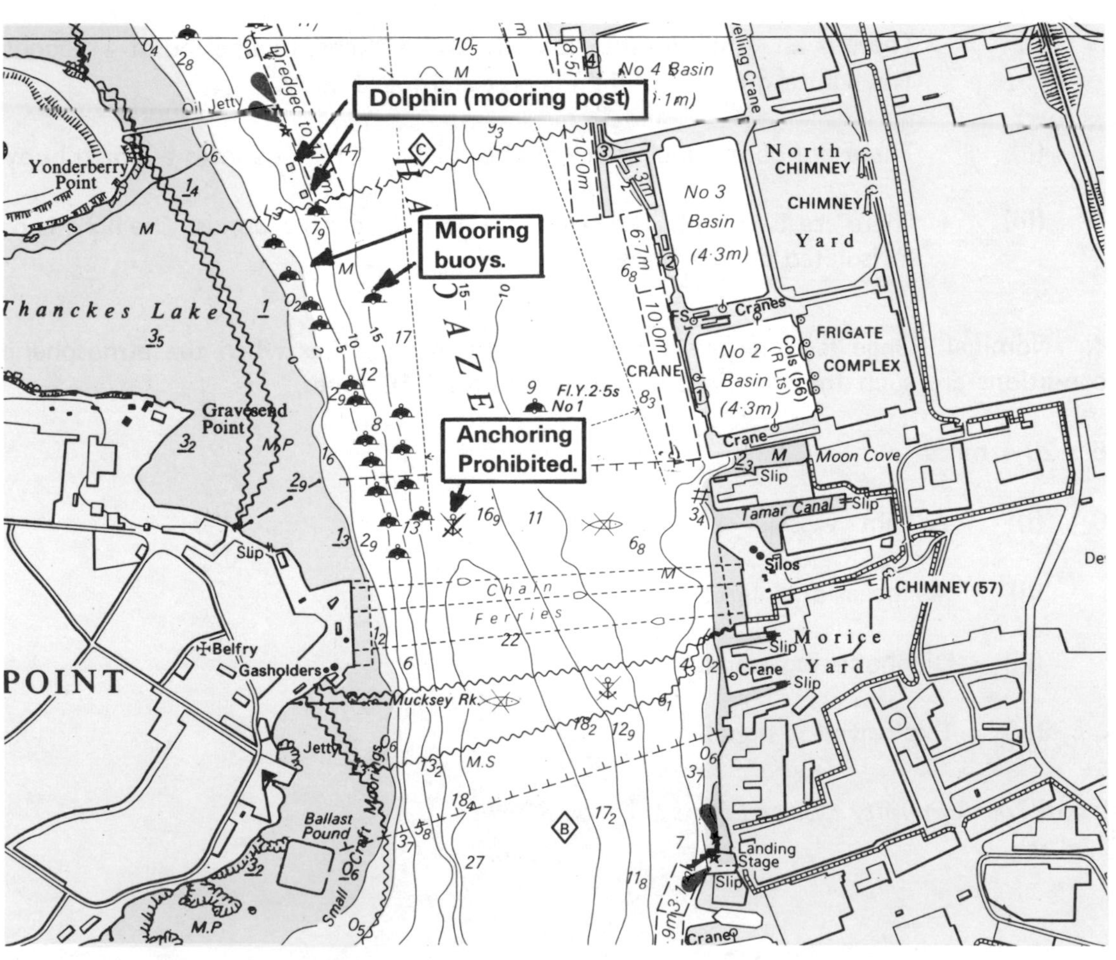

Related to the question of anchorage is the quality of the bottom. As you can see from the extract from chart 1267 shown below, this information is given in abbreviated form at sounded points over the sea area. The full list of abbreviations is given in *Symbols and Abbreviations used on Admiralty Charts* and a selection is given here.

S	–	Sand	*f*	–	fine
M	–	Mud	*c*	–	coarse
Sn	–	Shingle	*so*	–	soft
R	–	Rock			
Sh	–	Shells			
G	–	Gravel			

What is the quality of the bottom at the points indicated?

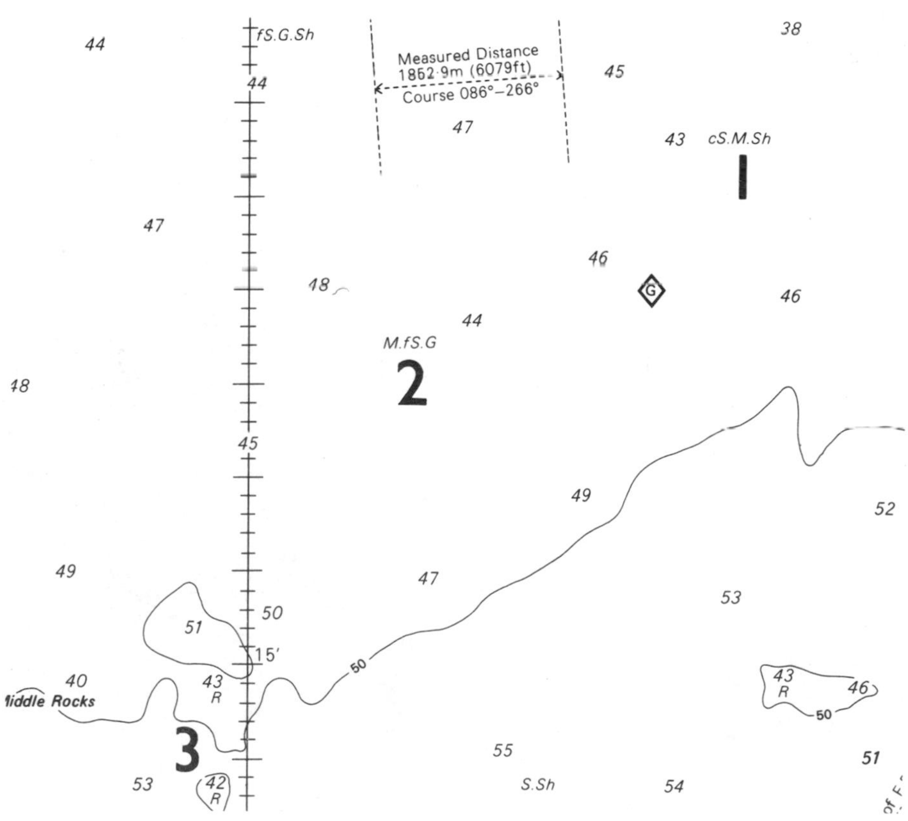

1. Coarse sand, mud and shells.
2. Mud, fine sand and gravel.
3. Rock.

What is the meaning of the symbols indicated?

1

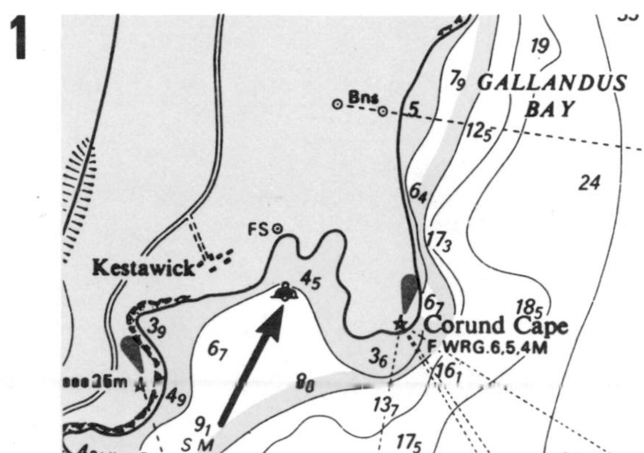

2

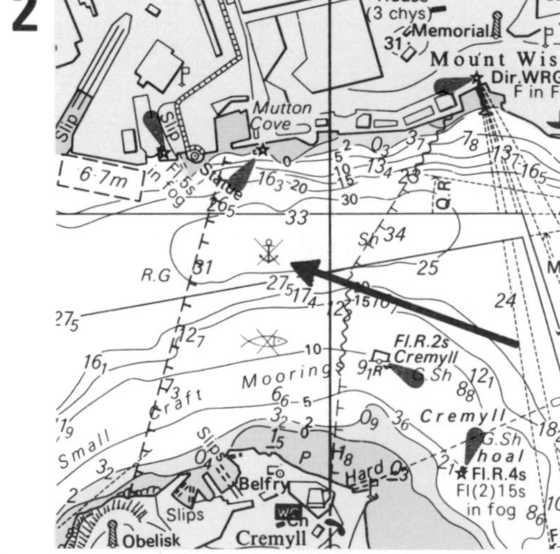

3

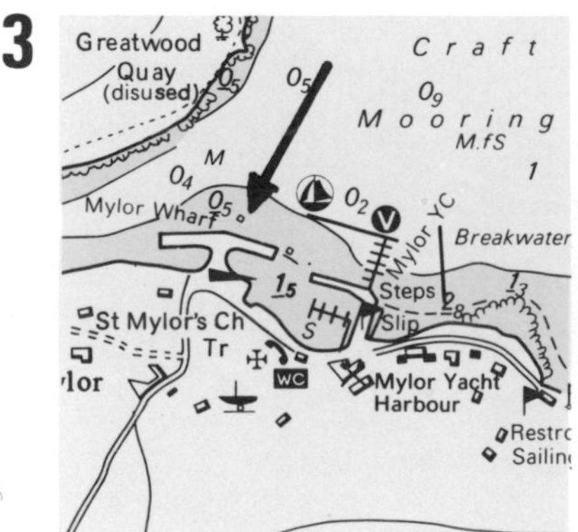

1. Mooring buoy. 2. Anchoring prohibited. 3. Dolphin.

The charts that you use for navigation have been based on surveys. The accuracy of a chart depends on whether it is a well-surveyed chart.

A

SOUTH AMERICA

EAST ENTRANCE OF

MAGELLAN STRAIT

FROM C. VIRGINS TO THE FIRST NARROWS.

BY CAPTAIN R.C. MAYNE, R.N. C.B.

Assisted by Navg Lieut. F. G. Gray, Lieut. J. H. Orlebar,

& Navg Sub Lieuts. J. T. Hoskyn, E. R. Connor, & J. W. Dixon, R.N.

H.M.S. 'NASSAU' 1867-8.

B

ENGLAND – EAST COAST

BLAKENEY TO FLAMBOROUGH HEAD

COMPILED FROM ADMIRALTY SURVEYS TO 1962.

With additions and corrections to 1965.

The Topography is taken chiefly from the Ordnance Survey

For Abbreviations see Admiralty Chart 5011 or Mariners' Handbook, S.D. 100

Underlined figures express in Feet Drying Heights above Chart Datum

All other Heights are expressed in Feet above Mean High Water Springs.

SOUNDINGS IN FATHOMS

(Under Eleven in Fathoms and Feet)

NATURAL SCALE 1:146,000 (at Lat 53°27')

Projection – Mercator

C

SCOTLAND — EAST COAST

FIRTH OF FORTH

ISLE OF MAY TO INCHKEITH

DEPTHS IN METRES

SCALE 1:50000

Depths are in metres and are reduced to Chart Datum, which is approximately the level of Lowest Astronomical Tide.

Heights are in metres. Underlined figures are drying heights, in metres and decimetres, above Chart Datum; all other heights are above MHWS.

Projection: Gnomonic. Positions are based on the Ordnance Survey of Great Britain (1936) Datum.

Authorities: Sources of the hydrography are shown in the source data diagram. The topography is taken chiefly from the Ordnance Survey.

Which of these charts would you consider to be based on the least reliable survey and why?

The survey of Chart A would be the least reliable because it has the earliest date of survey.

In deciding whether a chart is well-surveyed, the first point to notice is whether the date of the latest survey is reasonably modern.

The second point to notice requires a look at the chart itself. Which of these charts is the most trustworthy, and why?

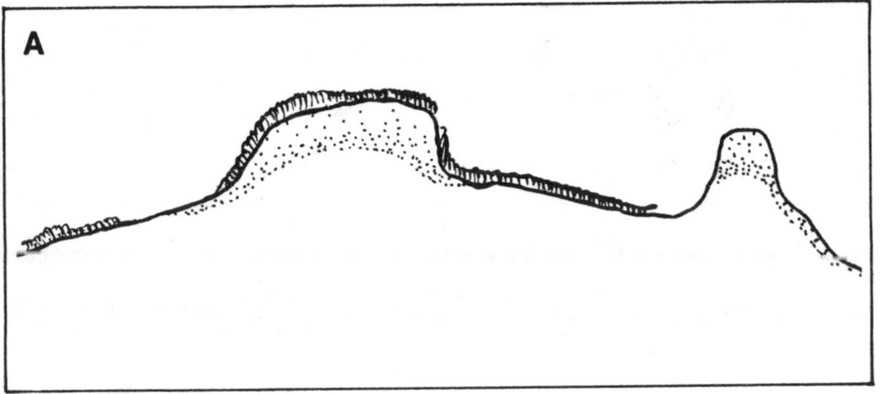

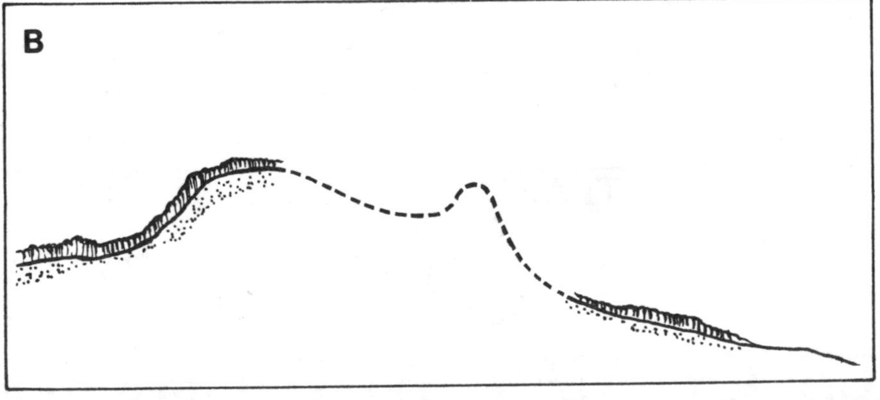

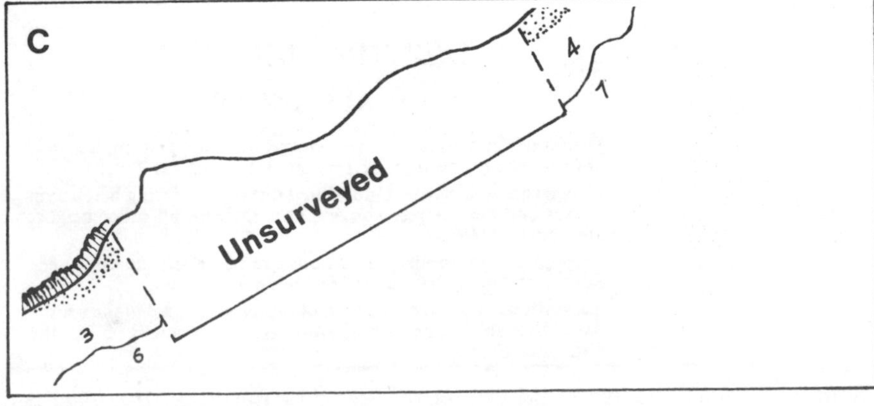

Chart A is the most trustworthy, because the other two contain areas which are unsurveyed.

A well-surveyed chart is one:

i) where the date of the last survey is reasonably modern.

ii) where there are no unsurveyed areas.

On this portion of chart you can see that part of the coastline is unsurveyed. There are other indications that this is not a well-surveyed chart– what information is lacking in the area that has been circled?

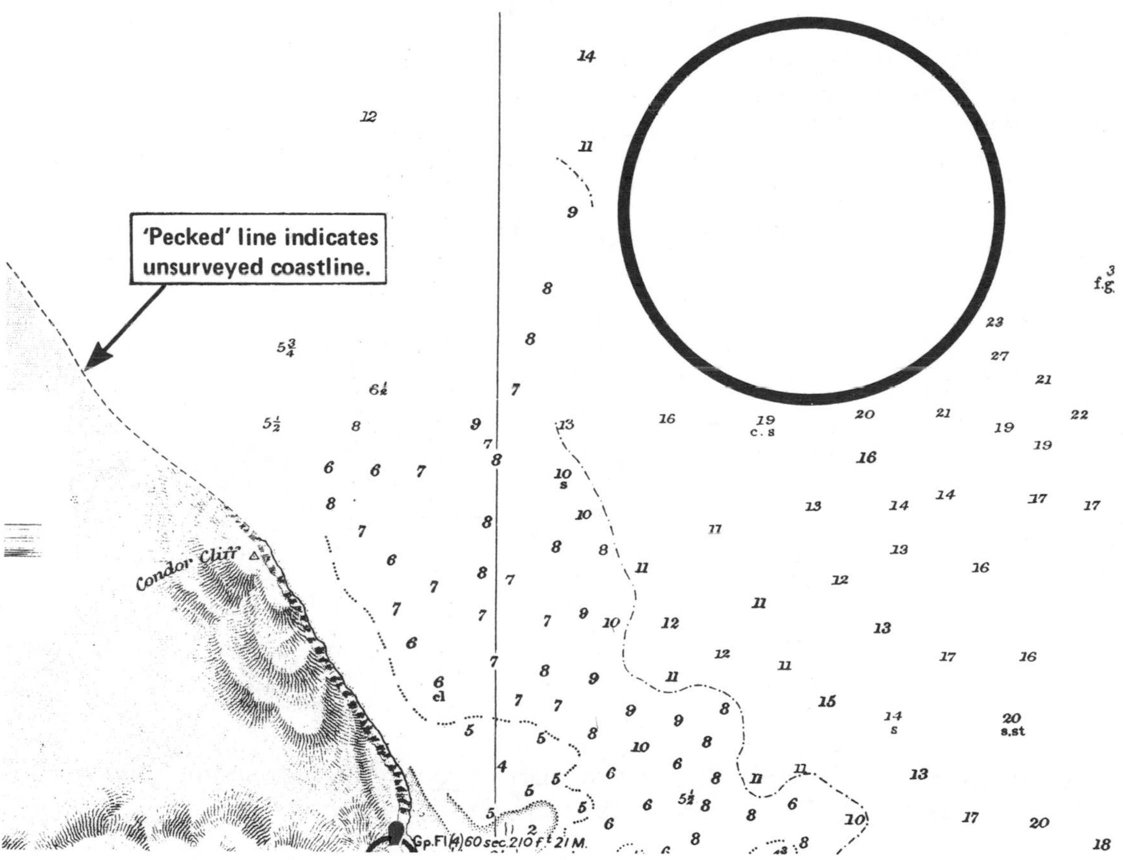

The part of the chart indicated has a blank space where no soundings are given.

This indicates that surveys have given either no information or insufficient information about depths in this area – showing that this is not a well-surveyed chart.

On most new charts an insert "Source Data" will inform the navigator of the dates of survey of that chart. This diagram shows the dates of survey of chart 1828.

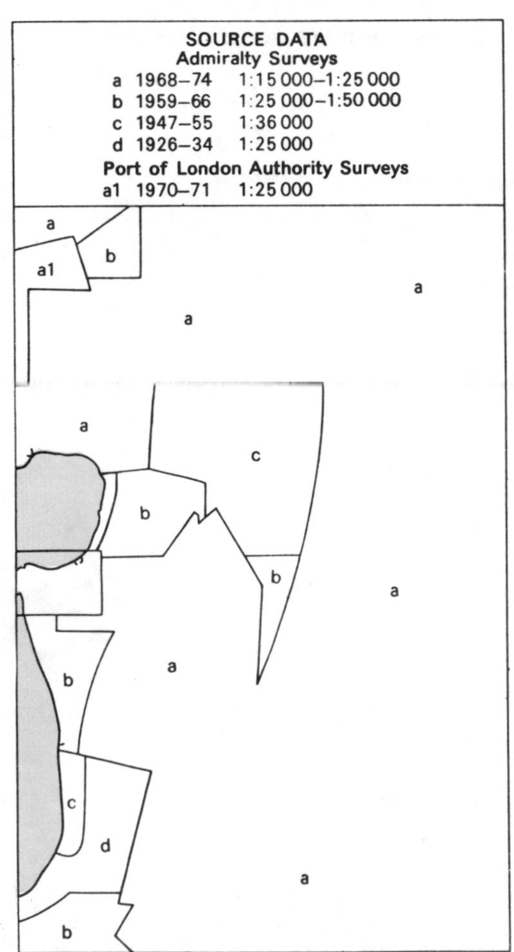

The navigator needs an indication on the chart of <u>continuity</u> of soundings. The portion of chart on page 179 fails to provide this because it shows incomplete____ ______ ____.

depth contour lines

There are thus four criteria used to identify a well-surveyed chart:

1. The date of the latest survey should be reasonably modern.
2. There should be no unsurveyed areas.
3. There should be no gaps in the soundings.
4. Depth contour lines should be shown.

One reason for requiring a recent date of survey is that features of the coast and sea will change continually. When you receive any chart from the Hydrographic Supplies Establishment, you will find that certain amendments have already been made by hand. These are 'small but important' corrections recording changes which have occurred and which have been inserted since the chart was printed. It is essential that the navigating officer sees that the chart is subsequently kept up-to-date in the same manner. The Hydrographic Supplies Establishment sends out a weekly *Notices to Mariners* which includes details of 'small but important' corrections needing to be made. On receipt of this, the corrections must be inserted at once in permanent violet ink on the appropriate charts.

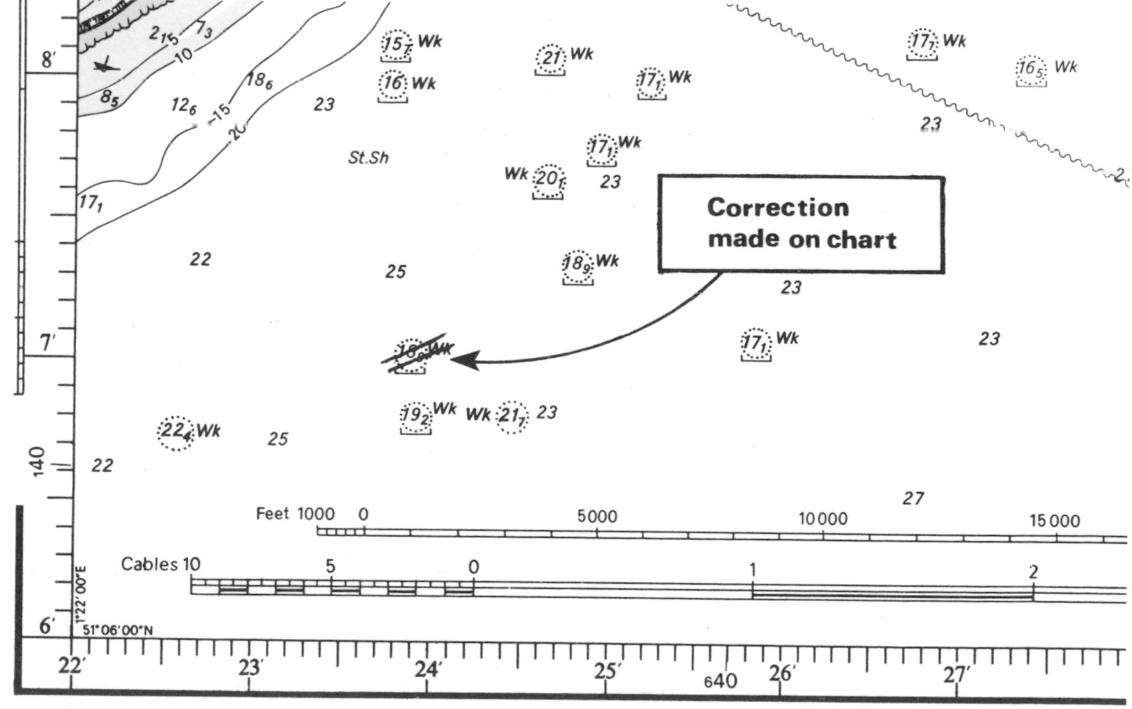

Small corrections 1984 -1317-1462-1526-2270-2275-2495-1985-572-573-697-1256-1514-1820-1827-1828-2047-2334 + 2486

The number of the correction is noted in the margin at bottom left on the charts

From what source will you receive corrections?

The Hydrographic Supplies Establishment: *(Notices to Mariners).*

These small corrections, whether already done in the chart store or made subsequently on board, are noted in the bottom left-hand corner of the chart, giving the date and the number of the *Notices to Mariners.*

Large corrections, on the other hand, are always done in the Hydrographic Supplies Establishment.

You will also receive from time to time urgent warnings which will also need to be noted on the chart. These will concern, e.g. derelicts, drifting structures, buoys out of position etc. In order that they may be received as soon as possible, they are promulgated by signal. These urgent corrections are noted in pencil on the chart since they are of a temporary nature.
What are the four criteria used to identify a well-surveyed chart?

1. The date of the latest survey should be reasonably modern.
2. There should be no unsurveyed areas.
3. There should be no gaps in the soundings.
4. Depth contour lines should be shown.

Section 8 : Self-test

1. How are chart corrections normally received?
2. What action should be taken on receipt of them?
3. How are urgent temporary corrections received?

Now turn to page 184 for answers.

Section 8 : Answers to Self-test

1. They are issued by the Hydrographer. They are printed in *Notices to Mariners.*

2. They must be inserted immediately on the appropriate chart.

3. They are promulgated by signal.

Section 9: Fixing the Ship's Position

It is essential that the navigating officer is able to establish accurately the ship's position. But how can he do this? The surface of the sea is not criss-crossed with lines of latitude and longitude! Nor is he in the same situation as the motorist who has only to follow the right road to reach his destination.

One method is to use landmarks. But these must be used accurately. It's no use the navigating officer saying, "We must be somewhere near the Eddystone Lighthouse." He must be able to pinpoint the ship's position <u>exactly</u>.

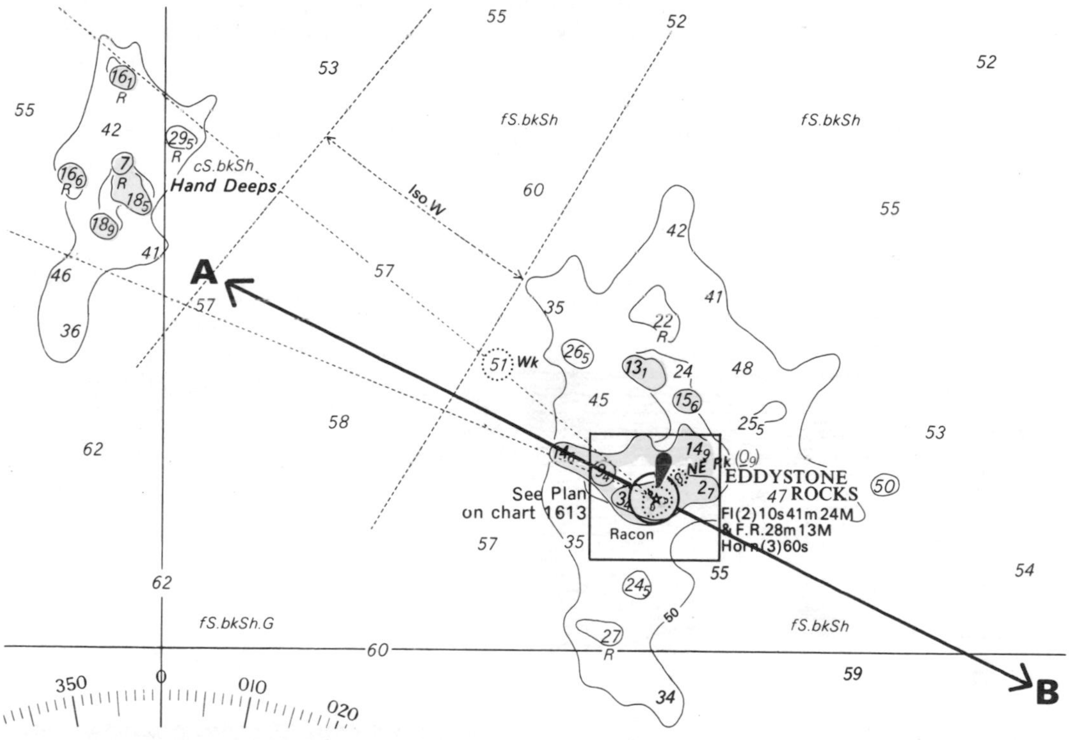

If a gyro-compass reading shows that the Eddystone Lighthouse bears 115° from the ship, on which line will the ship's position lie, A or B?

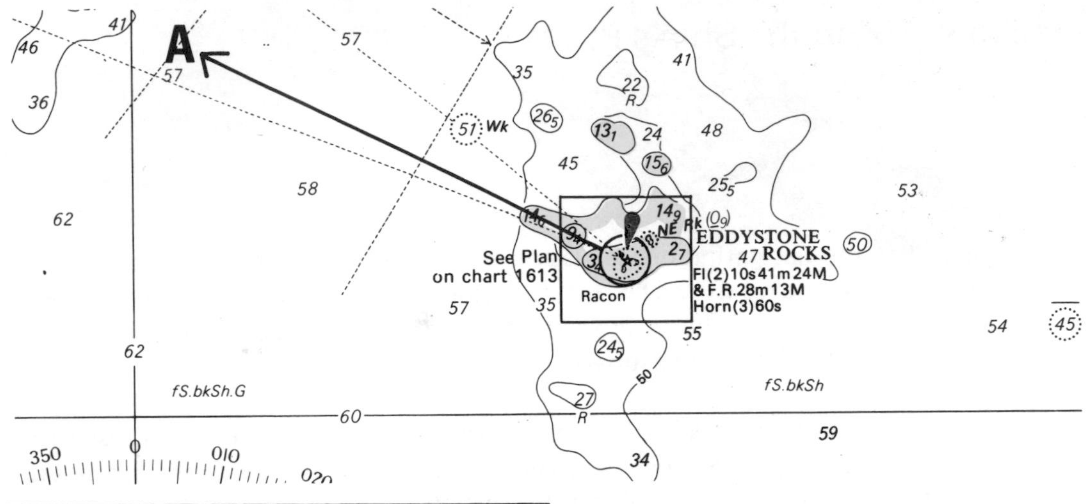

If the bearing of the lighthouse from the ship is 115° the ship's position will be somewhere on line A. Such a line is called a *position line* because the ship's position is known to lie on it.

The normal method of obtaining a compass bearing entails making use of the gyro-compass repeater on the bridge, known as the *Pelorus.* The reading is made after lining up the mark (in this case, a church) with the V-shaped sighting device.

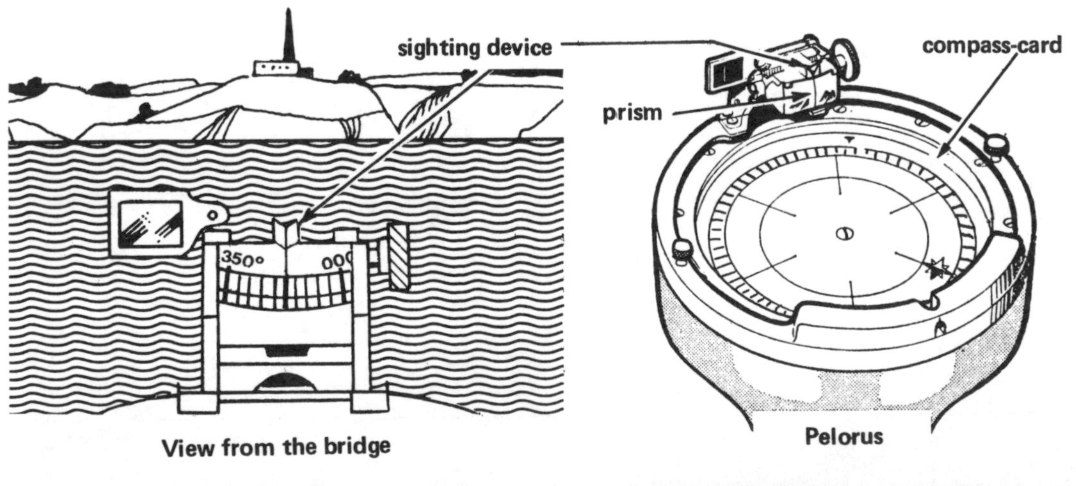

View from the bridge

Pelorus

The line of bearing is then plotted on the chart at the correct angle with a single arrowhead pointing away from the mark. The time is recorded alongside. Bearings are plotted by means of 'parallel rulers' which ensure accurate transfer of the bearing measured from the compass rose to the position line through the mark.

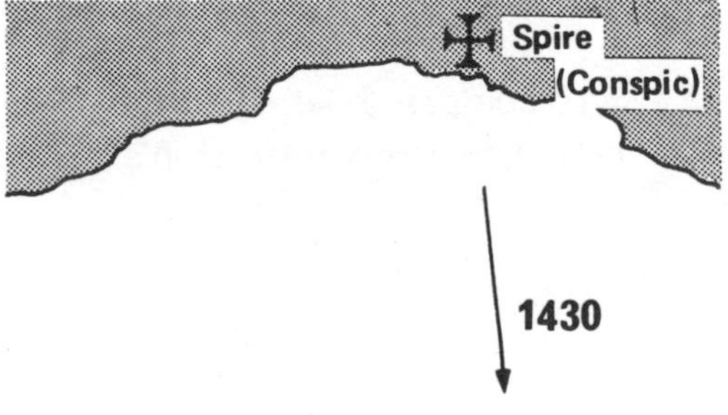

Plotted Position Line

Another type of position line can be obtained by finding the *range* of a mark i.e. finding how far away it is. This is normally done by using radar.

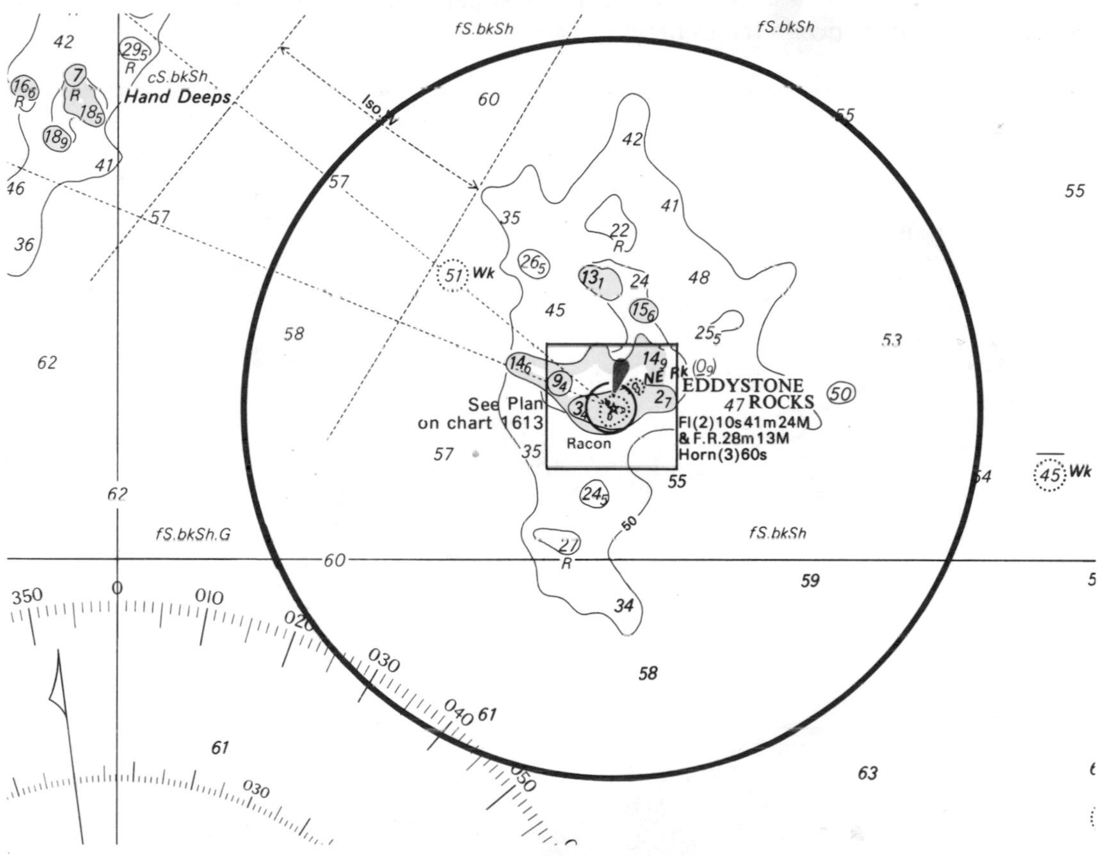

If you find that you are two miles away from the Eddystone Lighthouse, you know that your position lies on a circle which has a radius of two miles and whose centre is the lighthouse.

Having taken the bearing and range of the lighthouse at the same time — and they are known to be accurate — where can you be assured that the ship's exact position is?

Where the line of bearing and the range arc intersect.

A position thus obtained is called a *fix.* The navigator will only refer to it as a fix if he has complete confidence in its accuracy.

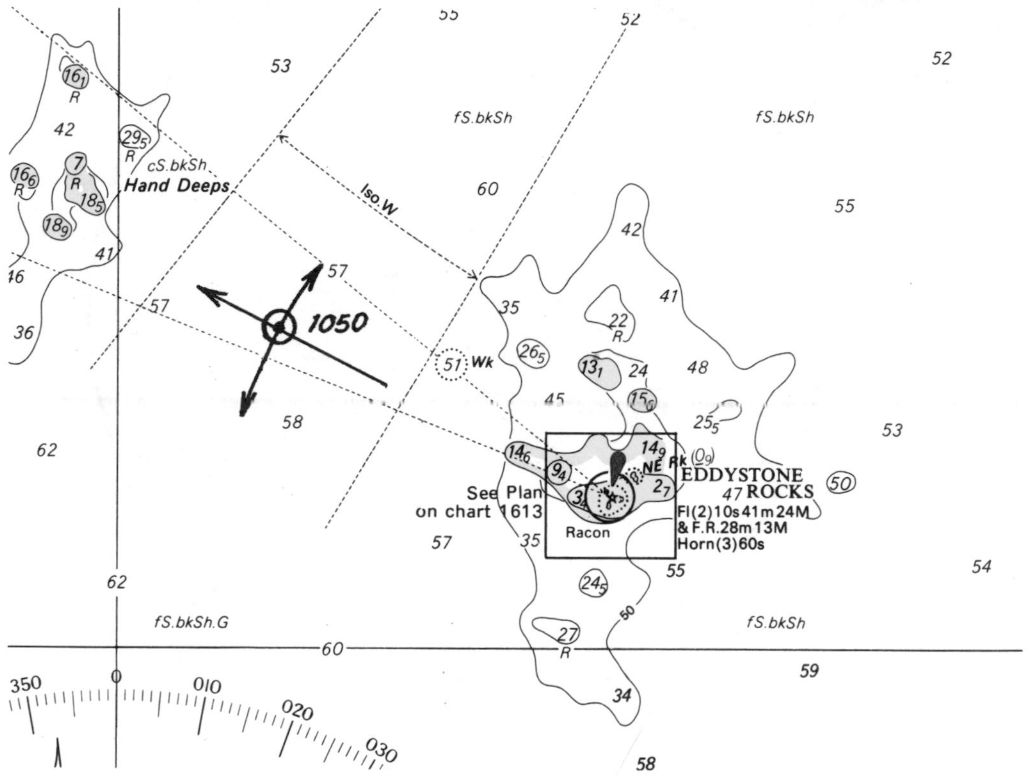

Look at the chart above where the fix is plotted, and then answer these questions.

1. How do you represent on a chart a position line taken from a bearing?
2. How do you represent on a chart a position line taken from a range?
3. How is a fix represented on a chart?
4. With what item of information is it essential to mark a fix?

1. A line with a single arrowhead at one end. ⟶
2. An arc with a single arrowhead at both ends. ⟷
3. A circle with a dot in the middle. ⊙
   (The position lines must also be shown.)
4. The time.

A bearing and a range is one method of obtaining a fix. Apart from this, how else might you obtain intersecting position lines to fix your position in the area below?

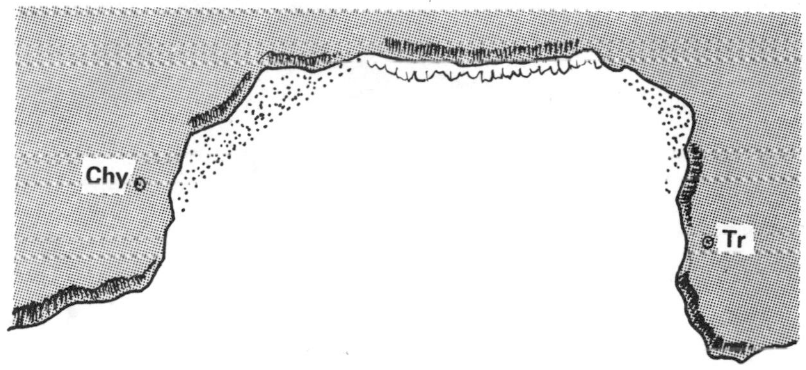

By taking two compass bearings: one of the chimney and one of the tower.

There are many ways of obtaining a position line. Those you have met so far are:

Compass bearing.

Radar range.

Any combination of two or more of these will give a fix, provided that they are taken in quick succession.

However, you will remember we said that the navigator has to decide if the position is to be called a fix. To make this decision he needs to be confident that there is no chance of error.

If you take two compass bearings resulting in a fix, like this-----------

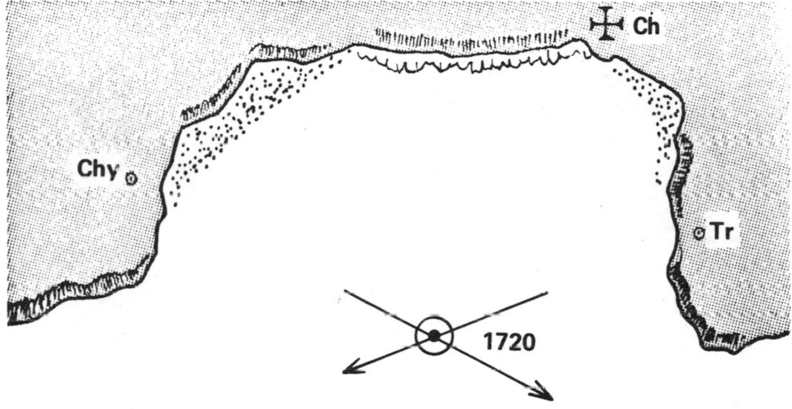

--------what can you do which will act as a check on the accuracy of the fix?

Take a third bearing (of the church spire).

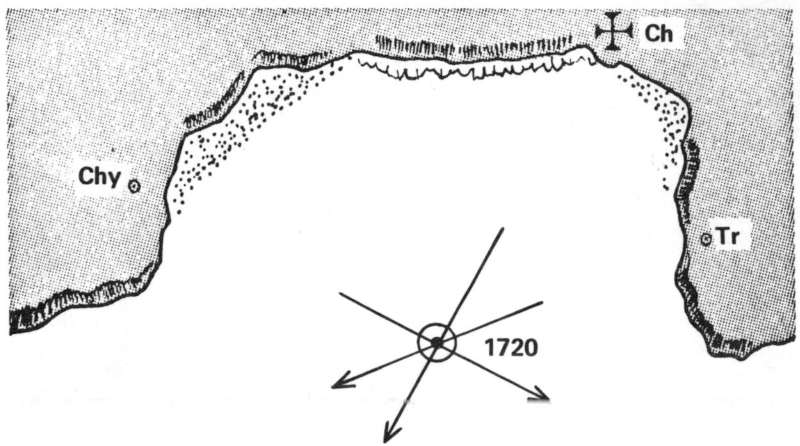

Two position lines, however inaccurate, will always cross somewhere (unless, of course, they are parallel). Only a third position line can make you certain of an accurate fix.

A further point to be sure of is that position lines cut at as great an angle as possible to reduce the error in position if the bearing is wrong. As a rule of thumb, position lines shall not be used if the angle of cut is less than 30°.

The three position lines above [provide/do not provide] a good angle of cut. Choose the correct alternative and then turn to page 193.

provide

As you have seen, the reason for using three marks is that an error in the position lines is readily apparent, because they will not cross in a point.

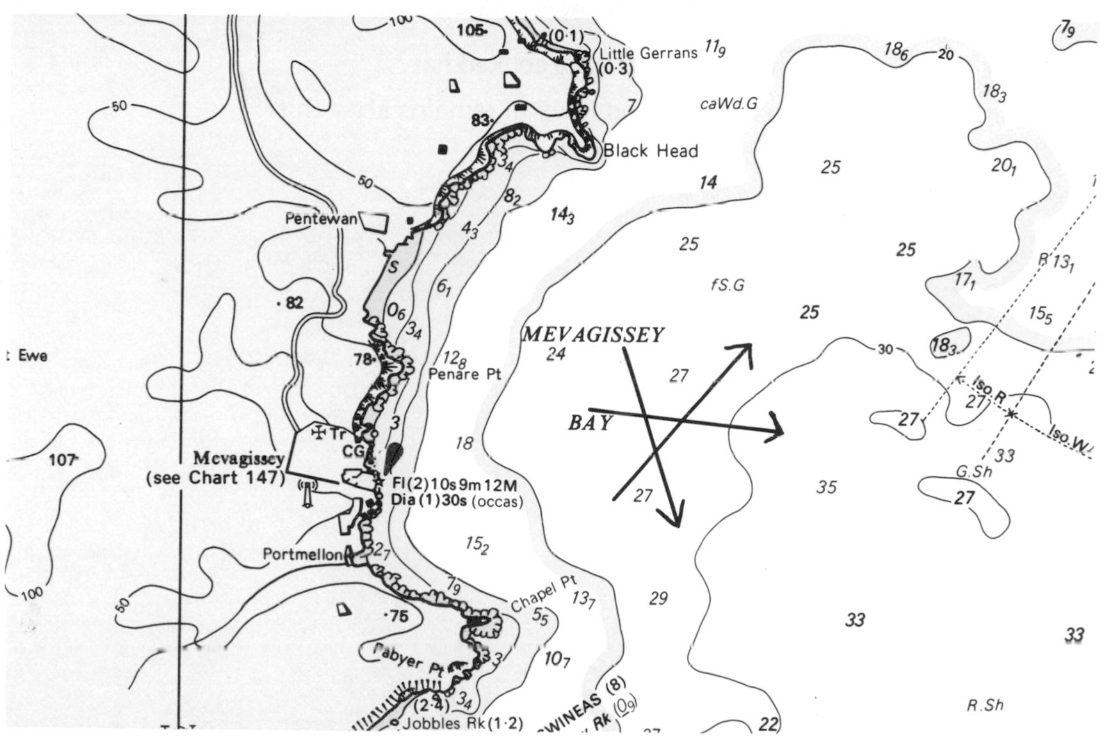

In this example the three position lines do not exactly intersect, they form a triangle. This triangle is known as a *cocked hat.* If it is a small one, then the centre of it can be marked as a fix. 'Small' is of course a relative term, and whether you decide to consider a particular cocked hat as a small one will depend on your distance from the nearest danger. (Make a note to discuss this with your Instructor or other experienced person.) When the cocked hat is a large one, you must check your plotting. If a large cocked hat still remains, you will have to take another fix.

You take three bearings and the position lines result in a cocked hat. What must you do?

You must first decide whether it is a small cocked hat.
(If you said that you must decide whether you are near to any danger, count your answer as correct.)

If you have a small cocked hat, mark the centre of it as a fix.

---

1. What must you do when there is a large cocked hat?
2. What must you do if a large cocked hat still remains after this?

Check your plotting.

Take the fix again.

In order to provide a continuous record of your observations and the ship's movements, entries are made in the *Navigation Record Book* in pencil. Every fix that is made should be recorded here.

A recommended layout for the Navigation Record Book is shown below. Note that horizontal lines should be drawn between the information in order to distinguish the different events corresponding to the times in the left-hand column.

DATE	30 JAN 85		WATCH FORENOON	OOW SCO
TIME	CO	SP	REMARKS	
1000	170	10	A/C 180	
1005	180	10	Portland Bill Lt 340	
			Shambles Lt 010	
			Anvil Pt 043	
1015	180	10	Sp 12	
1020	180	12	Decca Red A 16.0	
			Purple B 45.2	

The following abbreviations are commonly used when writing in the Navigation Record Book.

A/C	–	Alter course.
TS	–	Tidal stream.
SMG	–	Speed made good.
Sp	–	Speed.
CMG	–	Course made good.
Lt	–	Light
Lt.V.	–	Light Vessel.
Pt.	–	Point.

The Navigation Record Book must be neatly and accurately kept. It is the only complete official record of the ship's movement, and the Captain of your ship will inspect it regularly.

A fix obtained from bearings would be recorded in the Navigation Record Book with the mark being stated before the bearing (e.g., Rill Pt. 117°).

Conspicuous objects which are suitable for taking bearings will be marked on the chart (e.g., lights, church towers, chimneys). Quite often an edge of land like this would be suitable.

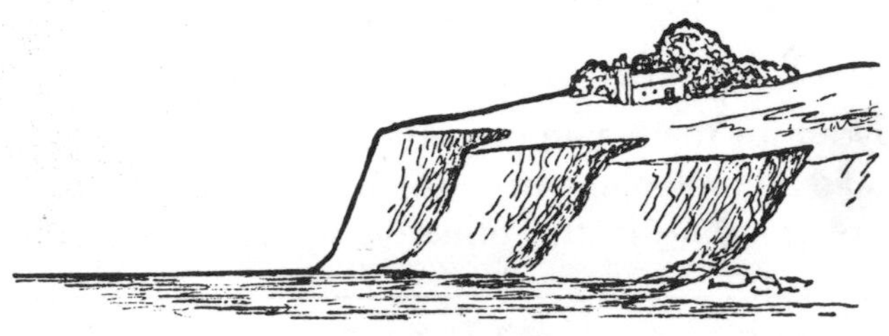

Whalley Point

This particular example is a left-hand edge i.e. the edge of land is to the left as you look at it from the ship. This would be recorded as ⇤—— Whalley Point. (The signs ⇤—— and ——⇥ refer to 'left-hand edge' and 'right-hand edge' respectively.)

At 1030 Dearman Bill (shown below as it appears to you) bears 175°. Canning Church bears 210° and Shipton Church bears 254°. Your course is 092° and your speed 15 knots. Write down this fix as you would record it in your Navigation Record Book.

Dearman Bill

1030	092°	15	RHE Dearman Bill 175° Canning ✝ 210° Shipton ✝ 254°

When you have obtained a fix, you may often need to report it. What two methods do you think could be used?

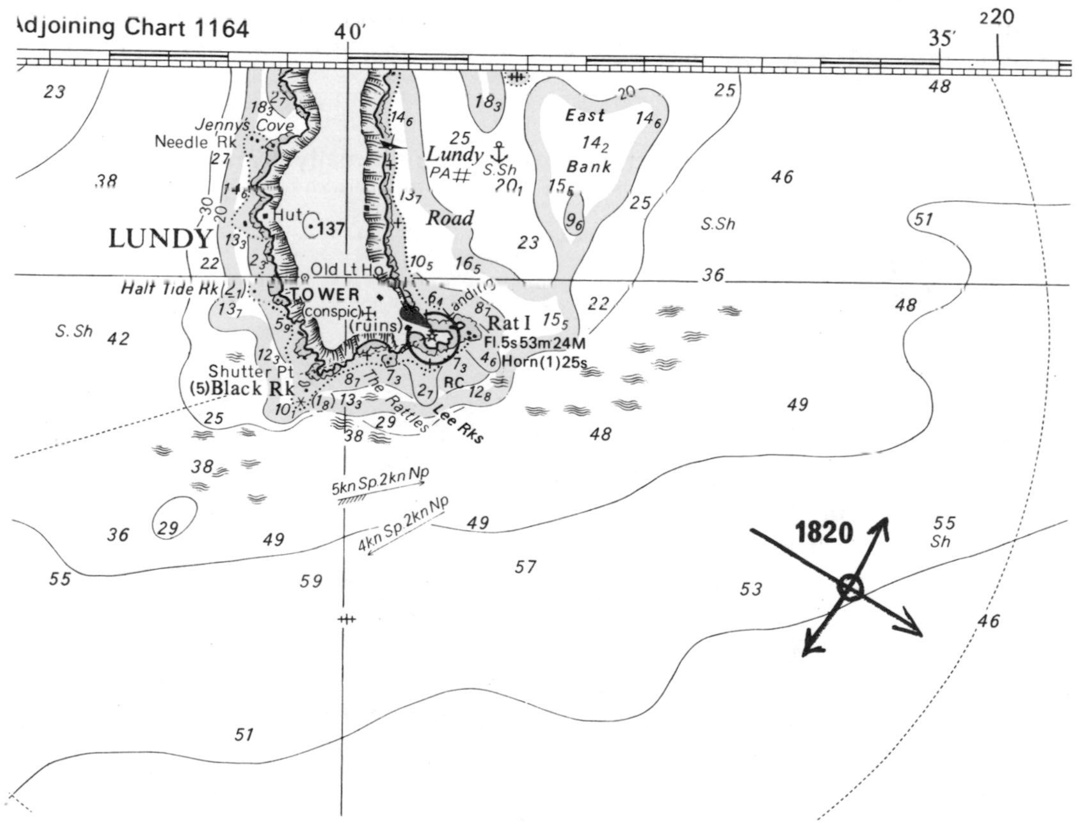

1. Latitude and longitude. 2. Range and bearing.

You already know how to express position by latitude and longitude. There are also conventions for expressing position as a bearing and distance from an object.

When you record a fix, you record the bearing of the object from you, because that is the bearing that you observe from the bridge. It is therefore possible to give your position by merely adding your distance away from the object:

e.g. Tongue LV 180°, 1′ means that the Tongue Light Vessel bears 180°, 1 mile from the ship. This is position A.

However the normal way of giving the position of the ship is to give the bearing of you from the fixed object, and then the range.

This makes sense if you assume the message is intended for an observer in another place who will start from the fixed object in identifying the position of your ship. To give your position in this way, you give first the bearing, then the name of the object, then the range.

If you were at position B on the chart, how would you normally give your position?

270° Tongue LV 1′0
Tongue LV 270°,1′0
090° Tongue LV 1′0
Tongue LV 090°, 1′0

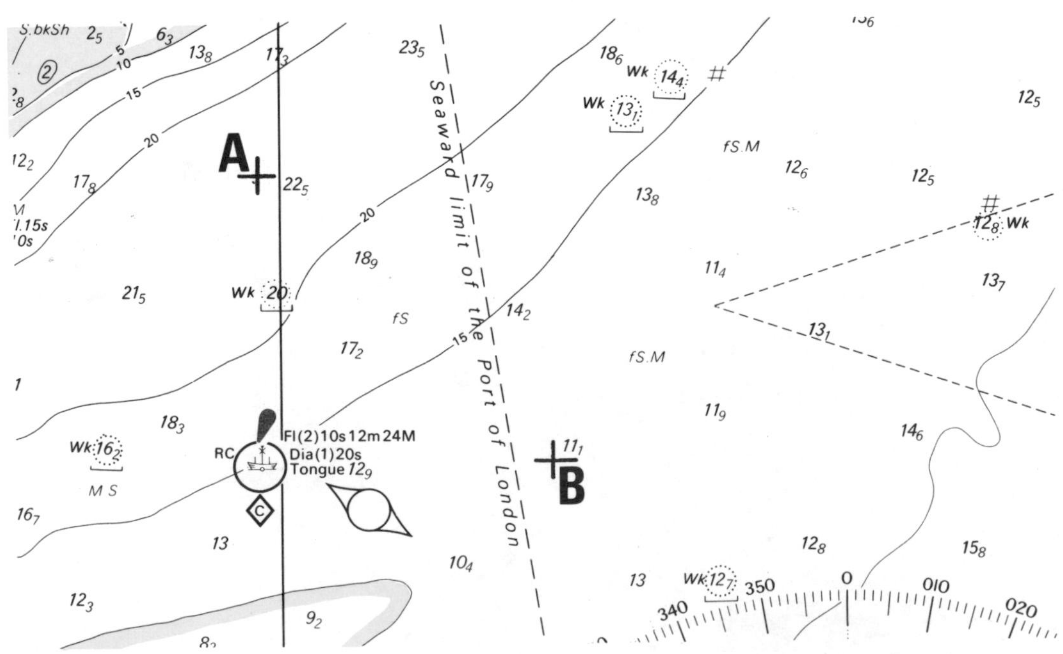

090° Tongue LV, 1:0

Another position line is the *transit.* If you take a bearing of two objects when they are exactly in line with one another ....

....then provided they are clearly charted, you can obtain their actual bearing from the chart. The symbol used in your Navigation Record Book to denote a transit is ɸ . Thus you would record the transit shown below as Island light ɸ|← Castle 340°, i.e. Island light in transit with left-hand edge of Castle, bearing 340°.

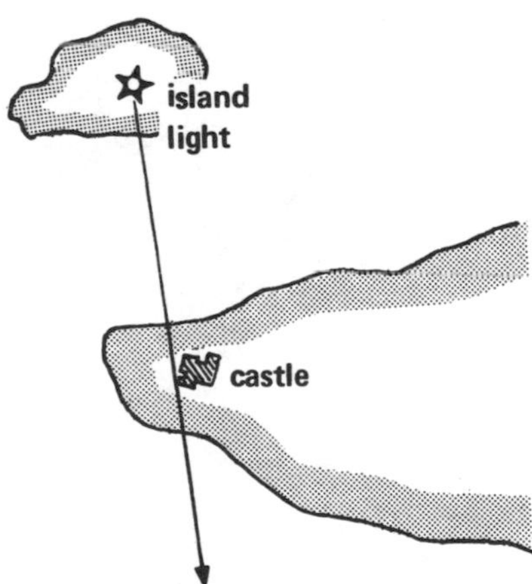

You can select your own transit provided that your marks are clearly charted and on the same level. Quite often transits are marked as such on the chart. For further information on transits see Chapters IV and V *Admiralty Manual of Navigation Volume I.*

Transits can also serve another purpose. What advantage can be gained by comparing the charted bearing of a transit with a gyro or magnetic compass bearing?

You are provided with a check on the accuracy of the compass or your deviation table.

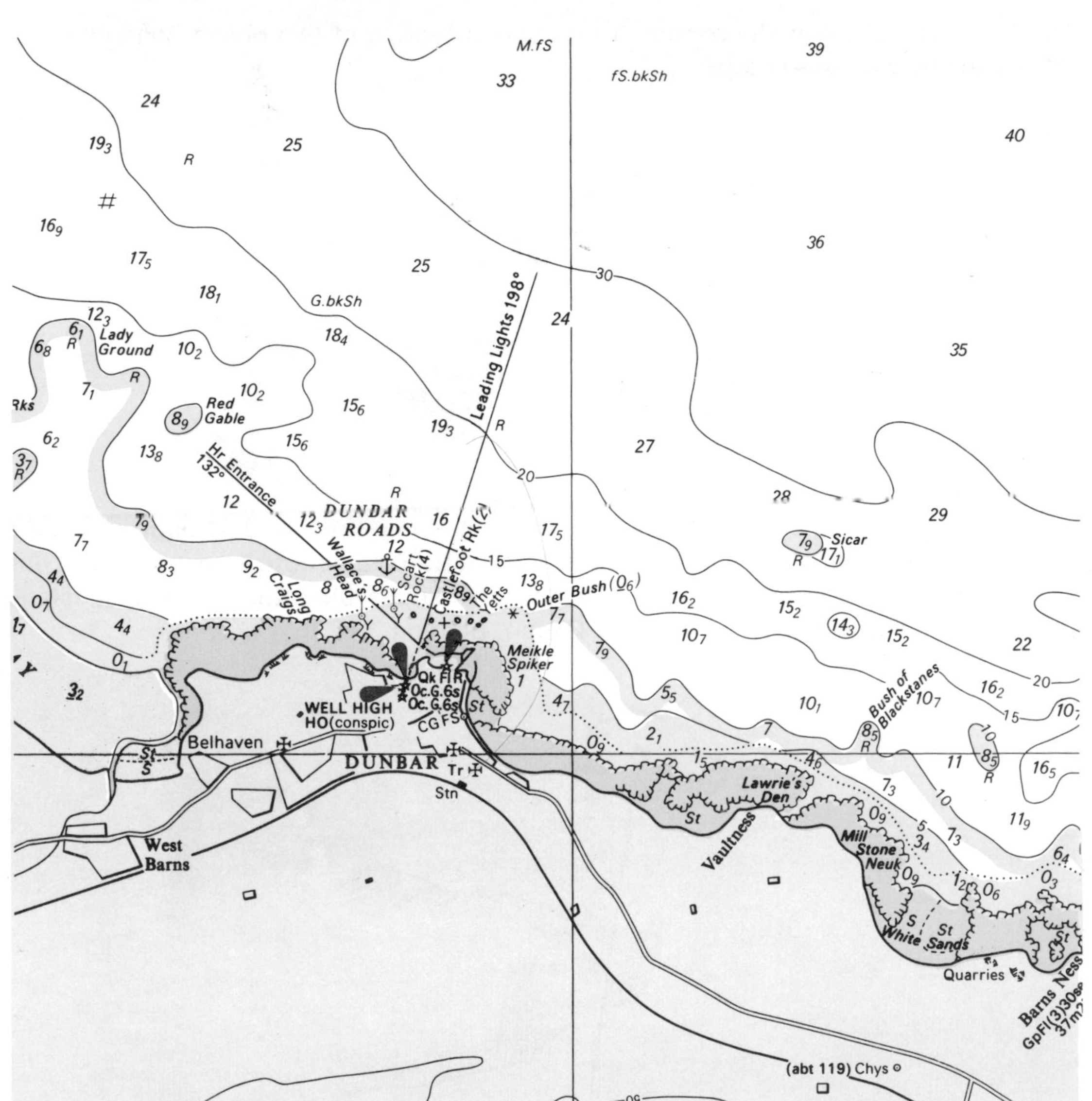

1. If you observed the Dunbar Roads Leading Lights in line bearing 197°, what would be the error of your compass?

2. If you wished to steer a true course of 270°, what would be your compass course? (Think carefully.)

1. Compass error 1°low (normally written 1°L). 2. Compass course 269° (not 271°).

Because of its importance we shall look more closely at one method of obtaining a position line, namely radar. For reasons which you will learn elsewhere, radar is not used to obtain a bearing, but only a range.

To get a reliable range there are three rules you should follow:

1. Select near objects in preference to far.
2. Choose objects which will reflect the radar beam well e.g., cliffs, rocky islands, rather than sandy shores.
3. Make sure that the objects you choose are spread angularly.
   (The angle of cut should be at least 30°.)

With these rules in mind, choose three objects for a radar fix at 1000. (Assume your position is close to the point marked X.)

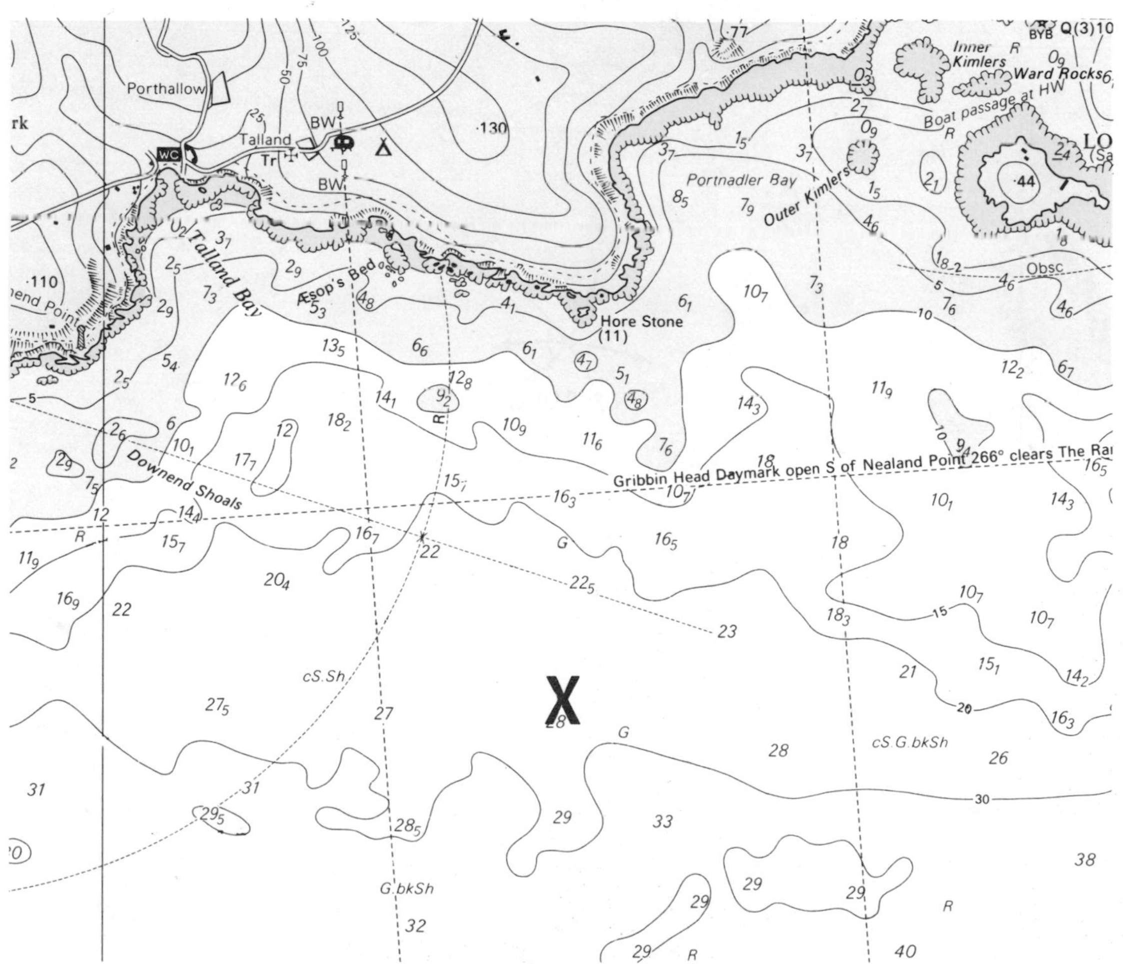

Suitable marks would be: Downend Point

Hore Stone

Looe Island

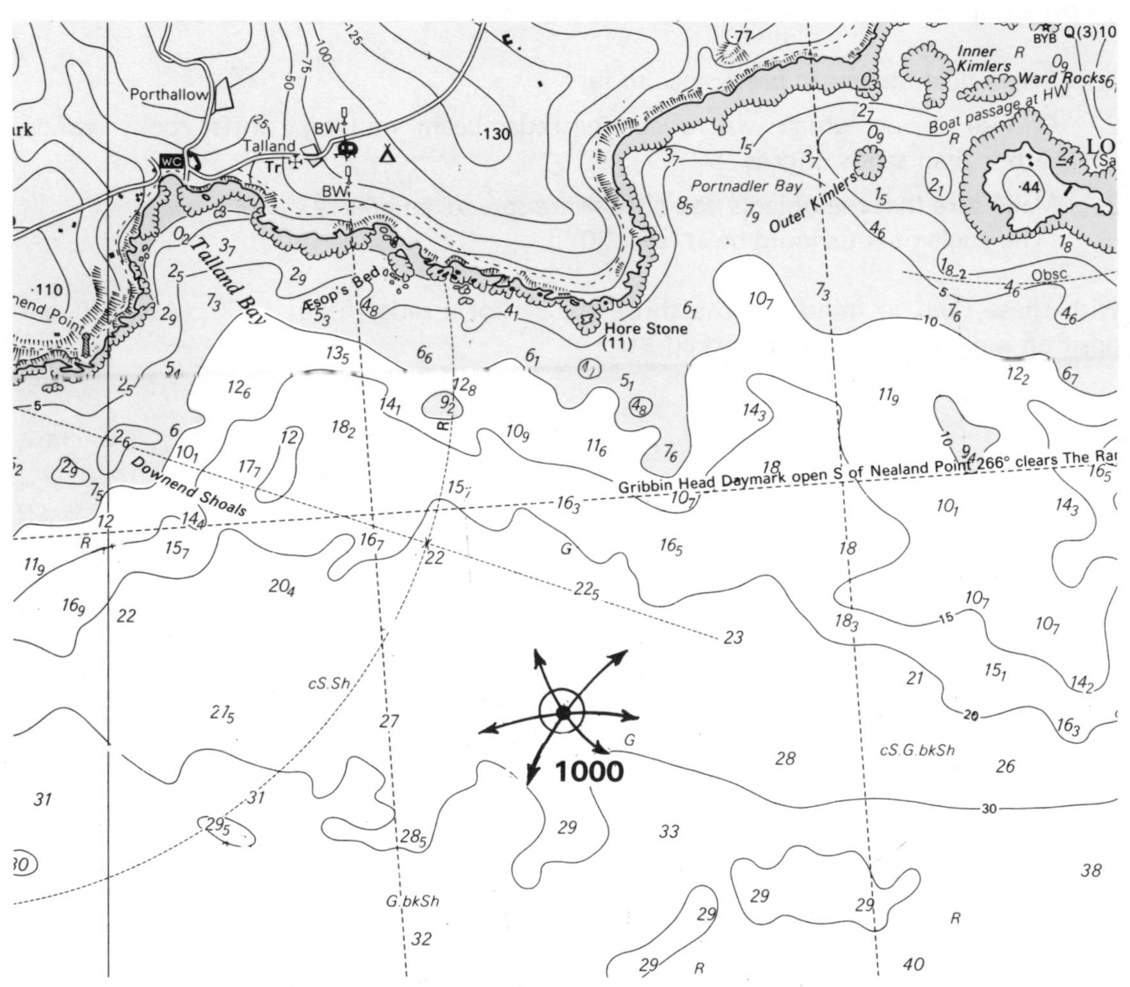

Radio can help in fixing the ship's position. There are various radio fixing aids which the navigator can utilize, but we shall only deal with one of them in this book.

For those ships with the appropriate receiver, a radio fixing aid known as the *Decca Navigator* (Decca for short) can be used in coastal waters. Readings are taken from dials on the shipborne receiver, and are then plotted on a coloured lattice which is overprinted on all charts which have L(D) before the chart number.

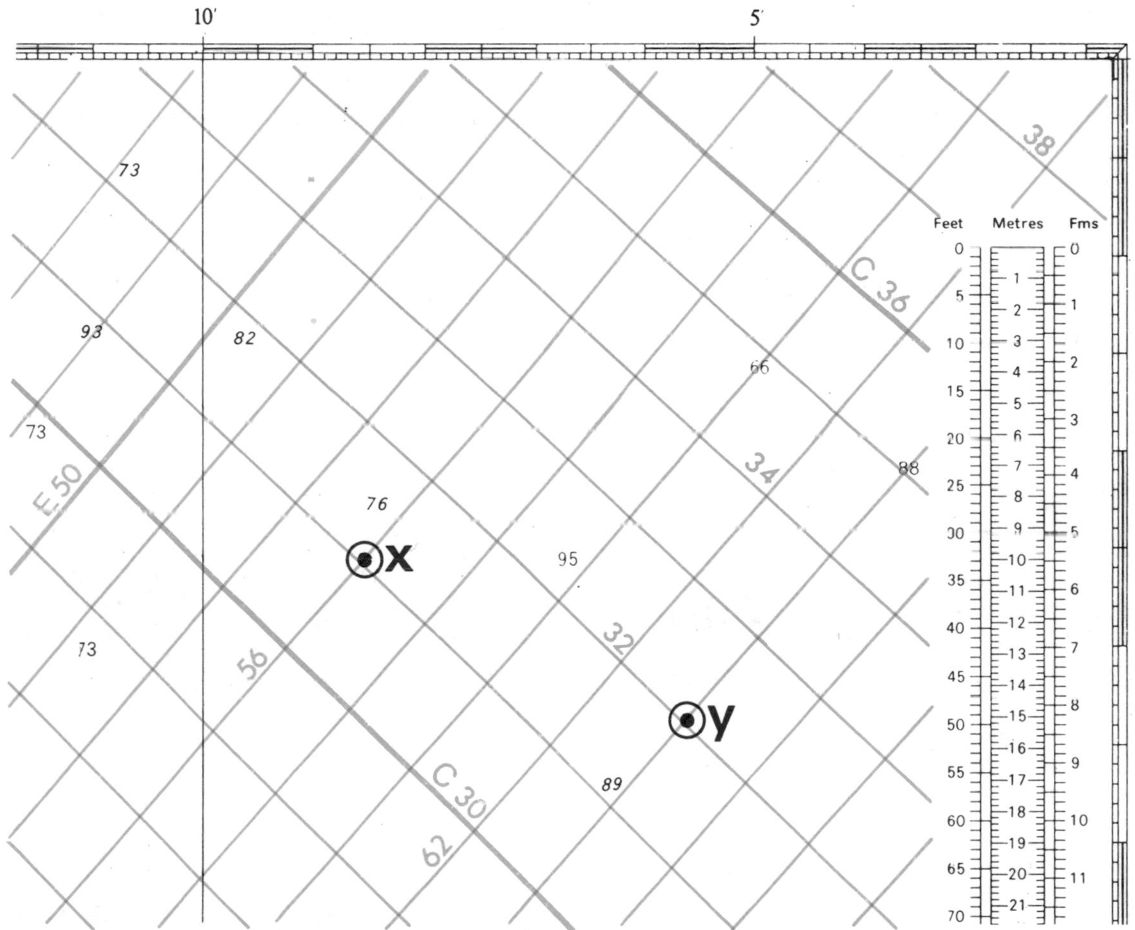

On this chart which position, X or Y, is a plot of these readings?

Purple E 56·0
Green C 31·0

Position X is a plot of readings Purple E 56·0 and Green C 31·0.

In practice, readings from the decometer dials must be corrected before they can be plotted on a Decca chart. In most areas the radio waves are distorted slightly as they pass over the terrain, and the amount of distortion in different areas must be obtained from *The Decca Handbook.* For instance, *The Decca Handbook* tells us that the correction for the area shown below is Purple + 0·35 and Green + 0·12. So after applying these corrections to the readings we have obtained, we draw two lines parallel to the lattice lines and mark the intersection as a fix like this:

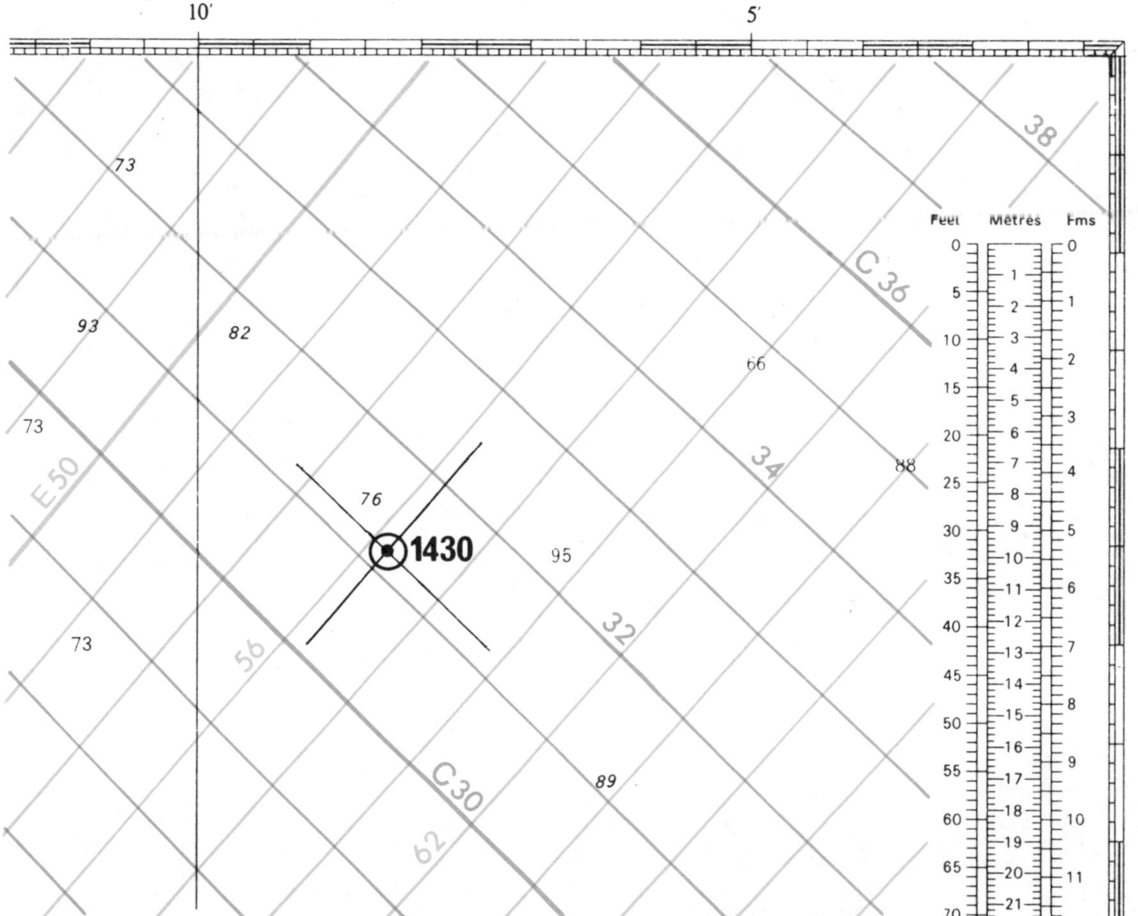

Note the symbol for Decca fix: the position lines do not have any arrowheads on their ends.

What has just been described is a fixed error, and a correction for it is straightforward. However, decometer readings are also subject to variable errors, due to interference from the skywave reflected by the ionosphere, especially at night. Because of its variable nature, the error in position can only be estimated, and you should refer to *The Decca Handbook* for guidance.

In certain circumstances, a depth contour line can provide a substitute for a position line. If you are on the course shown below you should be able to note the moment when the echo sounder shows 30 metres. You know that you are somewhere on the 30 metre contour at this time, (2130). In tidal waters, however, you must allow for the height of tide to obtain an accurate fix. In this example if the height of tide was 5 metres your position would be further to the north west of the plotted 2130 position.

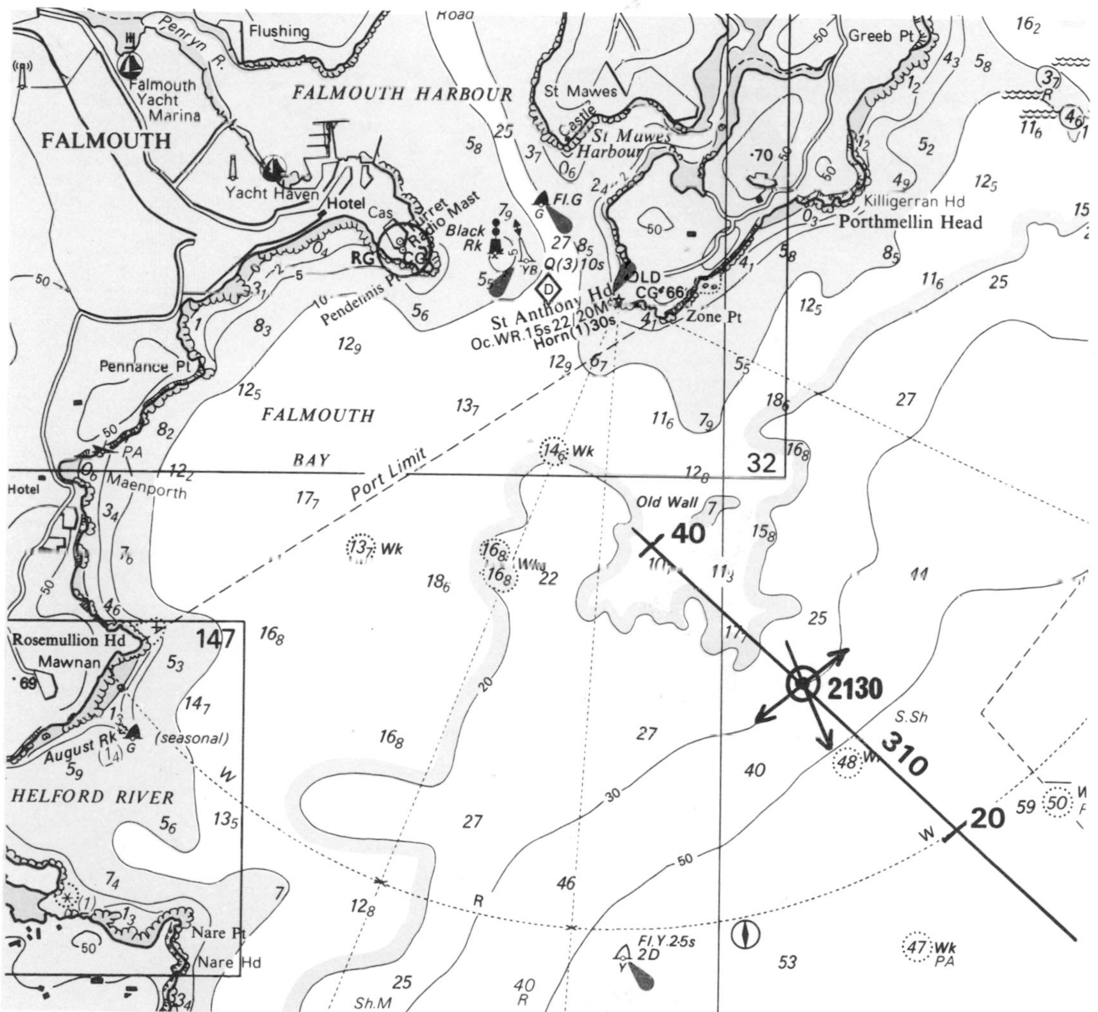

Note the symbol for this position line — a line with an arrowhead on both ends.

For the position line to be a good one, the sea-bed should possess one characteristic. Can you suggest what this characteristic is?

It must shelve steeply.

This method can only be used provided the ship is crossing the depth contour line at right angles (or nearly so), and provided that the sea-bed shelves steeply (so that there is no doubt of the exact time of passing across the contour).

Section 9 : Self-test

1. Define a position line.

2. If you are at position X on the chart, which of the following would be the best way of expressing your position?

   Elie Ness Lt 175° 2:0

   175° Elie Ness Lt 2:0

   005° Elie Ness Lt 2:0

   Elie Ness Lt 005° 2:0

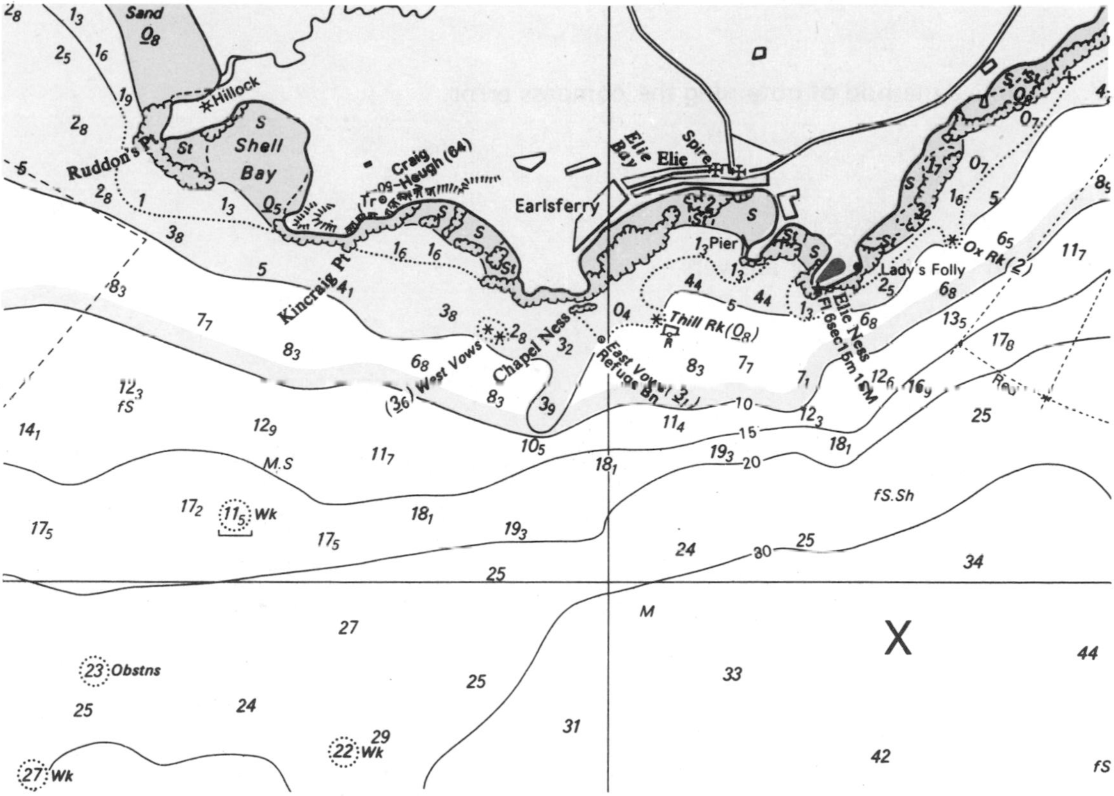

3. What do these conventions represent?

   i) 

   ii)

4. What does this represent, and what is missing from it?

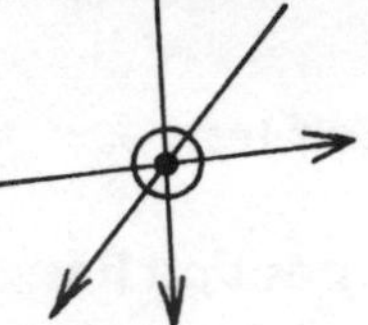

5. Name four ways of obtaining a position line in coastal navigation.

6. i) What is this called?
   ii) In the case of a small one, what would you do?
   iii) In the case of a large one, what would you do?

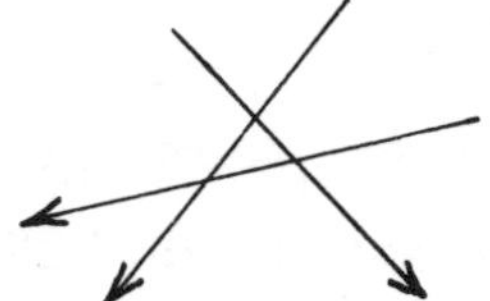

7. Name a method of obtaining the compass error.

Now turn to page 209 for answers.

Section 9: Answers to Self-test

1. Any line, straight or curved, on which the ship's position lies.

2. 175° Elie Ness Lt 2·0

3. i) A position line from the bearing of a terrestrial object.
   ii) A position line from the range of a terrestrial object.

4. A fix. It should have a time.

5. Any four of:
   A bearing of a terrestrial object.
   A transit.
   A radio fixing aid (Decca).
   A radar range.
   A depth contour line.

6. i) A cocked hat.
   ii) Make the centre as a fix.
   iii) Check your plotting, and if a large cocked hat still remains, take another fix.

7. By transit.

Section 10: Dead Reckoning and Tidal Stream Problems

Having obtained a fix you must immediately forecast the future position of the ship. This can be illustrated by an example.

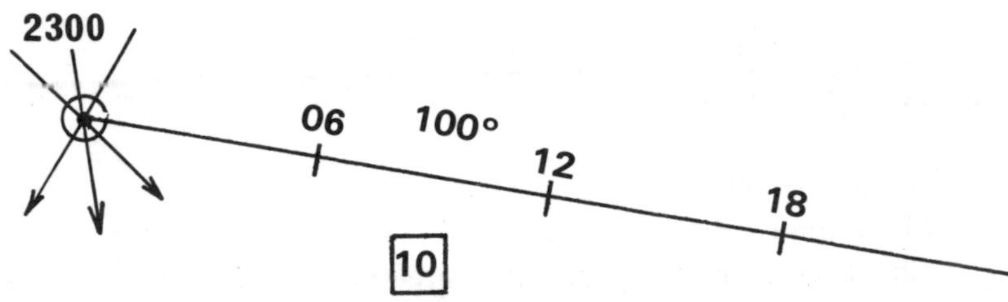

A fix obtained at 2300 is plotted on the chart. From the fix the navigator then draws a line representing the course that is being steered, in this case 100°. The ship's speed, as recorded by the ship's log, is 10 knots: this works out at 1 mile every 6 minutes. So at one mile intervals on the line he has drawn the navigator marks the ship's forecast positions with a cross (as shown above).

These forecast positions are called *Dead Reckoning* positions (D.R. positions). On what two factors are they based?

1. The course steered by the ship.
2. The speed of the ship.

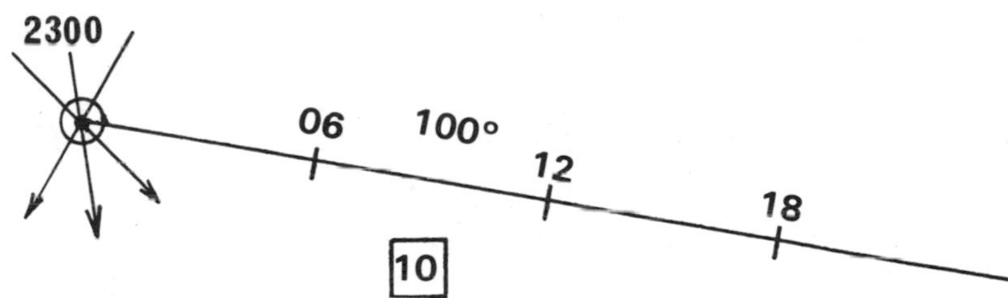

Note that the course being steered is written alongside the line on the chart and the speed is shown in a box. In addition, the Dead Reckoning (D.R.) positions must always be accompanied by the time. Use 2-figure times except for the first D.R. in a new hour.

In this case we have chosen to forecast the ship's future positions at 6 minute intervals. What interval you will use depends on circumstances – check this point with your Instructor – but 6 minutes is a very convenient interval, allowing you to divide the ship's speed by 10. For example a ship's speed of 19 knots represent 1·9 miles travelled every 6 minutes. Many navigators use this system, which is sometimes called 'the 6-minute rule'.

You have the following information:

Latest fix – 1140

Course steered – 270°.

Speed – 8 knots.

Make a sketch showing the fix and the D.R. positions for the next thirty minutes. (Use the 6-minute rule.) What is the distance between each of your D.R. positions?

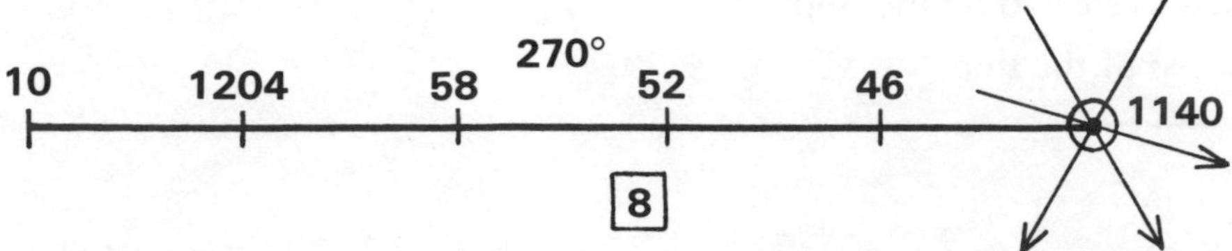

Distance between each D.R. position is 0·8 miles. (Did you record the course 270° and speed 8 knots alongside the course?)

Let's now look at an example where a fix can be obtained by using the D.R. position.

This type of fix is called a *running fix* and it is useful when only one fixing mark is visible.

If you obtain two bearings of one object at different times, say 0900 and 0930, like this...

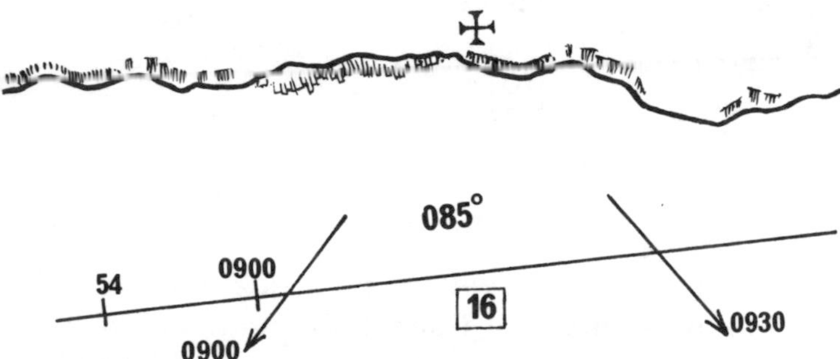

... then you can transfer the 0900 position line through the 0930 D.R. position, and the point where it cuts the 0930 position line is your fix.

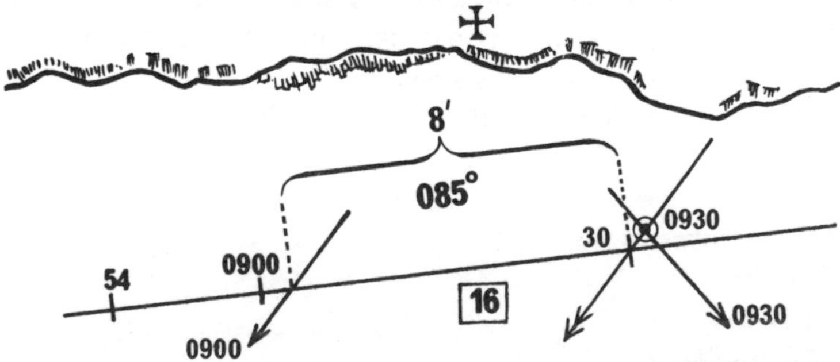

Note that the time of the D.R. position used in the construction of the fix must be the same as the time of the second bearing or position line.

Your 0930 D.R. position must be accurately plotted on from the first (0900) position line, and the transferred position line (which is parallel to the original one) must pass through this D.R. position. Note also that the symbol for a transferred line is a double-headed arrow.

You have the following information:

1030 Bearing of tower 180°.

1100 Bearing of tower 200°.

Course and speed of ship 125°, 20 knots.

In what direction and for what distance would you transfer the 1030 position line to get a running fix at 1100?

Direction 125° for a distance of 10 miles.

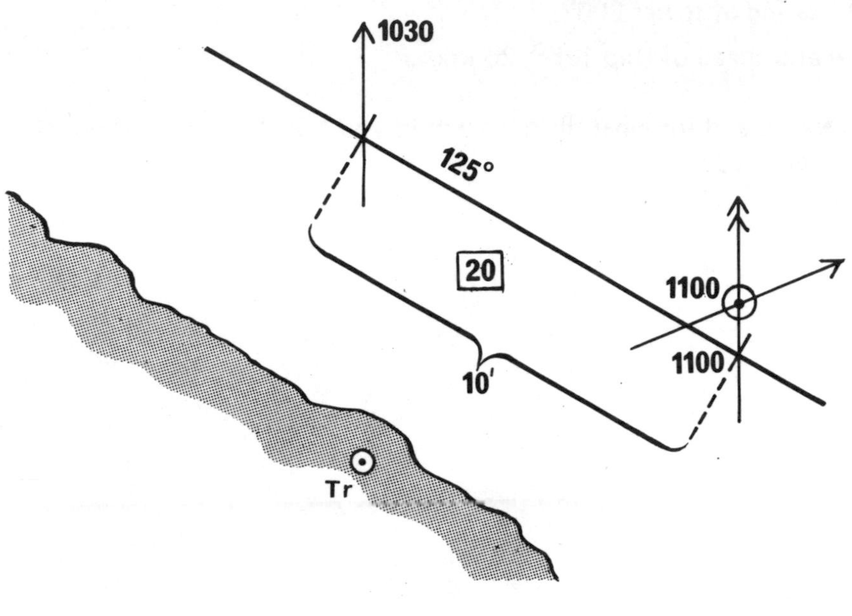

As you have seen, D.R. positions are most important as they give the only indication of the ship's present and future positions – because by the time a fix has been plotted the ship has moved on. The forecast of the ship's position (i.e. D.R.) must be updated when it is clear that the ship has been set well off the planned track. Look at the example below.

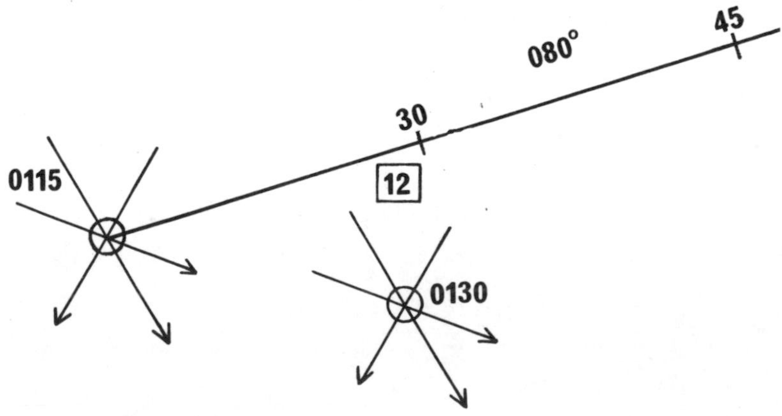

A fix at 0130 shows that the D.R. position at that time is no longer accurate. What must the navigator do immediately?

Forecast the future positions of the ship, using the new fix.

The forecast is made by marking the D.R. positions like this:

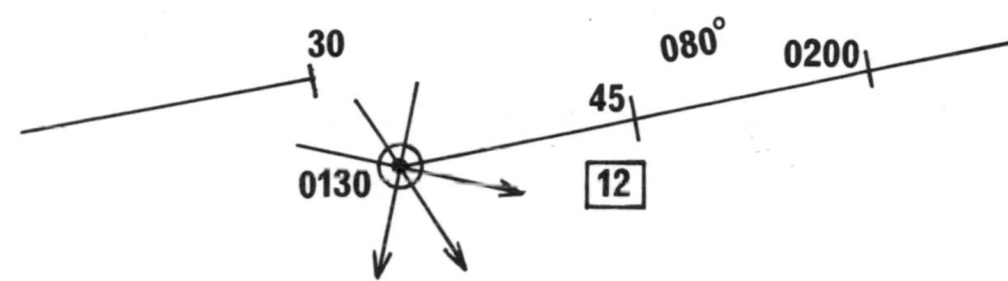

However, in order to have a really effective forecast, the navigator needs to make the best possible estimate of the ship's future position. Such a position is called an *Estimated Position* and is marked thus: △.

In the problem below a fix was obtained at 0115 and the D.R. positions calculated using this fix. A fix is subsequently obtained at 0130, as shown. You do not alter course or speed and you want to calculate the 0145 Estimated Position. Choose where you expect it to be, and turn to the appropriate page.

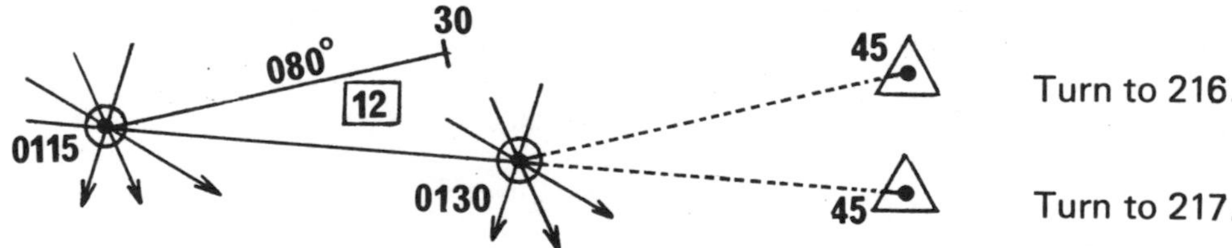

Turn to 216.

Turn to 217.

You chose:

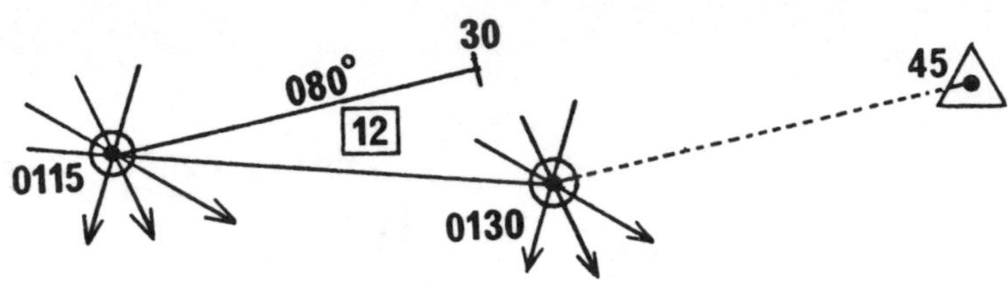

as showing the most likely 0145 E.P.

In the absence of other evidence it is more likely that the ship will continue to be carried down to the south (probably by a tidal stream) and therefore we would say that most navigators would assume that the speed and direction of the ship over the ground from 0115 to 0130 will probably be continued from 0130 to 0145 as shown below.

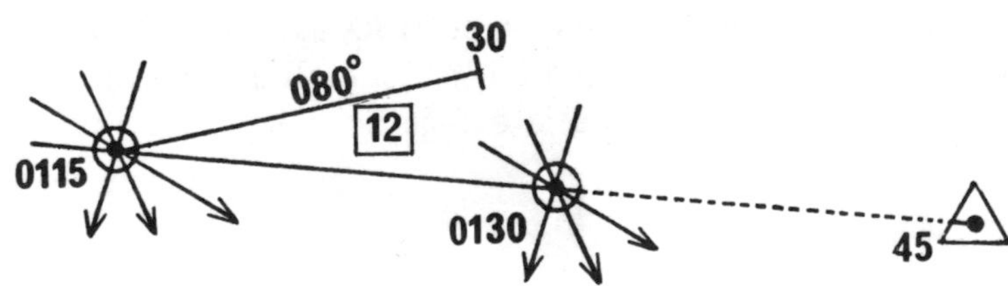

Turn to 218.

You chose:

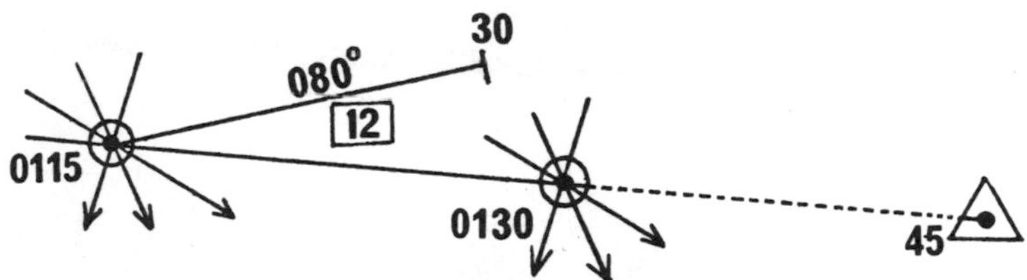

as showing the E.P. at 0145.

Yes this is the most likely position. The ship was obviously carried down to the south of her 0130 position (probably by a tidal stream) and in the absence of other evidence, will probably continue to be.

Turn to 218.

In the example below the D.R. position for 2020 has been forecast and a fix for 2020 obtained. For the purposes of this programme we will assume that the difference between the two (in this case the D.R. position for 2020 and fix for 2020) is attributable to the force of the tidal stream. (For large displacements this is the most likely cause.)

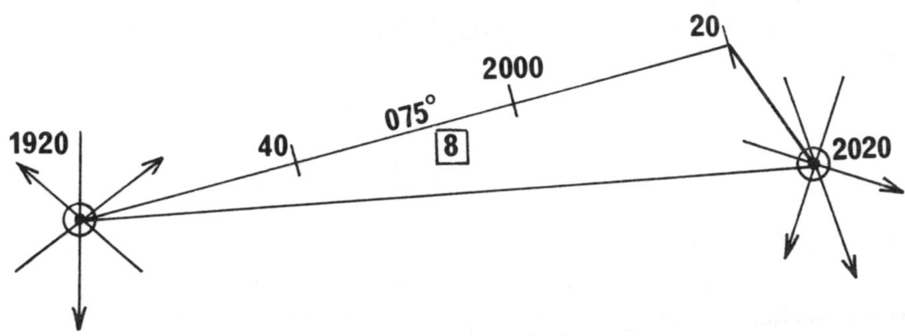

To understand how tidal stream affects the ship, do not think of it as pushing the ship somewhere – this implies resistance. Picture the whole surface of the sea moving in a certain direction at a certain rate and carrying the ship along with it like a man walking up an escalator, or on a Travolator strip at an airport.

Bearing in mind the effect of the tidal stream, you can see that the course steered by the ship is different from the actual track of the ship over the ground.

Which line on the diagram above shows the actual track of the ship?

The line joining the 1920 fix to the 2020 fix.

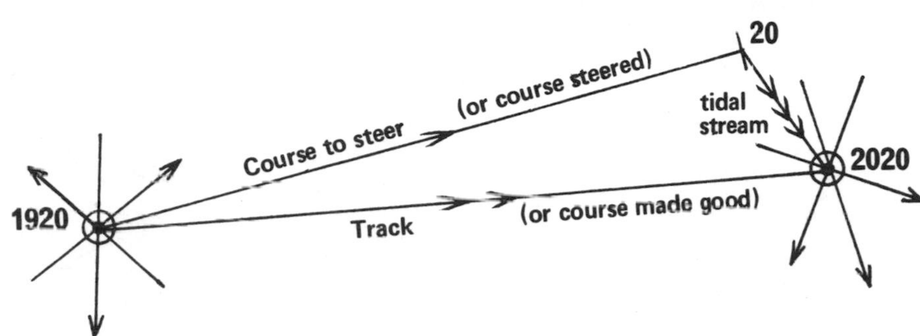

The three lines can be treated as vectors, making up a vector triangle. It will be useful at this point to learn how they are referred to and the conventions used to distinguish them.

Course to steer (or course steered)	–	This is the line giving the D.R. positions and is marked with a single arrowhead
Track (or course made good)	–	This is the line representing the ship's track over the ground and is marked with a double arrowhead.
Tidal stream	–	The line representing the tidal stream is marked with three arrowheads.

How would you refer to the line joining two consecutive fixes?

The track (or, course made good).

If we assume that the force moving a ship from its D.R. position is tidal stream we can find the direction and rate of the tidal stream, given the course steered and the ship's track.

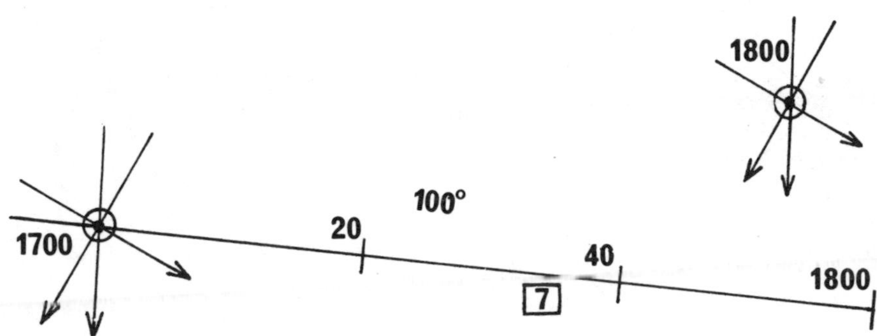

Make a rough sketch showing the vector triangle that you would draw in order to find the direction and rate of the tidal stream in this example. Use the correct conventions for arrowheads.

Your sketch should look like this:

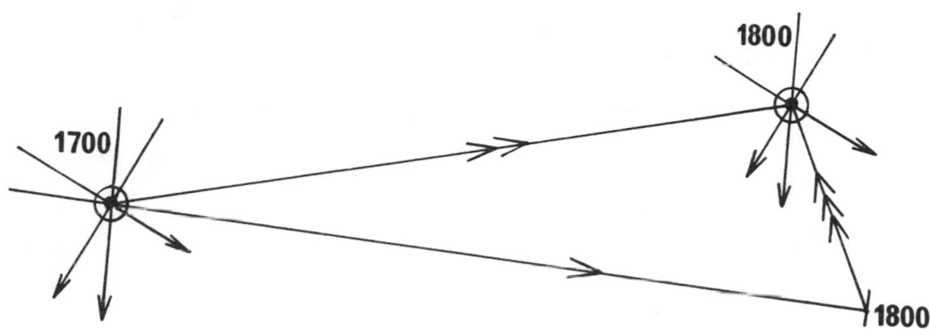

Check that the arrowheads are correct and are pointing in the right direction.

The direction of the tidal stream can now be found – by inspection it is approximately 340°. It can be measured accurately by using parallel rulers and a compass rose. The rate can be found by measuring the length of the tidal stream vector, say 2 miles – this means a rate of 2 knots if your vector triangle is for one hour as in this example.

Vector triangles can be used to find not only the tidal stream, but also the track and the course to steer to maintain a course allowing for tidal stream. This can be set out in table form:

GIVEN	FIND
Course steered and ship's track.	Tidal stream.
Course steered and tidal stream.	Ship's track.
Ship's track and tidal stream.	Course to steer.

If you know what the direction and rate of the tidal stream are likely to be, and then you draw a vector to represent it, like this.

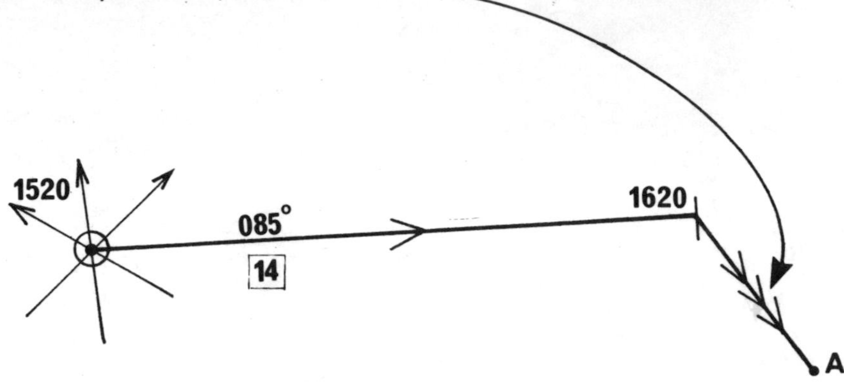

What is the name for the position (A) that you have now calculated?

The Estimated Position (E.P.) at 1620 (represented thus ).

We can now distinguish the D.R. position and the E.P.:

D.R. position – forecast position based solely on the course steered and speed through the water.

E.P. – forecast position based on all factors affecting the ship's movement (i.e., it includes tidal stream).

So far we have only used the vector triangle to find the rate and direction of the tidal stream and the E.P. We can also use it to find the ship's track.

You have the following information:

Course steered and speed through the water – 155° at 20 knots.

Direction and rate of tidal stream – 220°, 2 knots.

Which diagram, 1 or 2, is the correct one for calculating the ship's track? (Be careful!)

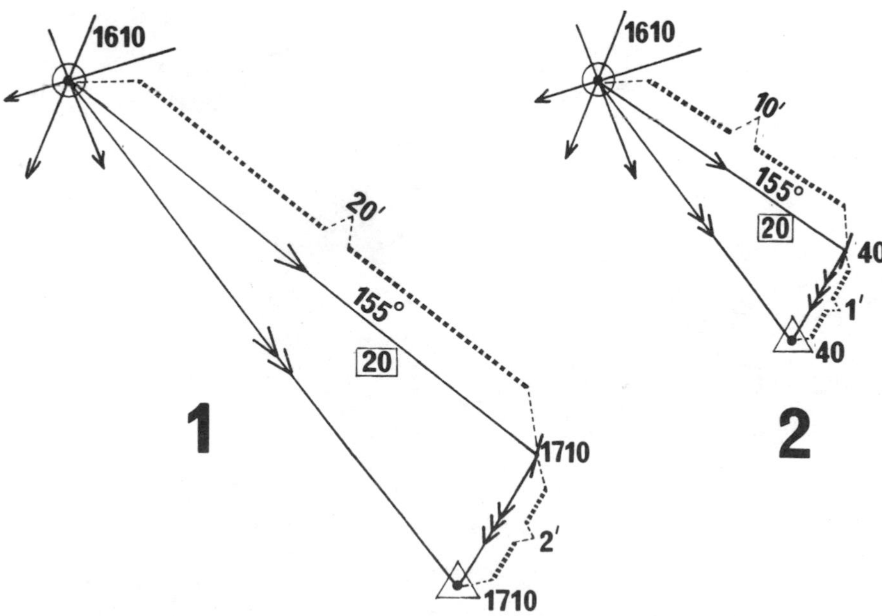

Either. (Provided the vectors are all drawn for the same duration of time any convenient time interval can be used, though an hour is the most convenient interval usually,)

In the problems you have tackled so far, the tidal stream is always plotted last in constructing the triangle. Now for a different problem: this time you have to find the course to steer to maintain a particular track.

You have to steer from point A to point B at 12 knots. The tidal stream is 335°, 4 knots. For this problem the tidal stream must be plotted first. This has been done on the diagram below, with an hour having been chosen as the appropriate interval.

Which diagram shows the correct construction to find the course to steer, to allow for the tidal stream?

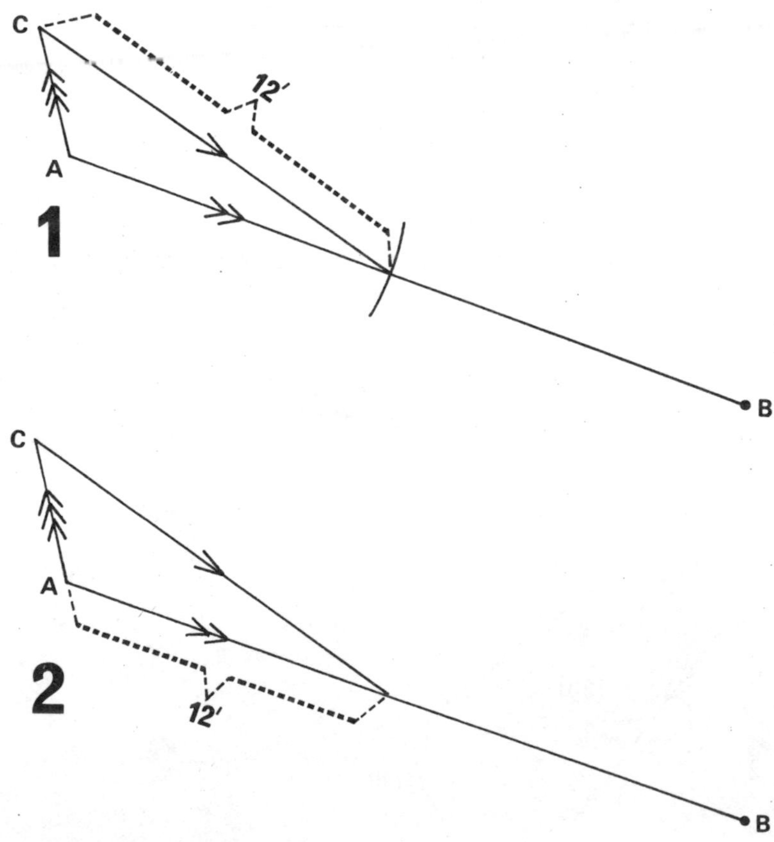

Diagram 1

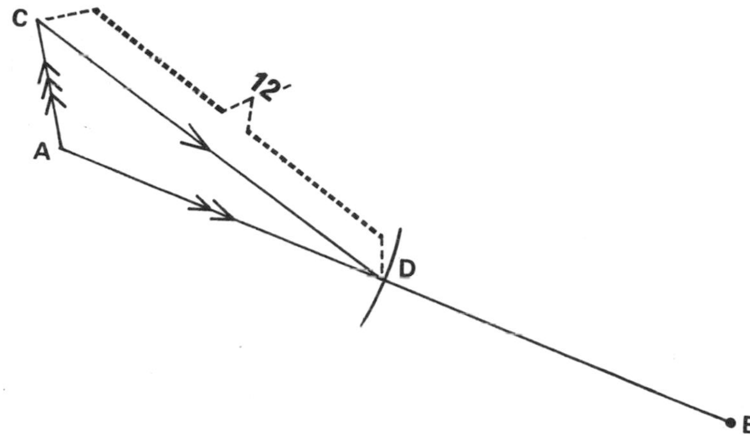

For those who may not have got this answer, let us explain more fully what was involved. You were told that the tidal stream is 335°, 4 knots, and that you had to steer from A to B at 12 knots. We chose to use an hour as the appropriate time interval. Hence we started by drawing a tidal stream vector 4 miles long in the direction 335°. Then we measured the ship's speed and drew a line 12 miles long from C to cut AB. This is done using a pair of compasses. Note that in those problems where you have to find the course to steer, you always plot the tidal stream vector first (at the beginning of the triangle) and then use the compasses set to the ship's speed to draw the arc cutting the track (line AB).

To find the speed that you will make good, you measure the distance AD – say, 11 knots in this example. It is clear that by steering into the tidal stream the ship will make less than 12 knots.

To take the last problem a stage further: if the distance from A to B was 40′, and if you left A at 0900 and had to arrive at B at 1100 then obviously you need to do 20 knots along the track. This is called making good 20 knots.

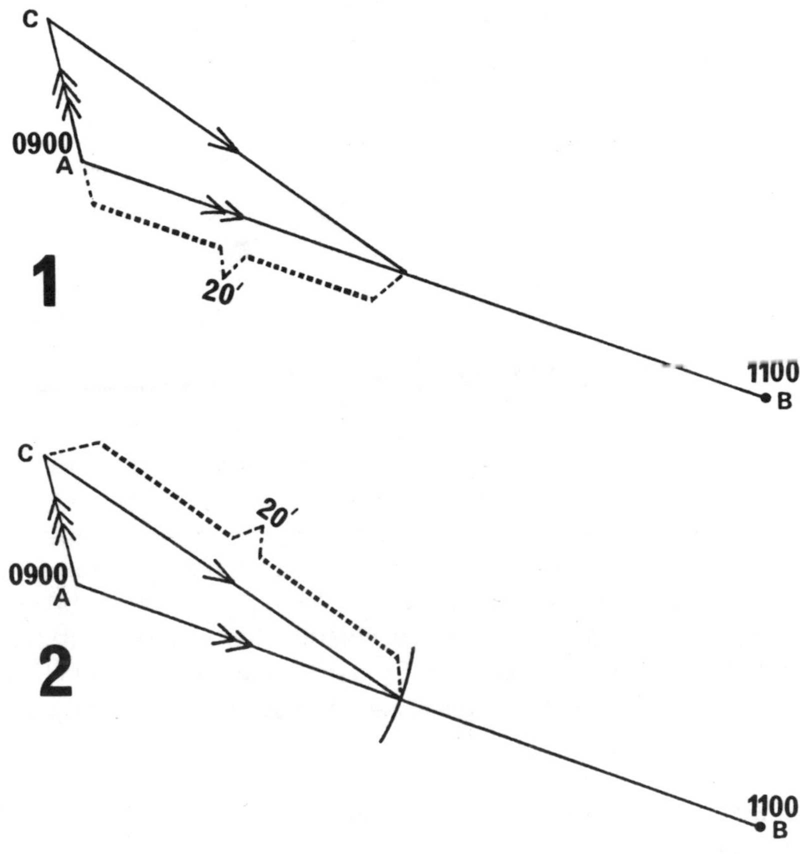

Which diagram shows the right construction to determine the course to steer and the speed required to make good 20 knots from A to B?

1 is correct. Making good 20 knots means covering 20′ in one hour <u>along the track.</u>

You will thus measure this vector ....

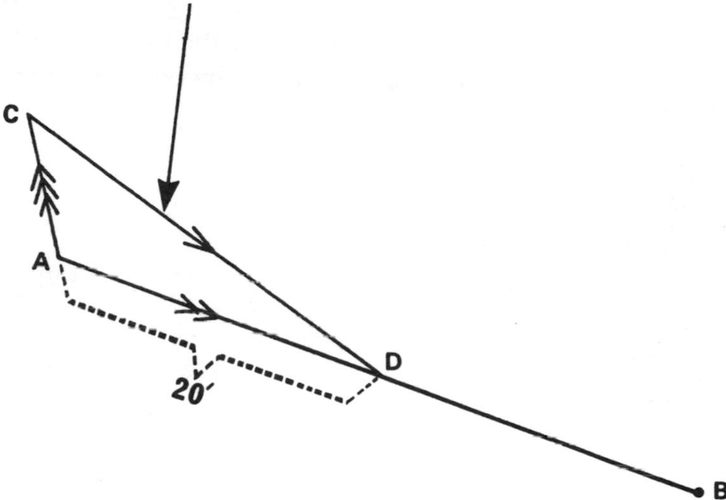

.... to find the speed at which you must steam.

The track from A to B, is also referred to as the *course made good.* The vector CD, therefore, represents the course to steer and the speed required.

Section 10: Self-test

1. What does this symbol mean? △ 1245.

2. If your course and speed are 060° 20 knots and the rate and direction of the tidal stream are 300° 2 knots, which diagram shows the correct way to find the course and speed made good?

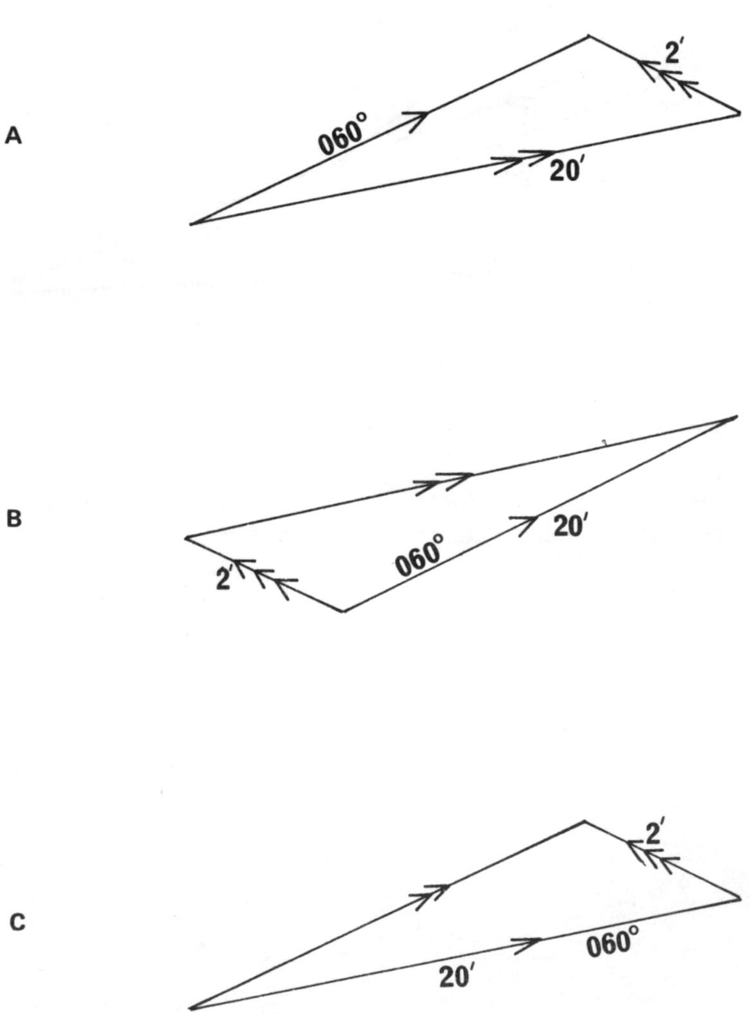

3. If your course and speed are 240°, 15 knots, and course and speed made good are 225°, 17 knots which diagram shows the correct way to find the rate and direction of the tidal stream?

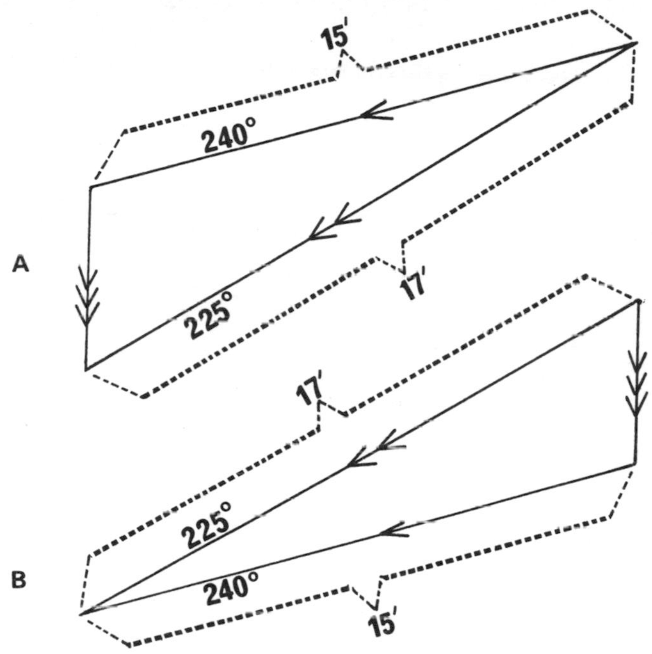

4. If the course to make good is 090°, ship's speed is 15 knots, and the tidal stream is 130°, 2 knots, which diagram correctly shows the way to find the course to steer to maintain the course 090°?

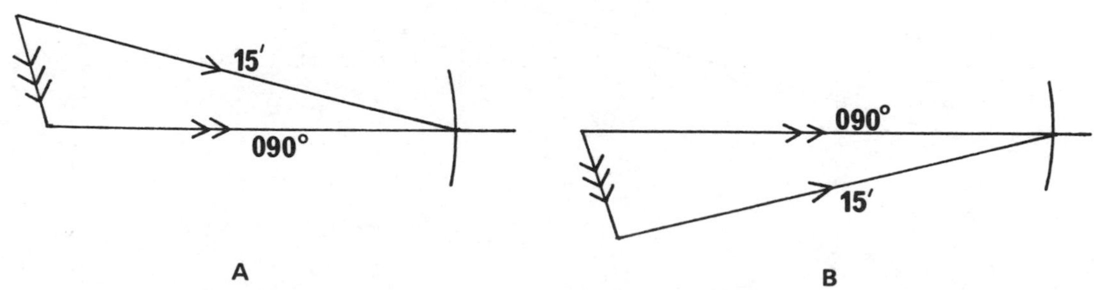

5. You wish to get from point X to point Y a distance of 40′ in 2 hours; the direction and rate of the tidal stream is 200° 2 knots.

Which diagram shows you how to find the course to steer and the speed at which to steam?

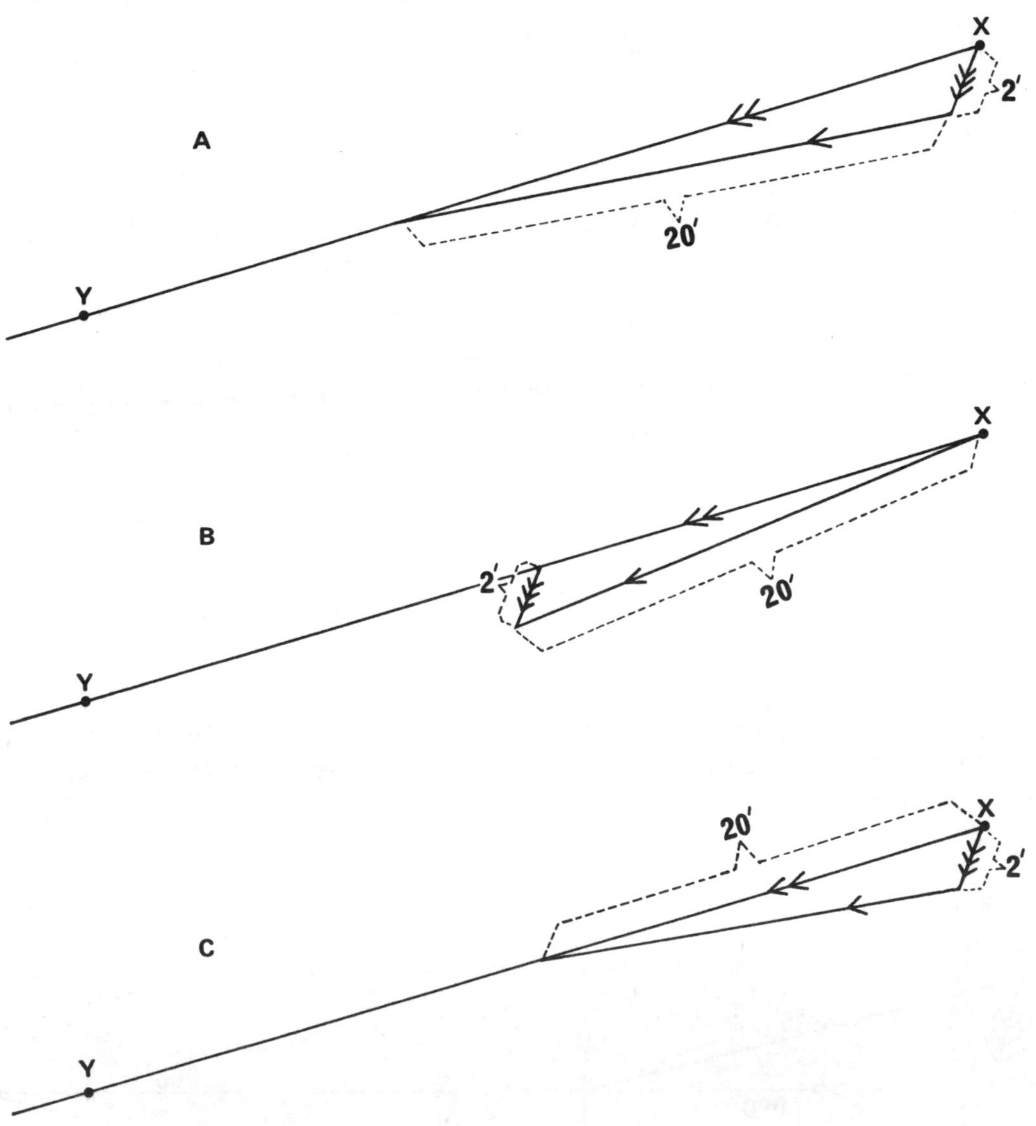

6. i) What type of position is shown at 1720 and 1740?

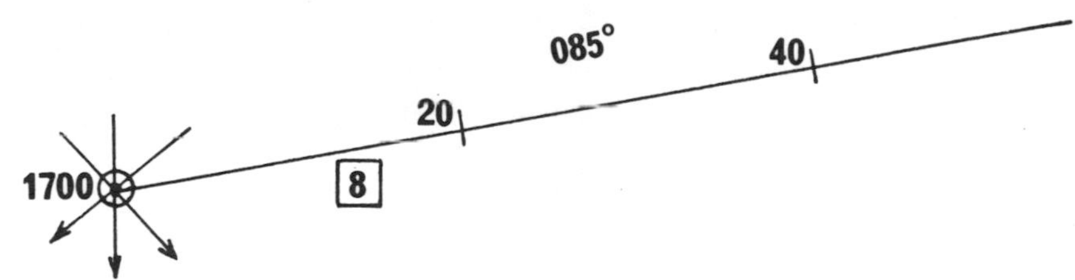

ii) How are these positions calculated?

7. You have the following information:

1300 Bearing of church 175°

1330 Bearing of church 100°

Course and speed of ship 220°, 16 knots.

Tidal stream is negligible.

i) How could you get a running fix at 1330?

ii) What name is given to the first position that you use to construct the fix?

iii) How is it represented?

8. What must you do on the chart after plotting any fix?

Now turn to page 232 for answers.

Section 10: Answers to Self-test

1. Estimated Position (E.P.) at 1245.

2. C

3. A

4. B

5. C

6. i) Dead Reckoning (D.R.) position.

   ii) By plotting ahead the course steered and by marking intervals depending on the ship's speed.

7. i) By transferring the 1300 position line for 8′ in the direction 220°.

   ii) A transferred position line.

   iii) By a line with a double arrowhead at one end.

8. Immediately forecast the position of the ship.